D0849728

Race and Affluence

An Archaeology of African America and Consumer Culture

CONTRIBUTIONS TO GLOBAL HISTORICAL ARCHAEOLOGY

Series Editor:
Charles E. Orser, Jr., *Illinois State University, Normal, Illinois*

A HISTORICAL ARCHAEOLOGY OF THE MODERN WORLD
Charles E. Orser, Jr.

ARCHAEOLOGY AND THE CAPITALIST WORLD SYSTEM: A Study from
Russian America
Aron L. Crowell

AN ARCHAEOLOGY OF SOCIAL SPACE: Analyzing Coffee Plantations in
Jamaica's Blue Mountains
James A. Delle

BETWEEN ARTIFACTS AND TEXTS: Historical Archaeology in
Global Perspective
Anders Andrén

CULTURE CHANGE AND THE NEW TECHNOLOGY: An Archaeology of
the Early American Industrial Era
Paul A. Shackel

HISTORICAL ARCHAEOLOGIES OF CAPITALISM
Edited by Mark P. Leone and Parker B. Potter, Jr.

LANDSCAPE TRANSFORMATIONS AND THE ARCHAEOLOGY OF
IMPACT: Social Disruption and State Formation in Southern Africa
Warren R. Perry

MEANING AND IDEOLOGY IN HISTORICAL ARCHAEOLOGY: Style,
Social Identity, and Capitalism in an Australian Town
Heather Burke

RACE AND AFFLUENCE: An Archaeology of African America and
Consumer Culture
Paul R. Mullins

A Continuation Order Plan is available for this series. A continuation order will bring delivery
of each new volume immediately upon publication. Volumes are billed only upon actual
shipment. For further information please contact the publisher.

Race and Affluence

An Archaeology of African America and Consumer Culture

Paul R. Mullins

George Mason University
Fairfax, Virginia

Kluwer Academic / Plenum Publishers
New York, Boston, Dordrecht, London, Moscow

Library of Congress Cataloging-in-Publication Data

Mullins, Paul R., 1962-
    Race and affluence : an archaeology of African America and
consumer culture / Paul R. Mullins.
        p.   cm. -- (Contributions to global historical archaeology)
    Includes bibliographical references and index.
    ISBN 0-306-46089-0
    1. Afro-Americans--Maryland--Annapolis--Antiquities. 2. Afro
-Americans--Material culture--Maryland--Annapolis. 3. Annapolis
(Md.)--Antiquities. 4. Afro-Americans--Maryland--Annapolis--Social
conditions. 5. Afro-Americans--Maryland--Annapolis--Economic
conditions. 6. Ethnoarchaeology--United States--Case studies.
7. Afro-American consumers--History--Case studies. 8. Consumption
(Economics)--United States--Case studies. I. Title. II. Series.
F189.A6N46   1999
975.2'5600496073--dc21   99-12107
                                                                     CIP

ISBN 0-306-46089-0

© 1999 Kluwer Academic / Plenum Publishers
233 Spring Street, New York, N.Y. 10013

10 9 8 7 6 5 4 3 2 1

A C.I.P. record for this book is available from the Library of Congress.

Printed in the United States of America

Preface □

The growth of racial ideology and the emergence of consumer culture were perhaps the two most pivotal threads of American life and thought between the mid-nineteenth century and the Depression. Scholars have extensively documented nineteenth-century racial ideology and the informal and legalized racial segregation that structured public privileges well into the twentieth century (e.g., Franklin 1967; Gossett 1963; Ignatiev 1995; Lott 1995; Roediger 1991). An equally prodigious volume of research has studied the transformations in material consumption from the late nineteenth century into the 1930s. These social and material shifts in emergent "consumer culture" included changes in mass advertising (e.g., Lears 1994), marketing (e.g., Leach 1993), gender ideology (e.g., Abelson 1989), commodity packaging (e.g., Strasser 1989), and leisure (e.g., Kasson 1978), among numerous other things (cf. Agnew 1990; Bronner 1989; Horowitz 1985; Purser 1992; Susman 1984; Williams 1982). Nevertheless, there is a vacuum of scholarship linking the dramatic shifts in race and consumption, and few, if any, scholars have been willing to place race, racism, and White privilege at the heart of American consumer culture.

This book examines the relationship between race and materialism by investigating African-American consumption between 1850 and 1930. Rather than simply approaching racism as one of many social and material processes influencing consumption, I probe how consumer culture was fundamentally structured by race and racism. Race was a social mechanism that ensured that emergent consumer culture's mass markets, public discourses, and economics never were utterly egalitarian, classless, or blind to ethnic and social distinction. This reality stood in stark contrast to the widely embraced pretense of "free market" access in an affluent national marketplace, a transparent ruse that evaded how race structured market privileges and obscured inequality among all consumers. All Americans fashioned distinctive positions within emergent consumer culture, but after the Civil War such positioning persistently was accented by efforts to appropriate empowering White privileges or to evade demeaning racial caricatures. Consequently, race was an inescapable structuring element in all Americans' consumer experience.

This book uses archaeological material culture to investigate the concrete consumption of African Americans in Annapolis, Maryland. When African-American archaeology began in Annapolis in 1989, predominant archaeological thought suggested that African-American assemblages would reveal a self-evident and clearly distinct material pattern. However, the quite subtle or enigmatic distinctions that we identified illuminated a problematic notion of African-American difference grounded in the racialized notion of bounded, "unique" identities. It was evident that African-American archaeology required a more sophisticated framework that probed race as a contested and politicized subjectivity, not as an essential cultural mindset or imposed ideological identity. Our initial archaeological goal was simply to include African Americans in the mainstream Annapolis histories from which they were excluded. This was not an unworthy ambition, but it did not confront our "mainstream" notions about racial difference or consider that those histories, and archaeology itself, were grounded in problematic assumptions about White identity. This study envisions archaeology as one modest but meaningful space in which Americans can commonly confront how and why we construct race and transcend persistent White denial that such construction continues, or is not a reasonable way to define people. An archaeology that examines race and consumption should illuminate pervasive material and social contradictions that have significantly influenced American life in the past 150 years.

Chapter 1 outlines the book's basic research questions and sources of insight, including some background information on Annapolis and the specific archaeological sites that will be most extensively examined in the book. The second chapter discusses the variety of politicized connotations of material consumption in emergent consumer culture and suggests how this study relates to historical archaeologies of race and African America. Archaeological knowledge is inevitably politicized, but precisely what it means to be "politicized" is not self-evident. To define how I will assess politicization, the chapter outlines a series of concepts basic to my framing of racism, consumer culture, and material symbolism.

The third chapter examines the spectrum of racist surveillance that shaped African-American consumption. While this includes well-studied practices, such as Jim Crow legislation and racist violence, our conception of racism must expand to include a wide range of everyday racialized disciplines in advertising, store window display, body management, and comparable practices that seem relatively disconnected

from racism. These racial disciplines shaped the reproduction and contestation of various consumer rights by constructing a Black caricature
that rationalized White-exclusive civil, labor, and material privileges.

Chapter 4 surveys the market space that African-American Annapolitans faced from the mid-nineteenth century into the Depression. To
illuminate African-American consumer options in Annapolis, the chapter focuses on neighborhood marketers; the challenges to an African-
American entrepreneurial community; merchants, such as Jewish marketers, who catered to African Americans; and the development of chain
stores.

The fifth chapter examines the link between labor, genteel morality,
racial caricatures, and African-American consumption. Late nineteenth
century moral ideologues constructed a vision of laboring "character"
that attempted to link personal subjectivity to racialized labor. For these
thinkers, consumption threatened to unseat their own social, material,
and moral influence, so they approached labor as a space that fashioned
genteel character. That character was denied to African Americans
through the racialization of labor, making certain types of work nearly
exclusive to Blacks. The stigmatization of particular labors and consumer goods had a complex effect on African Americans who desired to
be full Americans with all the rights of consumer citizenship.

Chapter 6 focuses on a series of consumption "tactics," systematic,
but consciously unplanned or unstructured, consumption patterns. The
chapter focuses on a series of tactics used by, but not exclusive to,
African-American domestic laborers. Domestics in private homes and
Annapolis workplaces (e.g., hotels) were astute observers of the shifting
boundaries of White dominance, and in these positions they honed
considerable acumen about commodities, marketing, and the interstices
in White domination. African Americans used this knowledge to secure
some of the benefits of a White consumer space that was intended to
deny African America any significant privilege.

The seventh chapter examines some of the seemingly innocuous
forms taken by African-American material desire and social aspiration.
Consumer space was one in which a variety of ambiguous desires were
entertained, and African Americans often used material goods both to
negotiate anti-Black racism and to secure the privileges of consumer
citizenship. African Americans consumed such goods as bric-a-brac,
brand goods, and chromolithographs as a means to defy racism and
racist caricatures, while securing the right to aspiration that commodities harbored.

African Americans forged a distinctive range of positions both
within and against American society, from which they variously ig-

nored, embraced, participated in, critiqued, and openly rebelled against emergent consumer culture. Not surprisingly, no monolithic Black experience emerged in, or was reflected by, African-American consumption. Yet uniquely marginalized by anti-Black racism and sensitive to the inequities of racially structured social privilege, African-American consumers fashioned a distinctive array of tactics to secure a share of affluence and condemn or circumvent racism. African Americans were at the heart of consumer culture as laborers, entrepreneurs, and consumers: African Americans were central to maintaining American consumer space and often eager to reap its benefits, even though they were marginalized by racial ideologues who aspired to make public rights and privileges exclusive to Whites. This position both within and outside American consumer culture produced a rich range of African-American voices that delivered resounding critiques of White privilege, questioned the concrete benefits of materialism, and sometimes embraced the potential of affluence. To ignore those voices evades race and racism's centrality in American consumer culture and hazards ignoring its persistence in contemporary consumer space.

Acknowledgments

This book is a patchwork of ideas influenced by many colleagues, teachers, strangers, friends, and family. Intensive critiques, scholarly advice, research assistance, and random conversations all have shaped the final product in ways I likely can never completely appreciate. Nevertheless, I can clearly identify some people who influenced my thinking and helped me carry this research to this stage.

Bob Paynter planted the seeds for this book as he directed my dissertation research and allowed me to do a project that reflected my somewhat chaotic curiosity. Helán Page emboldened me at critical moments, prodding me to write more assertively and to tackle the most complex dimensions of every problem. Daniel Horowitz was the model of a good teacher; he read these ideas in their early forms and then advised me on how to integrate whole new bodies of scholarship and primary literature that transformed my approach.

Many of the ideas in this study are distilled from conversations I have had with Mark Warner. Besides sharing his original research, Mark has been a sounding board for a host of misdirected hypotheses, research musings, and debate about the state of professional sports. I am grateful to Chuck Orser for encouraging this research and treating me and this book with meticulous attention and scholarly respect. Mark Leone encouraged my research from the outset and furnished fundamental intellectual departure points for my own thinking.

A host of individuals helped me along in various intellectual and practical ways that they may not recognize. Chris Matthews listened to many of these thoughts in the field, obliged me to provide citations, and receives special karma for reading a shaky first draft and offering a sympathetic commentary. I am indebted to Amy Grey for preparing the graphics for this volume and reading the text closely and critically. Hannah Jopling generously provided me with her oral history transcripts and talked through her ideas about common research issues. When I began thinking through this material, I was fortunate to be included in a School of American Research seminar; seminar members Terry Epperson, Mark Leone, Ann Smart Martin, George Miller, Chuck Orser, Parker Potter, Margaret Purser, and Alison Wylie sharpened

many of the basic ideas used throughout this book. Eric Larsen and
Mike Lucas provided drafts of their bottle and ceramic analyses from
the Courthouse site. Mame Warren graciously provided a disc copy of all
the oral histories conducted under her direction in the "Annapolis I
Remember" project. Philip Brown and James E. Bean, Jr. graciously
provided me with photographs from their own collections. Eliot Werner
shepherded the book through Kluwer Academic/Plenum Publishers.

A predoctoral grant from the Wenner-Gren Foundation for Anthropological Research funded the newspaper research and bottle analysis
at Maynard-Burgess (grant no. 5671). A Winterthur Research Fellowship supported my research in their archives; Neville Thompson and the
Winterthur library staff were the model for how a research library
should always work. A Grant-in-Aid of Research from Sigma Xi, the
Scientific Research Society, funded my ceramic sherd analyses at the
Maynard-Burgess House. A Graduate School Fellowship from the University of Massachusetts provided funding during my final year of dissertation writing. Ann Palkovich and Joe Scimecca graciously searched
out sufficient funds to cover the photo copyrights.

The Banneker-Douglass Museum's staff, particularly Barbara
Jackson-Nash and Laurence Hurst, supported and improved this research. Many African-American Annapolitans gave their time to our
project in all sorts of capacities—as founts of memory, sympathetic ears,
and voices of critique—making our archaeology into something socially
relevant and empirically sound. Orlando Ridout IV and the Port of
Annapolis Board of Directors were instrumental in involving archaeologists in the initial excavation of the Maynard-Burgess House. The
Historic Annapolis Foundation's president, Ann Fligsten, ensured the
preservation of the house and committed the organization to the archaeology of African Americans.

Many other people contributed in ways I cannot completely articu-
late, but they should take my word that they helped along the way:
Janice Bailey Goldschmidt, Brett Berliner, Claire Carlson, James Delle,
Amy Gazin-Schwartz, Susan Hautaniemi, Liz Kryder-Reid, Mary Anne
Levine, Barbara Little, George Logan, Nancy Muller, Mary Praetzellis,
Rita Reinke, Blythe Roveland, Neil Silberman, Paul Shackel, Mary
Corbin Sies, Sharon Stowers, Jackie Urla, and Martin Wobst all contrib-
uted support and/or intellectual advice to this study.

My dad has been proud to have an academic in the family and eager
to add this book to his collection. My brother has been persistently
curious and eager to see what will come of all that library research. My
mother-in-law, Pat Pearson, is as delighted with my research and this
book as if I were her own son. My mother was proud of her son, the

archaeologist, and her spirit wanted to see the completion of this study, but her body was unable to stick it out.

My wife, Marlys Pearson, has listened to numerous incarnations of every thought in this study. She has patiently and quietly suffered my raging at imperfect paragraphs, computer breakdowns, lost files, and impenetrable writing, and put my frustration and impatience in perspective. My son Aidan respectfully pondered the pile of paper, hoping that I would produce something with the lyricism, intellectual weight, and graphic magnitude of *Green Eggs and Ham*. I never really expected to fulfill Aidan's expectations, but perhaps he and these other folks can take some satisfaction from their contributions to this book.

Contents

Racializing Consumer Culture | 1

In February 1900, the editor of Annapolis, Maryland's African-American newspaper *The Negro Appeal* celebrated the citizen rights he and many other Americans envisioned in material abundance. African-Methodist-Episcopal (AME) Pastor S. Timothy Tice observed "I have no patience with that old-fashioned way of owning nothing. Religion is all right. The more one gets of it the better, but material wealth, houses, and lands help along very well.... Get all the religion possible but get material wealth also" ("Some Sound Sense," 1900).

By the 1920s, most Americans would admit that they shared Timothy Tice's repudiation of material asceticism, and they at least tacitly conceded his circumspect confidence in religion's force in an increasingly material world. During the late nineteenth and early twentieth centuries, Tice was among a score of American consumers who shared a remarkably consistent mass prophesy that material affluence harbored inevitable social empowerment. Department stores, movie theaters, a surfeit of exotic mass-produced goods, extensive advertising, decreased labor hours, and increasing wages formed the groundswell of an emerging mass culture focused on material consumption. This emergent consumer culture reflected the transformation of once-private material desires into publicly shared expectations of mass standards of living (Agnew 1990). An increasingly vast range of Americans like Timothy Tice vested profound sociopolitical hopes in consumer goods, rather than religion, nationalism, labor, or any other totalizing discourse. Even at the height of the Depression, many Americans zealously sustained this somewhat enigmatic faith in material affluence (Edsforth 1987).

American consumers' optimism inelegantly evaded the profound contradictions of apparent mass affluence. Perhaps the most fundamental ideological cornerstone of the ostensibly democratic consumer culture was that its mass standards of living and public politics were White. Myriad architects, agents, and benefactors of racial ideology patrolled public consumer space by imposing racially based rules on entry and participation. Codified as well as assumed, reaching from market spaces to workplaces, those rules restricted African America's

economic leverage and labor opportunities and portrayed African Americans as social and genetic inferiors to Whites. Nevertheless, stung by a
partisan political system that had gutted Reconstruction, sobered by
the turn-of-the-century resurgence of Jim Crow racism, and systematically denied labor and material opportunities, many African Americans believed consumer space harbored genuine possibilities for social
and material change. Tellingly, Timothy Tice divined African America's
social and material prospects in real estate, perhaps the most empowering of all African-American commodities: African Americans routinely
were denied real estate through racist housing codes, Whites' unwilling-
ness to sell choice residences, and a racially based labor structure that
afforded African Americans few substantial economic opportunities to
accumulate the capital needed to purchase a house. Rather than take
aim at political power, religious uplift, or labor inequality, Timothy Tice
instead focused his sociopolitical aspirations on the symbolic and practical benefits of "material wealth, houses, and lands."

Timothy Tice was not alone in his sense of material culture's power.
John Trowbridge ventured South in the wake of Emancipation, aware
that many White Northerners believed African Americans were unsuited to the full rights of citizenship. Yet, for Trowbridge (1866:333),
African Americans' consumption demonstrated that

> There was another side to the picture. At every stopping-place, throngs of
> well-dressed blacks crowded upon the train. They were going to Memphis to
> "buy Christmas,"—as the purchase of gifts for that gay season is termed.
> Happier faces I have never seen. There was not a drunken or disorderly
> person among them,—which would have been a remarkable circumstance
> had the occasion been St. Patrick's day, or the Fourth of July, and had these
> been Irish or white American laborers. They were all comfortably clad,—
> many of them elegantly,—in clothes they had purchased with money earned
> out of bondage. They paid with pride the full fares exacted of free people,
> instead of the half fares formerly demanded of slaves.

As Trowbridge's observation indicated, simply achieving the status of
consumers realized a significant privilege prized by many African
Americans. Beyond the public consequence of consumption, the goods
themselves had profound implications as well. In 1890, the Washington,
D.C. African-American newspaper *The Bee* noted that "The quickest
way to solve the Negro problem is for the Negro to purchase property....
The white people are opposed to us because we have no money, no
education and the like. These are the barriers to the race's success.
Take our advice and buy property" ("Now is Your Chance," 1890). Not
simply mundane reflective indices of wealth or social association,
homes, their contents, and shopping itself were inescapably politicized

signs of African-American ambition, accomplishment, and suitability to full consumer and civil citizenship. Rather than fetishize such commodities and ignore consumer culture's concrete inequities, African Americans probed the relationship between consumer space's racist underpinnings and the economic, labor, and political implications of African-American consumption. In 1885, for instance, *The Bee* starkly concluded that African Americans must "place higher estimates upon our labor, and contend for living wages, and not be so easily flattered out of our money by the white citizens.... the greatest estimate which we place upon life, is fine dress, and the only people benefitted are the whites" ("Weakness of the Colored American Citizens," 1885). In 1918, *The Crusader* went further, rejecting the suggestion that "white men would learn to respect and honor Negroes as soon as Negroes acquired sufficient property and education" ("The American Race Problem," 1918:12). Instead, the journal's editors argued that Whites would never surrender racial privileges simply because African Americans were model consumers: "The South has long since proved the fallacy of the theory that the ownership of pigs (and other property) will secure one in the rights of life and property." In 1904, *The Bee* emphasized that the material inequality structuring consumer culture was based in White supremacy, arguing that "the white man owns the offices; the Government; the machinery, and everything the earth affords. What then can the negro expect? He owns nothing; he produces nothing and from nothing nothing comes. He must be a producer to make him an independent consumer" ("Oppress Him," 1904). For many African Americans, material consumption harbored the concrete and symbolic privileges of citizenship and fueled a complex swath of aspirations; nevertheless, consumer culture clearly had an underside grounded in White supremacy, and it was unlikely to willingly concede human rights to African Americans simply because they went shopping.

The extensive popular discourse surrounding American material affluence was more than a superficial debate over what to buy, where to shop, or how to define the symbolism of commodities. Instead, it encapsulized, yet never confronted, modern American society's foundation in White racial privilege. Consumer culture's vast material disparities were minimized, ignored, and legitimized by pervasive discourses on affluence that trumpeted the accessibility of consumer goods, hyperbolized consumer culture's ever-expanding capacity to provide goods and services, and brazenly heralded the civil and moral benefits of prosaic commodities. In the face of this alluring promise of affluence, obvious social and material inequalities were rationalized through monolithic racial categories. Racial groupings subsumed class, cultural, and social disparities and formed the fundamental contradiction of the consumer culture that emerged during the 1870s and reached fruition in the 1920s. A genteel White consumer culture rested upon the simultaneous marginalization of African America, working-class WASP investment in White racial superiority (an investment gradually made by European immigrants), and the protection of a prosperous minority's material affluence and social domination. These inequalities were circumvented, if not effaced, by reducing material and social contradictions to an essential racial difference gauged by distance from a White ideal.

Two fundamental facets of race are examined in this study. American consumer culture was, in one sense, *racist* in its regulations, structural socioeconomic inequality, and anti-Black animosity. Racism refers to the more or less consciously apprehended, structured regulation of color-based ethnocentrism, such as public segregation, labor exclusions, and racist caricatures, that remains familiar to all but the most naive contemporary Americans. In another sense, American society was *racialized* by the implicit reduction of all social, class, and cultural distinctions to racial differences. Racial "subjects," such as Blacks, Indians, and various recently arrived Europeans (e.g., Jews and the Irish), were simply caricatures that provided oppositions to an ambiguous, ever-present, and unquestioned White ideal (Lott 1995; Page 1990). These racial subjectivities were social and material constructions that disciplined Whites and "aspiring Whites" (e.g., European immigrants) by demonstrating the inverse of genteel Whiteness. By subjectivity I mean seemingly coherent, albeit ever-hybridizing, identities that mediate the tensions between group and personal consciousness on the one hand, and material conditions and power relations on the other. Consequently, the genesis of racial subjectivities cannot be traced to personal experience, dominant ideology, cultural consciousness, biology, or objective structure alone.

All American consumers were racial subjects defined by their distance from, and reproduction of, the ideal, tacitly White consumer, regardless of whether they articulated their identity in purely racial terms. Blacks and Whites occupied opposing ends of a racial spectrum used to resolve and legitimize social and material inequalities through reference to a contrived amalgam of biology, history, culture, and behavioral discipline, among other things (cf. Harrison 1995:58–59). Racist ideologues hoped that the stigmatization of particular racial subjects would police aspiring White working classes, restrict access to resources, reproduce the fiction of White racial unity, and legitimize

White elite privilege. Until very recently, racialization was so widely accepted that it simply was beyond contemplation. Even today, many people who reject racism inadvertently accept a notion of essential differences that diverge very little from race. Pervasive investment in a racialized America has ensured that the conflicted instability of White identity remains an unexplored and relatively undefined subject (Lipsitz 1995).

RACISM AND CONSUMPTION
IN ANNAPOLIS, MARYLAND

My examination of race and materialism focuses on the experience of consumers in Maryland's capital city, Annapolis. Annapolis is a relatively small Chesapeake Bay port city 30 miles east of Washington, D.C., and roughly the same distance southeast of Baltimore (Figure 1). A center of gentry consumption during the eighteenth century, nineteenth-century Annapolis was reduced to a quiet bureaucratic town bypassed by extensive industrialization. The city served government employees and legislators, and the Naval Academy's establishment there in 1845 provided an additional stabilizing influence on community labor and socioeconomics.

A border state during the Civil War, antebellum Maryland was divided by northern and southern factions distinguished by both geography and philosophy (Brackett 1969; Fields 1985). In general, the sentiments of these factions ran from cool to slavery in the north, to fanatically proslavery in the south. Annapolis was the urban center for the overwhelmingly rural southern Maryland, and the city's staunchly pro-Southern antebellum residents shared far more economically and socially with their southern Maryland neighbors than their acquaintances to the north (Hurst 1981). Abolition never enjoyed much viability anywhere in Maryland, but northern neighbors were ambivalent about slavery or opposed to it altogether (Fields 1985). Despite these regional rifts, in the wake of the Civil War, Maryland legislators were bitter critics of Reconstruction and African-American freedom. The state was a post-war bastion of anti-Black Democratic party politics well into the twentieth century.

The ambiguous position of slavery in Maryland was magnified by the largest percentage of free African Americans in any slaveholding state's population (Clayton 1987; McConnell 1971). Annapolis always had a large African-American population and sizable free Black community: African Americans have composed more than a third of An-

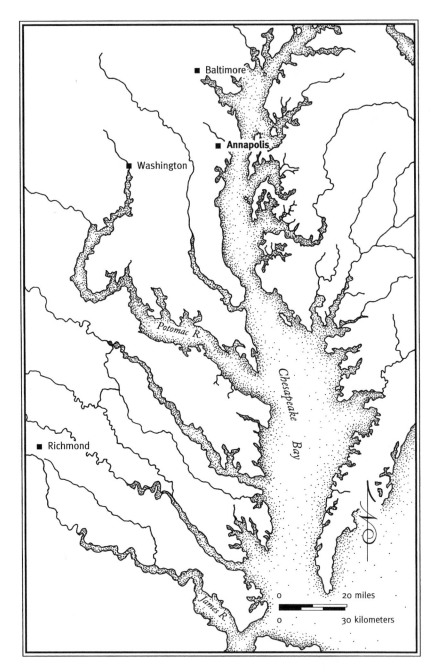

Figure 1. Chesapeake Bay region and Annapolis (courtesy of Amy E. Grey).

Table 1. Annapolis Population by Race, 1790–1917

Year	Black (free/slave)	City population	Percentage black
1790	120/670	2170	36.40%
1800	273/646	2212	41.54%
1810	333/558	2185	40.77%
1820	393/505	2260	39.73%
1830	458/578	2623	39.49%
1860	826/475	4529	28.72%
1870	1862	5744	32.41%
1880	2211	6642	33.28%
1910	3205	8611	37.21%
1917	3373	8769	38.46%

napolis' population since the late eighteenth century (Table 1). Nearby Baltimore and Washington also were homes to large African-American communities before and after Emancipation—communities that included some of the most influential African-American aristocratic circles in the nation (Gatewood 1990). A handful of African-American Annapolitans were connected to these aristocratic cliques by kinship or association, and many other African-American Annapolitans had friends and family in these cities.

This book studies a wide range of popular discourses on race and affluence and probes how dominant racial and material ideals were reproduced, as well as transformed, in communities like Annapolis. Dominant racial and material discourses were transmitted to myriad consumers and communities in a process that constantly reproduced, modified, and resisted prevailing material standards and racial subjectivities. Historical interpretation of racial construction overwhelmingly has focused on popular texts, including advertising (e.g., Ewen 1976; Lears 1983, 1994; Richards 1990), fiction (e.g., Agnew 1989; Tate 1992), and academic or state surveillance literature (e.g., Horowitz 1985), rather than material culture. Considerable period ink was devoted to popular analyses of African America that ran the gamut from virulent fictional tracts to naively measured empiricism to highly subjective travelers' insight. These authors, most of whom were genteel Whites, brought a variety of political and moral bents to their interpretations, but they never questioned that race was the appropriate framework for analysis: This maneuver placed racial subjects and Black caricatures at the center of their discourse without ever examining the concept of race itself.

Like most Americans, the vast majority of African Americans left behind few written records, but African-American writers did leave an enormous volume of writing, crossing genres from fiction to journalism to academic scholarship. African Americans like W.E.B. Du Bois, Booker T. Washington, and Marcus Garvey were simply the most prominent figures to articulately chart a course toward African-American social self-determination and material rights. The blueprints of these and other writers varied considerably, advocating everything from willing incorporation to utter economic autonomy to ascetic forbearance. The counsel of African-American thinkers is key because it articulated a framework of broad, increasingly conscious socioeconomic goals. Nevertheless, many African-American writers were well-educated elite or aspiring bourgeois whose professed privilege to "speak for the race" concealed a tangle of class, social, and individual agendas. The explicit politics of such authors are of a quite different kind than those of African-American consumers shopping in myriad markets, laboring in scores of racially structured workplaces, and discarding seemingly meaningless material artifacts into their yards. Consequently, an archaeological study of African-American consumption should complement histories of race and materialism, yet it also should illuminate the diverse everyday forms of African-American consumer agency and their underlying interests.

ARCHAEOLOGY AND AFRICAN-AMERICAN ANNAPOLIS

The research in this book was conducted as part of a long-term archaeological project known as "Archaeology in Annapolis." In historical archaeology the project is perhaps best-known for its focus on capitalist ideology in both the past and present, examining the range of historical interests reproduced by material culture and the ways in which archaeological knowledge itself can serve the interests of various contemporary social groups (e.g., Leone et al. 1987; Potter 1994). From its inception, Archaeology in Annapolis studied the city's famous historical personalities, as well as "forgotten" men and women such as craftspeople and middling merchants, yet the most prominent and unacknowledged Annapolitans have been African Americans. In 1988, archaeologists first met with African-American scholars at the Maryland Commission on African-American History and Culture to discuss the potential for an archaeological project focused on African-American life in the city (Logan 1998:73). The African-American researchers posed three basic questions that frame the African-American archaeology project (Leone et al. 1995:112). First, they wondered if there actually *was* an archaeological record of African Americans in the city (ironically, the parking lot around their Annapolis office is one of the archaeological sites examined in this book). Second, they directed us to study African America outside slavery and to emphasize the "success stories" in the African-American past. They argued that historians fixate on servitude, ignore antebellum free Black and post-Emancipation communities, and focus on the instrumental oppression of African Americans. Finally, they wanted to know if archaeology could demonstrate the persistence of African culture. Those questions continue to guide Archaeology in Annapolis' research on African-American Annapolitans.

Initial discussions between White archaeologists and African-American Annapolitans established that it was essential to secure the insight of African Americans at all stages of the project, from research design planning to excavation and analysis to public presentation. Many of my insights come directly from, or were influenced by, oral history projects conducted with African-American Annapolitans. This archaeological research uses oral testimony to outline what various African-American Annapolitans consider most critical about their histories, rather than simply to inform us where privies were located, trace genealogies, or any other number of conventional relationships between archaeologists and constituents. Archaeology in Annapolis' first interviews were conducted during the excavation of the Courthouse Site in 1990 (Warner and Ford 1990). Six African Americans who had grown up in the neighborhood were interviewed on a wide range of specific archaeological questions, such as placement of structures, as well as broader social issues, such as Annapolitan race relations. As part of her dissertation research on community in African-American Annapolis, Hannah Jopling began ethnographic research in 1991 among African Americans who had lived at the Courthouse Site and Gott's Court. Her project has focused on neighborhoods that have been studied archaeologically, and oral historical evidence has been used in museum exhibits organized by Archaeology in Annapolis researchers and African-American Annapolitans (Jopling 1998; Leone et al. 1995; Logan 1998). Jopling's research included single-person interviews with former residents of the Courthouse Site neighborhood, and she conducted two focus group interviews with a dozen former residents of Gott's Court in 1992 (Jopling 1991, 1992). These interviewees were born in the period between World War I and the early 1930s. We were initially directed to them by researchers at the Maryland Commission on African-American History and Culture; subsequently, others have become part of the

project through Jopling's research in the community. Jopling also directed interviews with 23 former residents of the ethnically mixed
neighborhood of Hell Point, which was examined archaeologically in
1993. Another oral history program was conducted as part of a broad
community history project known as "Annapolis I Remember." Annapolitan scholar and native Mame Warren directed interviews with a
wide range of Annapolitans, including African Americans, in 1989 and
1990 as part of the Annapolis I Remember research (Warren 1990).
Warren's oral histories are single-person interviews with Annapolitans
born between World War I and the 1930s that range across a vast array
of subjects, from marketing to the civil rights movement.

African-American Archaeology Sites in Annapolis

I will most closely examine three archaeological sites in Annapolis
that were all African-American residences (Figure 2). The site I will
discuss most extensively is the Maynard-Burgess House, a circa 1850–
1980 African-American home. Excavated in 1990–1992 under the co-
direction of myself and Mark Warner, the home initially was the resi-
dence of John and Maria Spencer Maynard (Mullins and Warner 1993).
Annapolis is located within Anne Arundel County, where John was born
free in 1810. In 1831, the 21-year-old Maynard received his certificate of
freedom in which he was briefly described as 5'5" tall with a dark complexion and a scar over his left eye (Anne Arundel County Certificates of
Freedom 1831). A waiter throughout his life, Maynard married the
enslaved Maria Spencer in about 1834. Maynard purchased 19-year-old
Spencer's 3-year-old daughter Phebe Ann Spencer in 1834 for $80.00,
and in May 1838 John purchased Maria as well for $350.00 (Anne
Arundel County Chattel Records 1839; Anne Arundel County Manumission Records 1840, 1857; McWilliams 1991).

John Maynard almost certainly was working at Annapolis' City
Hotel. Located directly across the street from the Maynards' future
Duke of Gloucester Street home, the City Hotel was Annapolis' premier
lodging throughout the mid-nineteenth century. In 1845, John and
Maria purchased Maria's 48-year-old mother Phebe Spencer from City
Hotel trustee James Iglehart (Anne Arundel County Chattel Records
1857). Two years later, Iglehart sold Maynard the Duke of Gloucester
Street lot, lending strong circumstantial evidence to argue that May-
nard likely worked in the hotel.

The Maynards lived in Annapolis since at least the 1830s, and
they purchased the lot at 163 Duke of Gloucester Street "with structures" in 1847 for $400.00 (Anne Arundel County Land Records 1847).
The nature of these "structures" is unclear, but the average value of an

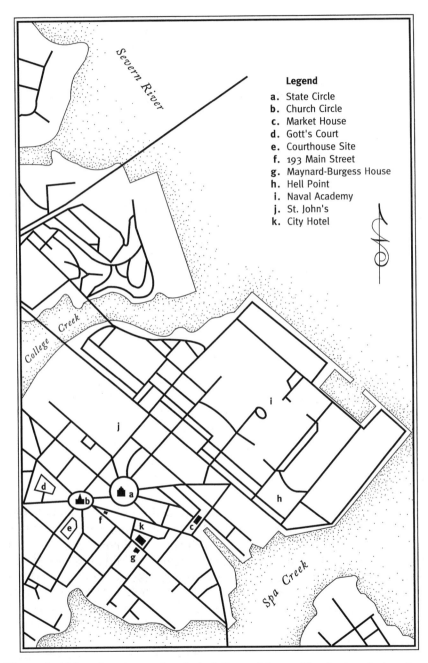

Figure 2. African-American archaeological sites and Annapolitan landmarks (courtesy of Amy E. Grey).

improved Annapolis lot in 1849 was $1640.00, suggesting that any structure at the address was quite insubstantial (Russo 1990). The Maynards likely built the central block for the home that stands there today between 1850 and 1858. Artifacts and property values support this dating; in 1860, the value of the lot had increased to $1,000 from the 1847 purchase price (and subsequent 1850 assessment value) of $400, which was also the 1850 assessment value of the lot. The structure originally was a single-story, two-room block with a central chimney, with a rear addition added sometime between 1874 and 1877 (Wright 1991). The main block and its rear addition were raised to the present two-story height with an attic by 1891.

The Maynards' Duke of Gloucester Street home was located in a neighborhood that did not include many African Americans in the 1850s, but some African Americans did live on the surrounding blocks. The Maynards' home sat at the corner of Duke of Gloucester and Market Streets. By 1870, 24 African-American households were located along Market Street, neighboring 23 White households on the same street (Ives 1979:135). The neighborhood clearly contained a stable African-American residency, but it never became exclusively, or even predominately, African American.

The Maynards apparently were among Annapolis' more affluent African-American families in the mid-nineteenth century, although they were not particularly prosperous. An 1849 tax book for 344 accounts in the city listed 19 African Americans, including John Maynard, who was assessed at $525.00 personal property (Davis Collection 1849). Ten of the 19 African Americans who paid taxes were assessed values less than Maynard, and 103 Whites (29.94% of the 344 accounts) were assessed values less than Maynard's $525.00 (McWilliams 1991). While over 200 Annapolitans were more wealthy than the Maynards, the household was economically more stable than many of their African-American and White neighbors.

John Maynard died at 64 years of age on July 10, 1875, and his son John Henry died between 1876 and 1880 (McWilliams 1991). In 1880, the household was headed by Maria Spencer Maynard and included John Henry's widow Martha Ready Maynard, granddaughter Maria Louisa (John Henry and Martha Ready Maynard's child), and three boarders. One of the boarders, Martha Ready Maynard's brother Willis Burgess, would eventually purchase the home. Maria Spencer Maynard died sometime between 1880 and 1900. Her daughter Maria Louisa married barber Upton Cooper between 1900 and 1908, but the family's fortunes declined. In July 1908 they defaulted on their mortgages, and the family sold the lot adjoining 163 Duke of Gloucester Street in

October to raise $1,000.00 (Anne Arundel County Land Records 1908). Eventually a firehouse was built there between 1913 and 1921. Upton Cooper died in January 1910, and Maria Louisa again defaulted on her mortgage. In 1914, the property was purchased at public sale by Maria Louisa's uncle, former boarder Willis Burgess (Anne Arundel County Land Records 1915). Willis Burgess died in 1935, and his daughter Ella lived there until her death in the 1980s. Today the house is owned by the Historic Annapolis Foundation, which conducted archaeology as part of the house's restoration.

The second archaeological site discussed in the book is the Courthouse Site, an African-American neighborhood from the mid-nineteenth century to the 1960s (Aiello and Seidel 1995; Warner and Mullins 1993). The block bordering Franklin (formerly Doctor), Cathedral, and South Streets first became home to an African American in 1832, when Charity Folks purchased a lot in the block (Aiello and Seidel 1995:1:43). By 1880, the block contained 38 households with 133 residents, including 33 Black- or Mulatto-headed households and 106 Black or Mulatto residents. Between the mid-nineteenth century and the 1960s, the neighborhood was home to African-American renters and home owners with a variety of social and economic backgrounds. In 1874, Mount Moriah African-Methodist–Episcopal Church was built on the block along Doctor Street (later renamed Franklin Street), and some of Annapolis' African-American professional class, merchants, laundresses, and preachers alike soon called the block home.

The block contained an alley complex in the block's center known as Bellis Court, a series of connected frame dwellings rented by African Americans (Aiello and Seidel 1995:1:48). The complex's construction was directed by Sarah Ella Bellis, whose husband William Bellis had owned property in the neighborhood since the 1880s. William had a tailor shop on Main Street that he operated with his son, but in the early 1890s he became mentally ill and was institutionalized (Aiello and Seidel 1995:1:48). His wife apparently directed additions to several existing dwellings in the block interior, including the eponymous court, which was completed in 1897. In 1900, 27 African Americans were residents of the six units at Bellis Court. African Americans lived in the alley buildings until 1939, when the lot was sold to Anne Arundel County and the Court demolished. Today the Mount Moriah Church still stands and is home to the Banneker–Douglass Museum, which focuses on African-American history in Maryland. The remainder of the block is now occupied by a parking deck and Courthouse addition.

The third of the African-American sites examined in this book is a 1907–1952 alley community known as Gott's Court (Figure 3). Gott's

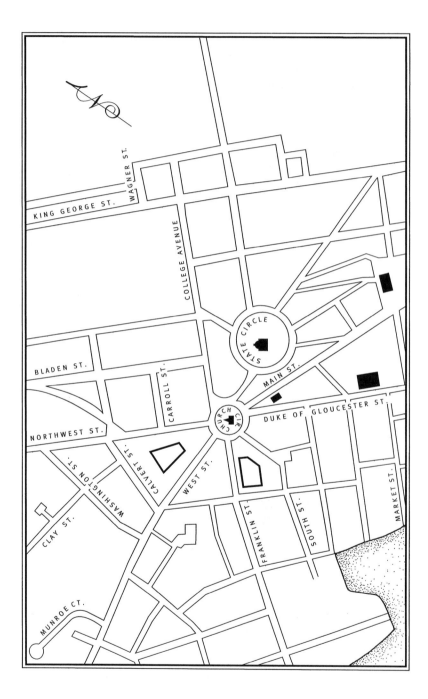

Court was a group of 25 connected frame homes rented by African Americans in the block interior bounded by West, Calvert, and Northwest Streets. The block neighbors Church Circle, one of Annapolis' two central circles, and is roughly a quarter mile from the Maryland State House. The construction of Gott's Court began shortly after February 1907, when "contractor Charles W. Jess, who has just finished a house for Mr. David Klawansky and for Mr. Louis Baer, has contracted to build twelve houses for Messrs. Gott and Meredith on the large vacant lot between West and Northwest streets" ("Building in Progress," 1907). Winston Gott purchased Casey Meredith's share of the 12 West Street houses in 1907, and a 1909 assessment of the parcel was the first reference to the community as Gott's Court (Russo 1987:8). In 1910, 23 households were listed as tenants of Gott's Court, all African American. Of 18 families living at the Court a decade later, only two addresses included the same occupants. The court consisted of two rows of two-story frame houses that faced an open dirt area on which families gathered, children played, and cars were parked (Figure 4). Each unit had an enclosed back yard area with an outhouse (Figure 5). The use of such privies well into the twentieth century was not particularly uncommon in Annapolis; a 1938 Housing Authority study reported that 27% of all homes in the city had no indoor plumbing (Brown 1994:23–24; cf. Home Owners' Loan Corporation 1941). Various households put in their own electricity, which was not provided by the Gotts. In the 1938 study, only 13% of homes in Annapolis did not have electricity. Each unit at Gott's Court was a two-level four-room plan with internal pumped water and either a wood, coal, or gas heat source. African Americans lived in the units until 1952, when Gott's son sold the Court to the city and the buildings were razed for a parking lot. Today a parking deck sits where the Court was located.

"IF WE WERE BLACK": THE POLITICS OF NAMING

Racists and antiracists alike have constructed a variety of terms to describe various groups. A 1879 *Maryland Republican and State Capital Advertiser* editorial defended the most hateful racist labeling, but the editorialist's raw malice is symptomatic of how many Whites

←————————————————————————————————————

Figure 3. After the mid-nineteenth century, many African-American Annapolitans settled in neighborhoods off West Street, including Gott's Court (outlined in block bordered by West, Calvert, and Northwest Streets) and the Courthouse Site community (outlined in block bordered by Franklin, Calvert, and South Streets) (courtesy of Amy E. Grey).

Figure 4. Looking into Gott's Court, circa 1940 (courtesy of James E. Bean Jr., Family Photo Collection).

attempted to contain Black subjectivity through language. The paper lampooned African Americans who asked to be called "colored" instead of "Negro" or its diminutive "nigger," because

> The word nigger is immortalized in a thousand songs that awaken kindly and tender thoughts of the darkey. The plaintive melodies dwell in our ears. And the nigger lives on their sympathetic strains. If we were black we would insist on being called a nigger (" 'Niggers,'" 1879)

The recent collapse of Reconstruction may have emboldened the editors to publish such hyperbole, but the anonymous editorial brazenly demonstrates that certain racial labels lent a distinct inflection to Black subjectivity. The *Republican* editor betrayed an anxiety that calling African Americans "colored" would impart a different social status than the paper wished to ascribe through other terms. With ridicule, the editorialist mused, "Colored papers! Just think of it! Colored papers! And we read about Colored bands, Colored schools, Colored votes, and all kinds of colored things." Indeed, the construction of new racial labels like "colored" reflected an increasingly adamant African-American attempt to portray themselves as Americans with rights and aspirations.

Figure 5. Gott's Court backyard, 1939 (courtesy of the Maryland State Archives; Special Collections, Annapolis, I Remember Collection, MSA SC 2140-104).

This was a chilling notion to many Whites, and they responded with chilling language and violence.

"White" is itself as much of a construction as "Black." Both were well-understood identities by the turn of the century, despite the instability of their meanings. Generally "White" refers to WASPs and "Black" refers to African diaspora, but there is no universal link between ethnicity, skin color, and racial subjectivity. In various times and places, Blackness and Whiteness alike have had a vast range of definitions and sociopolitical implications, though they always have had some connection to one another. The diverse social applications of both typically attempt to conceal the instability of racial subjectivity, the vast conflict within each subject position, and the precariousness of White supremacy. Both terms appear throughout this study as they were, and still are, used; that is, as social constructions, rather than reified racial truths or monolithic references to all WASPs or African Americans. I use the labels Black, White, and Mulatto in instances where period commentators defined social differences in those racial terms. I have capitalized Black and White to emphasize that I am attempting to use those terms in a way that is consistent, but not in agreement, with their dominant usage.

I have referred to African diaspora in the Americas with the label African Americans. This, too, is a diverse subject position, and it should not be read as a monolith of its own. It is a provisionally collective subject position that recognizes that many Americans of African descent share both real and perceived cultural associations and historical experiences, and not merely spatial or cultural points of origination. Using the term "African American" provides a concept to recognize shared social and cultural subjectivity, but it is not intended to ignore vast cultural, class, gendered, and social variation within African America.

RACE AND CONSUMPTION

Rather than reduce consumption to a series of marketing transactions of symbolically insipid goods, this book examines how consumption was an African-American sociopolitical statement of civil aspirations, material desires, and resistance to monolithic racist caricatures. Many African Americans viewed consumption as a significant symbolic and concrete privilege that augured a possible progression in African-American labor and civil privileges. In some cases the hope vested in consumption was idealistic or naive, yet consumer space offered precious possibilities for African-American socioeconomic self-determination.

Consumer ideologues viewed Black and American as profoundly incongruous identities, yet African-American consumers labored to demonstrate that they could be both Black and American. This book probes the illusion of essential racial subjects and examines the process by which consumers used material culture to see themselves as, or opposed to, racial subjectivities. Rich with symbolic possibilities and carrying the tacit promises of citizenship, material goods provided a seemingly innocuous, yet meaningful, mechanism to reposition African Americans in opposition to racialized inequalities. At the same time, African Americans defied the racist connotations ideologues labored to impress on commodities and consumer spaces, creating a distinctly African-American symbolism out of ostensibly "White" commodities. To overlook how a racialized consumer society attempted to materialize White supremacy—and to evade how African America resisted that marginalization—is to ignore one of the most fundamental aspects of American consumer culture.

The Politicization and Politics of African-American Consumption | 2

In 1852, the Democratic party met in Baltimore to nominate a Presidential candidate. Held in the midst of complex party and regional conflict, the convention and the years leading up to it were symptomatic of deepseated national divisions on the eve of the Civil War. Certainly the most profound impact of those regional economic, social, and political divisions was the ensuing national conflict, yet these 1850s divisions shaped the sociopolitical position of African Americans well into the twentieth century. By the eve of the Baltimore Convention, now-familiar racist attitudes regarding African America's labor marginalization, citizenship, and relationship to other Americans were outlined or assembled. By midcentury, the Democrats, their political competitors, and the authors and audiences of popular racial discourses had begun to forge a powerful, lasting vision of Black Americans that attempted to deny African Americans White-exclusive privileges in labor, consumption, and public space.

The nation's midcentury dissension smoldered within the Democratic party's own ranks. Material, social, and partisan conflict boiled to the surface in the mid-1840s, when regional factions jockeying for political supremacy and economic influence battled over the legal status of slavery in territories acquired during the Mexican War. In 1846, before the Mexican War even ended, a circle of northern congressmen, led by Pennsylvania Representative David Wilmot, proposed that slaveholding be prohibited in territories acquired during the war. Bitterly attacked by Southerners, the Wilmot Proviso died in the Senate, but it unleashed a pitched political and popular debate over slavery, labor, economics, and regional influence. Crystallized by the proposal's near-victory, a faction of disaffected Northern Democrats and Whigs defected in 1848 to form the Free-Soil party. By advocating the landholding rights of "Free Labor" over the political power of slave states, the Free Soilers' antislavery sentiments magnified White working-class interests and pushed racially based labor and citizen rights ever-closer to the surface of partisan political discourse (Fogel 1989:346).

Some of the deserting Free Soilers returned to the Democratic party before the Baltimore Convention, persuaded by a string of measures intended to soothe regional hostilities (e.g., the Compromise of 1850; Holt 1992:72). Despite their return to the Democratic fold, the Free Soilers' secession infuriated proslavery Southern Democrats and alienated Northern Democrats who were cool to slavery but hostile to abolition. When these deeply divided Democrats arrived in Baltimore in the miserably hot Chesapeake summer of June 1852, none of the warring factions' candidates could garner sufficient votes to secure the nomination. On the 35th ballot, Franklin Pierce's name was submitted for consideration. An affable, albeit mediocre, New Hampshire lawyer who had served in the House and Senate, Pierce was a potentially acceptable compromise to Northern and Southern factions alike. Pierce openly abhorred abolitionists and championed Southern interests, convictions that secured critical backing from Southern Democrats. His New England party boss training and congeniality swayed sufficient Northern support. On the 49th ballot, Pierce received the party's nomination.

Pierce campaign operatives distributed a plethora of ribbons, medals, and various Franklin Pierce knickknacks to drum up the vote. Among these was a redware pipe recovered in excavations at the Maynard-Burgess House (Figure 6). The pipe proclaiming Pierce's 1852 Presidential run was recovered from the earliest layers of household refuse the Maynards discarded into their Duke of Gloucester Street back yard. Around the home's back door the Maynards deposited food remains, broken ceramic dishes, and domestic discards that were preserved by the construction of a rear addition between 1874 and 1877. The pipe itself was made and marketed as a partisan political symbol,

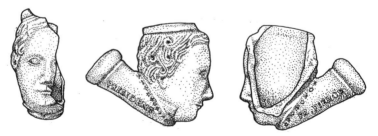

Figure 6. 1852 Franklin Pierce campaign redware pipe (courtesy of Amy E. Grey).

but it, and all of the artifacts under the addition, were politicized in the sense that their meaning was contested across discourses and groups (Fraser 1989:166). This definition of politicization expands on the narrow partisan notion of institutional public politics, and recognizes that subjects can be politicized in many forms and relationships and contested in seemingly innocuous material forms. The bottles, plates, bones, and other debris alongside the pipe reflected and mediated profound contradictions in the construction of African Americans as laborers, consumers, and citizens, inevitably politicizing their consumption.

This chapter examines the politicization of African-American consumption in artifacts ranging from the Franklin Pierce pipe to apparently mundane bottles, buttons, and other prosaic goods. Archaeologists appreciate that objects like the pipe are relatively meaningless curiosities if they are interpreted in isolation from broader social processes or outside their archaeological context. To be interpreted as *politicized* objects, it is necessary to define the relationship between goods in the assemblage and in the broader social context using a series of concepts outlined in this chapter. The chapter first discusses the Pierce pipe and two other pieces of partisan material culture from the Maynard-Burgess rear assemblage that illustrate the complex politicization of African-American consumption. The following section confronts the implications of politicized consumption and whether there actually was an African-American politics based on consumption. I then examine how consumption should be viewed as a process that attempts to mediate social contradictions and express social and personal desires. Such a definition of consumption envisions it as a social negotiation focused on desire, rather than a static reflection of essential identity, the result of imposed conditions, or a utilitarian need for material objects. The chapter outlines how the book defines desire, material symbolism, and agency in ways that frame consumption as a complex social and personal process. This approach to consumption requires rethinking any sort of essential identity that precedes material symbolism, a status often granted to cultural identity. I examine the dilemma of even unintentionally reducing material symbolism to a "natural" cultural identity, and suggest how this study integrates a clear, anti-essentialist understanding of power relations and subjectivity. The chapter concludes with an examination of how social position, defined as both conscious experience and dominant structure, can frame an interpretation of consumption that avoids essentialism, confronts the role of desire, recognizes the dynamism of consumption, and acknowledges the complex politicization of African-American materialism.

PARTISAN POLITICS AND AFRICAN-AMERICAN
MATERIAL POLITICIZATION

The Pierce pipe is politicized in a number of senses, providing both an interesting partisan political insight and a socially politicized commentary by free African-American consumers. African-American Marylanders like John Maynard could not vote in 1852, as could no American women, but the denial of voting privileges certainly did not render John and Maria Maynard disinterested in partisan politics. Increasingly stringent state laws regulating free African Americans clearly emphasized the Maynards' stake in the upcoming election, and it would have been difficult for any American to overlook bitter regional debates surrounding the 1852 contest (cf. Berlin 1974:210). A quandary in interpreting the pipe's partisan symbolism is that if African Americans had been conceded the vote, they would seem unlikely to support Pierce: The competition definitely was not racially enlightened, but Pierce was a vocal champion of Southern slaveholding interests and a vicious critic of abolitionists (Bilotta 1992; Freehling 1984:228). Pierce carried Maryland as part of a resounding electoral college victory, but the pipe trumpeted a campaign that lacked any substantial focus and an administration whose only legacy was the ill-conceived 1854 Kansas–Nebraska Act (Fogel 1989:342-343; Freehling 1984:232).

To complicate this interpretive quandary, the molded likeness of Pierce was found in a deposit with a striking juxtaposition of partisan material culture. The same deposit bearing the pipe contained an intact glass flask manufactured by New Jersey's Spring Garden Glass Works between 1851 and 1856 (McKearnin and Wilson 1978:666) (Figure 7). Mid-nineteenth century glass flasks often were embossed with socially charged symbols or political motifs, ranging from George Washington to Masonic shields. The Maynard flask was molded with a log cabin, a motif that surfaced in popular iconography in the 1840s, when Whigs introduced local log-cabin headquarters that stocked a barrel of hard cider for the party faithful (Fischer 1988:38). Log cabins often appeared on Whig campaign material culture as well as mass-produced objects, and the Maynard rear assemblage also included a second Whig campaign trinket, an 1840 William Henry Harrison campaign medalet (Figure 8). Emblazoned with a log cabin and cider barrel, the medalet heralded Harrison's victorious 1840 Presidential campaign (Holt 1992:170).

In their partisan symbolism and oblique politicization, these three artifacts illustrate the complex politics of African-American consumption. On the one hand, these artifacts were symbols that evoked partisan principles with which a person became allied through consumption.

Figure 7. Whig log cabin motif on flask produced by Spring Garden Glass Works, New Jersey, 1851–1856 (courtesy of Amy E. Grey).

Reducing these objects simply to institutional political displays is problematic, however, because it limits their symbolism to the contrived coherence of party platforms in an anti-Black political system. If we only consider partisan positioning, the attraction of these objects to free African Americans is somewhat mystifying: Despite significant policy differences, the Whigs and Democrats alike harbored no meaningful antiracist attitudes (Evitts 1974:21–22; Smith 1989:30). Once the most powerful party in southern Maryland politics, the Whigs were disintegrating as a state and national power by the time these objects were discarded. The party failed to respond to slavery when it emerged as the nation's most pressing partisan issue, and southern Maryland Whigs

Figure 8. 1840 William Henry Harrison campaign medalet (courtesy of Amy E. Grey).

swung to Pierce and the Democrats in 1852 and for years to come. Clearly, no midcentury political party harbored significant favor for African America or conceived of African Americans as an audience for their party designs.

On the other hand, the Maynards' partisan artifacts reflect a host of aspirations that were utterly politicized, yet had only a tenuous attachment to specific partisan positions. Rather than simply reflecting identification with Whig or Democratic sentiments, these tokens denoted measures of genuine nationalism, idealistic identification with the political process, and aspirations to participate as citizens. This interpretation of the Maynards' political artifacts casts their consumption as an effort to satisfy social and personal desires and negotiate contradictions, such as that between the Maynards' freedom and their incongruous denial of voters' privileges. These artifacts bespeak a desire for American citizenry rights, as well as a somewhat conflicted effort to mediate or ignore the racist contradictions in partisan politics.

This politicization of consumption places desire and the negotiation of social contradiction at the heart of consumption, rather than the satisfaction of material need. In contrast, the most conventional archaeological interpretation of the Maynard artifacts would reduce these objects to their functions (e.g., a pipe consumed for smoking) and unambiguous historical associations (e.g., display of Whig politics). Perhaps the Maynards were oblivious to some of the partisan symbolism in these artifacts, but the notion that African Americans consumed such objects purely for functional utility stripped of ideological weight and social symbolism is difficult to fathom. It is equally unlikely that the Maynards simply reproduced Whig and Democratic symbolism wholesale.

More importantly, African Americans could not evade the utter politicization of every element of their lives: No African-American right or public behavior was not impressed by racist obstacles and demeaning racial assumptions. All material consumption and symbolism inevitably negotiated racism, and such negotiation could have various sorts of politicized tenors. Reducing these objects to curious functional trinkets evades the significance of African-American meanings, and it denies how African America's deep-seated politicized social consciousness was shaped and reflected in material consumption. The issue is not *if* African-American consumption was political; instead, the question at the heart of this book is *how* different consumption tactics were political.

POLITICIZING CONSUMER CULTURE: THE POLITICS OF CONSUMPTION, OR THE CONSUMPTION OF POLITICS?

It is not particularly radical to suggest that material consumption is politicized in the sense that material meanings are points of contention that can contest power relations, fuel oppositional perceptions of subjectivity, or simply register discontent. Indeed, we can attribute some inchoate, if not conscious, politicization to virtually all consumption, regardless of whether it is conducted in modern commodity trade, nascent capitalist marketing, or any other exchange system for that matter. Yet it is quite another thing to argue that consumption itself is a politics, a practice that constitutes the public articulation and realization of a polity's shared interests. That is, beyond disagreement over material symbolism or consumers' critique of dominant social structure, precisely how can consumption itself provide the grounds for a concrete alternative social formation? Can consumption itself frame a tangible morals and philosophy to restructure society? This is a critical question: It is one thing to argue that African Americans foresaw social possibilities or critiqued power relations in consumption, but it is considerably more momentous to ascribe African-American consumption the status of sociopolitical alternative.

The question of consumption's political dimensions has been most articulately framed by Jean-Christophe Agnew (1990:15–16). Agnew does not question the fundamental shift in American mass culture that has occurred since the 1920s and, like many other historians, he sees materialism at the heart of such change. Warren Susman (1984) provides perhaps the most eloquent and influential insight into emergent consumer culture, arguing that from roughly the 1920s to World War

II the masses redefined the "American way of life" by focusing national identity on commodities. Various adaptations of Susman's basic insight cogently argue that Americans invested fundamental sociocultural values in a mass consumer culture whose vision of citizenship focused on commodity consumption (e.g., Cohen 1990; Curtis 1991; Denning 1987; Edsforth 1987; Fox and Lears 1983; Levine 1993:222–224). Yet, as Agnew (1990:16) argues, the polity envisioned by consumers was at best abstract; consumer culture placed consumption privileges at the focus of citizenship and at least obliquely criticized existing inequalities, but consumption ultimately has provided no alternative to the state. Consumption influenced our visions of who we may be, how we may fit into society, and even our civic consciousness, but it has not articulated a dramatically new polity. Consumption has been moralized and philosophized, but it seems unlikely to constitute a morals or philosophy unto itself.

If anything, focusing civil rights on consumption was a somewhat conservative, or even reactionary, political statement. For instance, Ronald Edsforth's (1987:223–224) study of consumption in Flint, Michigan concludes (as Susman did) that labor unrest after World War I often focused on securing employer and state commitments to protect working-class laborers' material consumption rights. Such strikes did not threaten to erect a socialist or egalitarian state in the space once occupied by consumer capitalism: Instead, they attempted to fortify labor privileges that protected workers' consumption. Even in the depths of the Depression, most working-class Americans remained deeply committed to the fiction of mass material affluence. Positioning consumption at the heart of collective social interests did not replace the state; if anything, it threatened to expand a producer class' power within a consumer state.

The expansion of consumer rights in visions of American citizenship—and the genuine politicization and politics of such consumption—raises several quandaries. First, why might African-American Annapolitans, in particular, and marginalized Americans, in general, have placed material consumption at the heart of their visions of citizenship? This question demands a close look at labor, social, and racist dynamics, that is, an examination of the historical contours of inequality that influenced how and why African Americans envisioned consumer space as politicized, if not political.

Second, this inquiry must probe how race constrained and enabled particular forms of radical, as well as reactionary, political action (cf. Gilroy 1987:246). We cannot dismiss race, despite its biological artificiality, and race cannot be reduced only to disempowering constraints or one collective form of African-American political agency. In the late nineteenth century, the historical confluence of Reconstruction optimism's collapse, the rapid expansion of consumer space, and the ascent of Jim Crow produced distinctive Black subjectivities and political tactics. We need to examine how Black racial subjectivities—specifically African-American resistance to them—enabled a rich range of African-American political agency in defiance of White racism, just as race and racism circumvented and defused other types of African-American politics.

Third, what was the genuine impact of African-American material consumption? Did African-American Annapolitans formulate any tangible sociopolitical alternatives in consumer space? Or, as Agnew suggests, is consumption more clearly politicized in another sense, offering less a concrete civic option than a consciousness-raising space? Scholars most often have studied politics as an emancipatory movement focused on the dissolution of structural inequalities. African Americans certainly formulated cohesive, formally organized material movements that conform to this notion of political formation, such as consumer boycotts and African-American business collectives. However, it would be shortsighted to neglect the utterly politicized social agency that disparate African-American consumers wielded against racism, even if that resistance appears spontaneous or lacking collective structure. Peter Lunt and Sonia Livingstone (1992:169) suggest expanding our vision of politicization by combining Anthony Giddens' (1991:214) concept of "life politics" with the conventional definition of emancipatory politics. Lunt and Livingstone define Giddens' life politics as the process by which ordinary consumers articulate "challenge not through protest but through taking control of the shape of their own lives in the negotiation of their personal identities." This vision of politicization assumes that individuals' negotiation of subjectivity has broad sociopolitical influence through its continual mediation of conflicting personal, collective, institutional, and state interests. Rather than assume the powerless isolation of individual African-American consumers (or, conversely, search for a universal class collective), we need to appreciate the myriad forms political agency may take.

There certainly is little indication that African-American consumption in Annapolis was a consciously calculated collective strategy that articulated goals pursued over time. Agnew argues that consumption itself never really was a coherent political activity for any Americans, so it is not surprising that we would be hard-pressed to divine an African-American political movement forged in the name of material consumption. Nevertheless, African-American consumption was a sig-

nificant patchwork of reinscribed dominant meanings and local innova-
tions with genuine, albeit diffuse, sociopolitical impact. This politicized
patchwork defended African Americans against racism and appropriated a variety of real and perceived opportunities in defiance of racialized labor structure, partisan political marginalization, and the ever-
present impress of public racism. Together these forces fashioned a
backdrop that attempted to circumscribe African-American rights and
aspirations and to demonstrate the racial exclusivity of citizenship. It
was against such forces and their construction of White racial privilege
that African-American consumer tactics were directed.

MATERIAL SYMBOLISM, SOCIAL
SUBJECTIVITY, AND CONSUMER AGENCY

Like every other object discussed in this study, the Maynard-
Burgess campaign trinkets were situated within particular consumers'
visions of society and their relationship both in and against that society.
Material consumption of objects like this partisan material culture,
critiques, masks, and resolves contradictions by invoking empowering
social possibilities. Consumption focuses on the daydreaming desire
that fans social aspiration and critique alike and distances consumers
from marginalization, though the distance is often more perceived than
real.

This definition of consumption departs from one that sees it as the
reproduction of essential identities lying beneath the surface of material symbolism. Like most social scientists, historical archaeologists
typically see material culture as a reflection of identity, which on its
surface seems a reasonable enough conclusion. In this vision of the
material world, objects mirror internal identities that are solidified,
accentuated, or masked by objects. This approach to material symbolism probably is best illustrated by various forms of structuralist analysis, such as James Deetz's (1990) argument that landscape similarities
throughout the Anglo colonial world reflect a bedrock English cultural
character (cf. Deetz 1977). This assumes that individuals have a coherent internal identity of some sort—be it cultural, ethnic, economic,
gendered, or whatever—that archaeologists are *really* studying when
they study material culture. However, the material world provides no
self-evident reflections of individual consumers' internal identity attributes, as though "who we are" is either mirrored or conferred by
particular objects. Quite the opposite, consumers use material culture to

imagine new social possibilities, mediate lived contradictions, and envision new personal pleasures, posing new relationships between consumers and society and portraying who we *wish* to be. Objects embody
relationships between producers and consumers, future and past, and
Black and White, but they are not mirrors for "real" identities. At the
same time, consumption is not a way in which shoppers instrumentally
fabricate identities; instead, it is an idealized, situational vision of social
possibilities and personal pleasures that consumers believe can be realized or entertained by possessing material goods (Campbell 1987:118;
Wylie 1996:441). Consequently, it is infeasible, on the one hand, to
reduce objects simply to reflective or mimetic mechanisms or, on the
other, to accord them absolute power to forge identity. Object symbolism
instead negotiates and reflects contradictions confronting a consumer,
so a fundamental dimension of material symbolism can only be defined
by probing the contradictions that shape particular consumers' lives.
    This paints a vision of material symbolism as thoroughly mercurial,
imaginative, local, and non-essential. Rather than see material symbolism as a mimetic representation of identity, an instrumental construction of self, or a mere satisfaction of "needs," consumers negotiate desire
and social position in a perpetually incomplete mediation of a host of
lived and structural contradictions. Race (or any other totalizing subject
category) is not a mechanism to explain material symbolism; on the
contrary, these identities are the problems to be explained.
    Archaeologists harbor a deep-seated sentiment that material sym-
bolism is circumscribed by the physical properties of objects (e.g., form,
function) and the intent of producers and marketing systems (e.g.,
maximization of profit). The physical attributes of an object, systemic
function, and intended use loosely circumscribe the symbolic possibilities of that object, but for the most part form and function do not
impose particularly profound limitations on meaning. An anthropological study of material symbolism should not fixate on how the object *itself*
limits meaning; put that way, analysis minimizes how consumers constitute a material object's social properties. Inquiry instead should
examine how social discourses enable and limit consumers' fabrication
of meanings; for example, what racial "truths" allowed particular Victorian Americans to define African-American and White materialism in
distinct ways?; or, how was affluence defined, what sorts of promises did
advertisers of affluence make, and how might such definitions and
promises have affected the materialism of various consumers?
    Rather than focus on the social contradictions that allow consumers
to divine a range of meanings in particular mass-produced goods, his-

torical archaeologists have labored to pin down the definitions of objects. For American historical archaeologists, price itself has been the single most important criteria constraining material symbolism. The central dilemma of this focus is that it implies that exchange value is the appropriate model for material symbolism and social relations, a perspective capitalists certainly have always championed. The most mechanical of these economically driven "status" approaches simply reduce artifact values to monolithic mechanisms that can be used to divine the objective relationships between consumers in an integrated hierarchical socioeconomic system (Paynter 1990:54). In such thinking, it is assumed that consumers primarily employed material objects in competitive envy displays of economic status, displays that focus on the assumed prestige of possessing costly or rare commodities (cf. Campbell 1987:49–50). Yet the suggestion that consumers in a coherent market system share a touchstone symbolism of any sort is highly debatable: Even costly material assemblages variously could signify self-determination, overcompensation, militant resistance, class legitimization, deceitful affectation, or any number of things.

The notion that objects can have a range of possible meanings is known as multivalence; that is, objects assume meanings drawn from a circumscribed range of symbolic possibilities (Perry and Paynter 1999; Tilley 1989; Wylie 1996:436–442). The range of meanings an object can assume changes over time and can differ from one consumption space to another, but it is always socially grounded and genuinely limited to some extent by physical form. Consequently, objects cannot mean anything: Even the most idiosyncratic material meanings are circumscribed by broader discourse, material form, and social structure. Yet multivalence emphasizes that there is no essential symbolic meaning that "proper" archaeological method inevitably will identify (cf. Rorty 1989).

Despite this slightly retooled definition of material symbolism, I do not diverge from standardized functional and stylistic descriptive conventions in any serious way: The minimum vessel counts, morphological descriptions of objects, minimum number of individual techniques, artifact categories, and methods in this book are standard fare. However, I have taken Christopher Tilley's (1990:333–334) suggestion to describe material objects' contradictory details and illuminate the incongruities between assemblages and social assumptions. This compels us to confront the multivalent meanings that various objects could assume. Such an approach may make for a somewhat more taxing read, but we should not expect to reduce the lives of real people to simplistic prose and preconceived patterns dictated by cookie-cutter research designs.

Desire and Consumer Subjectivity

My framing of consumption stresses the centrality of desire. Certainly, a dimension of consumption addresses concrete utilitarian purposes, and some consumers may acquire certain goods as a mechanism to realize a specific identity represented by particular material culture (e.g., a costly object that displays economic wealth). Most consumption, however, rotates around relatively inchoate desires that negotiate or envision new material meanings and social possibilities. Desires are defined here as socially conditioned, contextually distinctive, and idealistic aspirations played out in all material consumption (cf. Campbell 1987:89). As such, it is a misnomer to reduce consumer desire simply to an effort to address a "need" of some utilitarian or psychological sort. Consumer desire is not simply a never-ending cycle of articulating wants that are then satisfied with objects; it also cannot be reduced to conscious idealization that inevitably leads to disillusion because those ideals cannot be realized by goods. Instead, desire articulates social contradictions in a way that mediates, attempts to reconcile, or appears to resolve incongruities (cf. Brottman 1997:46). This mediation process occurs as consumers visualize and attempt to articulate new possibilities that will be secured through consumption, regardless of whether those possibilities are explicitly or vaguely articulated, plausible, or of grand or modest scale. We certainly should be skeptical of the genuine resolutions worked by consumption or consumers' capacity to articulate social contradiction simply through material goods. However, if we reduce consumption's significance merely to its capacity to satisfy utilitarian need, instrumentally transform social structure, or realize specific conscious goals, then we likely will reduce it to either the most hollow symbolism or self-destructive false consciousness. The "authentic" meaning of an object and its capacity to actually satisfy desires are essentially inconsequential, if not themselves illusory; what is significant is consumers' *belief* that an object will realize or contribute to some idealization when it is consumed. An archaeological analysis of consumption will illuminate the social contradictions that consumers negotiate, the social and individual aspirations reflected in certain consumption tactics, and why particular goods become vehicles for desire.

It is critical to link African-American consumer desire to broad struggles over the contradictions of racial subjectivity. That is, rather than simply refine the definition of African-American material patterns, we should scrutinize how such patterns were part of the construction and contestation of African-American racial subjectivity. I use the term "construction" because race is not a "natural" identity: Racial subjec-

tivities are forged to serve particular groups and mask social contradictions, a process that inevitably contests, limits, and expands the social
opportunities of various groups. There have been numerous disabling,
ambiguous, and empowering racial subjectivities over time, as there
have been shifting gender, cultural, or regional subjectivities whose
instability reflects the power relations within which identities are forged and resisted. This framing of subjectivity assumes that material
conditions and power relations form a context in which people negotiate
identities; those subjectivities are neither essential nor imposed, and
they cannot be reduced to either a disempowering or empowering status
(cf. Lunt and Livingstone 1992:24).

African-American struggles addressed personal desires and secured social opportunities in defiance of dominant Black subjectivity.
That approach places African-American agency against racism at the
center of analysis, but this is not agency simply in the sense of inten-
tional decision-making by individuals or collectives. Dissecting individual decisions is, at best, difficult to begin with; perhaps more significantly, fixating on conscious intentions hazards ignoring that all
seemingly autonomous decisions are shaped by social conventions that
structure possible forms of agency. Agency is active decision-making in
which the "truths" informing decisions (e.g., racial "truths") are themselves contradictory constructs that are not always self-evident or
clearly defined, so they often are assumed without self-reflexive contemplation. At the same time, they routinely are dismantled or radically
revised when their contradictions are recognized.

Cultural Organicism and Cultural Construction

A rethinking of the nature of material symbolism initially must
confront the prevalent assumption of a monolithic, clearly defined cultural identity that precedes such symbolism. Archaeology tends to mirror
most social sciences' romanticized notion of cultures as neatly bounded
homogenous entities that determine social and material meaning (cf.
Handsman 1995; Howson 1990; Wolf 1982). Robert Schuyler (1988:40),
for instance, captures this perspective quite clearly when he argues that
"culture comes to us in history in the form of 'packages,' functional
units with temporal and spatial boundaries." The dilemmas in similar
definitions of culture and material symbolism are clearly reflected in
African-American archaeology. Since the 1960s, historical archaeologists have been keen to demonstrate enslaved African-Americans' cultural integrity in the face of overwhelming domination. The most visible
thread of such research in African-American archaeology has focused on

"Africanisms," practices derived from African cultures. This archae-ological research provides unique insight into the common historical experiences of African Americans. Yet lingering anthropological roman-ticism for cultural "tradition"—and a wariness of consumer goods' meaninglessness—have produced an unbalanced and slightly contrived focus on African cultural practices and craft goods.

Leland Ferguson's (1992) examination of colonoware and its link to African cultural traditions is among the most articulate and persuasive of the archaeological studies of African cultural persistence in the New World. A low-fired, unglazed earthenware found on southeastern sites associated with African Americans, colonoware has been identified by Ferguson as a tangible indication of African cultural continuity. Like most scholars examining African culture in the New World, Ferguson certainly acknowledges change, or what Anne Yentsch (1994:302) calls "accommodation on both sides." Curiously, though, the vast majority of Africanism studies include no systematic examination of power rela-tions. Like many historical archaeologists, Ferguson's celebration of anonymous cultural agents attempts to counter sociological analyses that vest determining power in social totalities and dominant ideology. For Ferguson, domination is a given whose efficacy is overestimated: Even with the leverage of overwhelming oppression, society can never utterly rob individuals of agency and cultural integrity.

Though its underlying intellectual position is generally unstated, Robert Paynter (1990:53) argues that Africanisms research typically implies that White "hegemony over Afro-Americans impoverishes the surface features of the Afro-American material assemblage but leaves its essential structure unaltered." Paynter suggests that this "cultural-ist" position assumes a more-or-less unchanging cultural conservatism in the face of vast material change, as though a unique African always lurks within archaeological assemblages. Some archaeologists in this "culturalist" vein even argue that the discipline has exaggerated the impress of racism, as though racism simply produces a monolithic African-American powerlessness and material pattern (e.g., De Cunzo 1998:52).

Terrence Epperson (1990:35) argues that such archaeologies tend to reduce African-American agency to either autonomous African-American cultural practice or complete assimilation. Epperson argues that "over-emphasizing the autonomy of slave culture runs the risk of mystifying relations of power" and reifying the same separations that planters constructed in racialized social practice and material culture. A fixation on Africanisms without a clear confrontation of power rela-tions risks portraying African-American culture as an "organic" entity separable from the context in which it is expressed and constantly reworked. This predominant definition of African-American culture is organic in the sense that it is cast as an object with clearly defined and continuous roots in space and time, from preslavery Africa to plantation quarters. Theresa Singleton (1995:133) voices a comparable concern that archaeologists' single-minded quest for African continuities provides little or no means to probe African-American subjectivity's "discontinuity and reconfiguration." Instead of confronting racism and material domination, a considerable volume of archaeology examines euphemistic diffusion processes that either discount or evade the compromise and reformulation essential to negotiate inequality (cf. Shanks 1996:389). Dell Upton (1996:3) likewise approaches the search for material "authenticity" as an artifact of classic visions of bounded, organic culture, but he also faults the fixation on Africanisms on archaeologists' own unexamined compulsions to "find" a unique African-American culture (cf. Blakey 1997).

Along similar lines, Charles Orser (1996:32) argues that the dilemma lies in the presumption of culture as a preexisting reality, rather than ever-unfolding social relationships that constitute broad subjectivities we heuristically label "cultures." Orser advocates framing mechanically defined cultural research in more complex, "mutualistic" terms that conceive of society as chains of social relationships with a variety of local subjectivities. These cascading chains represent the active negotiation of power relations, not essential cultural identities surfacing in disconnected localities.

Essential cultural identity poses a significant quandary in the interpretation of mass-produced objects: In an interpretive model that views meanings emanating from culture, objects tend to be reduced to vastly different exotic goods or familiar goods produced and given a monolithic collective meaning by the dominant group. This reduces objects like colonoware to "authentic" artifacts counterposed to "artificial" commodities, with no concession to the vast range of meanings in between, or to the overlap between seemingly distinct types of goods (cf. Eagleton 1990:326).

Artifacts' meanings are not cultural any more than they are racial, even though they can be constructed as such by producers, ideologues, marketers, consumers, and even archaeologists. Ensconced at the center of African-American archaeological inquiry, cultural identity distills African-American subjectivity into a constellation of unique practices and traits shaped by an unrecognized cultural mindset and looming as a contrived source of all meaning. In effect, culture has become the fundamental tool archaeologists use to interpret African America, not the subject that the discipline aspires to explain. Culture is not what determined the meaning of African-American consumption; culture was the ever-evolving product of African Americans forging individual and social desires and negotiating racialized social structure. This negotiation continually reproduced, modified, and jettisoned preexisting practices, appropriated dominant practices, and focused upon tactical concerns of the moment. The complexity of changes in African-American subjectivity demands that we confront African America's unique social position in consumer space and conceptualize how African-American consumers stood in relation to dominant structure and a distinctive African-American cultural subjectivity.

COMPLICATING SOCIAL POSITION: CONSCIOUS EXPERIENCE AND DOMINANT STRUCTURE

Material symbolism is shaped by consumers' social position, which has two fundamental dimensions, loosely described as conscious and structural. First, social position is a conscious apprehension of the relationship between an individual, social collective (e.g., Blacks, African America), and society. Second, it is a location within a dominant structural formation that has various local manifestations but cannot be wholly apprehended (e.g., capitalist economics, world systems, class relations). Explicitly framing social position this way can, on the one hand, recognize group and individual experience, and on the other, acknowledge the structural conditions that shape local conditions and inform how that experience is perceived and articulated.

Social position can be traced to no isolable source in ideology, cultural mindsets, essential human nature, or individual perception. Michael Shanks (1996:390) develops a comparable conception of the relationship between individual agency and structure, arguing that any interpretation of material culture cannot be subsumed to dominant social processes or entirely separated from those processes. In historical archaeology, thought on how social position is determined tends to take one of two polarized forms that revolve around the sway of dominant groups. Some theorists place primary influence on social formations in the hands of classes and material processes (e.g., marketing) whose interests are reproduced through, for instance, systemic domination (e.g., South 1977) or ideologies (e.g., Leone 1984). For such thinkers, the enigmas of everyday resistance and individual agency are relatively insignificant factors upon dominant social structure. Indeed, scattered

negotiation of dominant interests tends to figure as static, with relatively little clear impression on the overall social formation. In contrast,
other archaeologists eager to valorize ordinary folk focus on difference
and resistance in order to defuse the implication that ideology or dominant systems impose identity or a "false" consciousness that effaces self-
identity (e.g., Beaudry et al. 1991). The critique of ideology is a crucial
corrective to the most deterministic definitions of social position, but
such criticisms tend to overcompensate for systems' apparently totalizing
determination of human agency; that is, they risk casting subjectivity as
mystically springing from some internal nature (e.g., ethnicity), or else
they pose it as a self-construction.

Most scholars have scrapped the vulgar vision of ideology as a
"false" identity imposed by class-interested ideologues. Generally, dominant ideology refers to prevalent discourses like racism that are rooted
in material inequality and tend to reproduce that inequality by distort-
ing competing groups' social interests (cf. Little 1996:56–58; Mullins
1998). The question is whether a "real" social identity is concealed by
ideological systems; that is, are there objective identities that are revealed upon dispelling ideology? Clearly some Marxian-inclined thinkers
once suggested as much, viewing race as a "false" consciousness that
would unleash an interracial class revolution once it was exposed. In
1919, for instance, African-American union leader Asa Philip Randolph
(1919:10) argued that capitalism

> does not apply to Negroes only. It is the common fate of the servant class,
> black and white. But they must not understand that their interests are
> common. Hence race prejudice is cultivated. Lynching, jim-crowism segrega-
> tion is used to widen the chasm between the races.

Randolph was correct that racism was an obstacle to collective political
action, but he overestimated the producer class' ability to hoodwink
White laborers. As David Roediger (1991:9) emphasizes, thinkers like
Randolph did not appreciate (or were unwilling to admit) that America's
White working classes consciously colluded with racism and understood
the social "wages" provided by White privilege. If White superiority
was a false consciousness, it was a falsity of which most White working-
class laborers were well aware.

Traditionally, political economy assumed a view of ideology as a
sort of veil that analysis can expose to reveal the objective structure of
social struggle. However, there are no neutral or "authentic" identities
and social relations that underlie ideology and should be our appropriate research targets (Foucault 1980:118; Hoy 1986:131). All identity is
constituted in concrete, fluid, and historicized power relations: Domi-

nant structuring elements like racism and class structure range across many different power relationships with diverse local meanings and material forms. This network of power relationships is not simply forged by any given faction or process; of necessity, it is a contested set of relationships that has some overall conformity, but never assumes uncontested homogeneity. Certainly some groups and classes achieve inordinate influence over structural relationships, but they cannot utterly determine the efficacy of dominant ideologies or completely circumscribe social possibilities.

Those archaeologists who hope to stress the lives of anonymous agents—in the process deemphasizing or discarding ideology—sometime focus on "experience," or the more anthropological "emic" perspective (e.g., Beaudry et al. 1991:160; Yentsch 1994). Commonly (usually implicitly), experience is cast as an individual or group's construction of self and society, a sort of conscious apprehension that provides the most appropriate basis for interpreting the past (cf. Scott 1992). Defined this way, experience risks posing as an essential identity that can explain the past, rather than as a historical problem in itself. The focus on conscious experience ostensibly avoids approaches whose apparent ideological, mindset, or systemic determinism reflects what Mary Beaudry et al. (1991:161) call a "fear of the emic." Ultimately, though, it hazards shifting deterministic capacity to "experience" and evading the influence of dominant social formations and material structure. All conscious apprehension of self and society is socially informed, and not an autonomous realization separable from structure; that is, consciousness does not simply spring from an individual's self-formulated perceptions, and there is no point at which it is "complete." Experience is a subjectivity constantly constituting, and in turn defining, how dominant discourses represent social and material conditions.

RACIALIZATION AND SUBJECTIVITY IN CONSUMER CULTURE

A focus on African-American subjectivity and agency diverges from an archaeology that purely documents the material evidence of difference, even one that recognizes the impact of racism. To concede racism as a barrier to African-American consumption and broader social privileges is a significant gesture, yet it needs to be pressed further to get at the roots of racialization, the persistent power of White supremacy, and the complexities of African-American subjectivity. Reducing race to a facile structural hindrance in consumer space casts it as ideological artifice and risks reproducing the illusion of a "free market" that simply must be unfettered of such gatekeeper practices. Consumer culture is inherently structured by concrete inequality: Capitalism and consumer culture are structurally unequal by design and tend to reproduce the domination of a minority, rather than mass affluence. The contradictions of inequality structure and influence consumer desire and are not simply by-products or structural details that can be cleanly unraveled from idealized marketplace economics.

In the late nineteenth century, consumer space was defined as a democratic social body, albeit one structured by individual character. Its real and supposed privileges were governed by racial subjectivity and each individual's ability to conform to a tacitly White genteel ideal. Black subordination and the guise of exclusive White privilege attempted to soothe those Whites who were eager to share affluence but slow to secure it, a maneuver that preserved the faith of marginalized non-Black consumers in their predestined affluence. For Americans who procured the moniker of "White," White supremacy held together their commitment to material affluence and conceded them the illusion of social privilege as they awaited a commodity bounty.

Placing racialization at the heart of consumer culture means that consumer and racial subjectivity are inseparable: Any Americans can be studied archaeologically as racialized consumer subjects. We cannot ignore race, even though it is utterly constructed, because racialization provided a lens through which all Americans perceived and articulated various "Others" and themselves. In this sense, racialization is more complex than imposed racist obstacles somehow separable from an essential underlying identity, a "false" ideological consciousness concealing objective identity, or completely self-constructed identities. Instead, racializing is a social process that shaped how all consumers experienced transformation, their own subjectivity, and their position within consumer culture.

A truly democratic consumer culture never surfaced and is quite unlikely to do so. Nevertheless, we should not simply dismiss consumption as a purely assimilative mechanism of dominant ideologues. Many Americans found genuine empowering possibilities within the niches of consumption. Certainly many consumers were disappointed by the realities of material possession: Despite commodities' articulate and implied promises, material objects rarely produce enormous change or realize radically new pleasures. Yet, curiously enough, consumer desire has never ceased.

Some moralizing theorists view social and material investment in consumption as an ominous sign of mass stupefaction, a reflection that the masses elect to go shopping rather than struggle for change in social structure (e.g., Ewen 1988). However, a study of consumer desire instead tends to reveal self-conscious consumers who voiced wholly meaningful social critiques. The collective social desire of consumption is more significant and truly transformative than the apparent herd instinct of mass consumption. The social transformations worked by consumption are indeed circuitous, as consumers remade society incrementally and obliquely, rather than in instants of focused revolution: Changes in consumer culture generally originated as situational negotiations geared to modify moments and local spaces, rather than systemic strategies designed to work radical transformations in the service of future goals. Yet in their cumulative impact, consumption tactics fueled a profound social transformation that vested our shared desires in the material world. What makes that transformation distinct, as well as somewhat disarming, is that it redefined public aspirations and rights in the form of material goods and occurred, in Jean-Christophe's (1990:14) words, "privately, imaginatively, and inconspicuously—in short, without discussion."

African Americans aspired to be full members of consumer culture, and their seemingly modest participatory appeals and business philosophies apparently posed little threat to its basic economic principles. African Americans generally shared the widespread belief in a *laissez faire* marketplace and saw success in the marketplace and wider society as a reflection of individual character. These were not revolutionary ideas—indeed, they were standard genteel ideology. Nevertheless, persistent African-American designs to rid consumer culture of racism (if not racialization) certainly were radical and cut to the very core of consumer culture's inequality.

Black subjectivity compelled African Americans to contemplate their contradictory position within and outside consumer culture, and African Americans carved a range of complex social positions uniquely against and within dominant ideologies. In their vision of consumer space as a site to express social ambition, African Americans certainly were not alone. Indeed, by the 1920s a rich range of consumers felt their aspirations were most likely to be fulfilled in consumer space. Unlike other consumers, though, African Americans took aim at the racial exclusivity of American consumer culture, launching a subtly politicized, yet profound, critique of the very basis of American social privilege.

Material and Symbolic Racism in Consumer Space

Perhaps the most compelling show of turn-of-the-century consumer affluence was the plate-glass shop window. Plate-glass window scenes encouraged consumer desire through often-dazzling displays of goods amidst lights, color, mirrors, and myriad mechanical contraptions. Window displays implied universal access to a social ideal that could be realized by consumption within the premises (for Annapolis examples, cf. "The City Drug Store," 1893; "New Goods," 1873; "Our Merchants," 1870). Abba Goold Woolson's 1873 study of American women noted that "on every fair day they throng the dry-goods stores, and stand in mute, admiring crowds before windows where the latest fashions are gorgeously displayed" (Woolson 1873:105–106). Such shop windows were public spaces that ostensibly democratized the desire of all the consumers who peered into them.

The window decorators' vision of material affluence was a calculated effort to merge fantasy and reality, confounding the boundaries of consumer space and projecting genteel discipline and producers' social interests beyond the sales floor. In 1910, Bertha June Richardson (1910:65) voiced her apprehension of such displays, noting that

> Stronger than printing, because more convincing than a picture, is the influence of the shop window. There one sees the marvelous combination of bed, bookcase, dressing table, and hatrack actually worked by an attendant who moves too rapidly for you to grasp the mechanism, but conviction follows. There one gazes into parlors, bed-rooms, bathrooms, kitchens, and many suggestions are received and acted upon which are useful and helpful, many which are not. In these windows women see themselves as they resolve others shall see them, and to some it is a lesson well learned; to others it brings a wrong discontent.

Richardson recognized that window displays disciplined women to their role as primary household consumers and impressed them with the social and moral connotations of an appropriately outfitted material assemblage. Yet she feared that women would be rendered "discontent" by their inability to reproduce display ideals, forever laboring to duplicate shifting and poorly defined material norms.

Black caricatures were among the racialized disciplinary ideals that were materialized in shop windows. In 1888, for instance, *The Bee* directed its readers' attention to

> a ridiculous representation of their race, in the show windows, by the pro-
> prietors of the Boston Dry Good house.... It is a fact that these proprietors
> have a large colored patronage to their firm in this city, and if ridiculous
> charactercatures [sic] of the colored race must be exhibited as adverti-ing
> [sic] cards we would advise them to purchase their goods elsewhere. ("Ne-
> groes for a Show," 1888)

In a store with the undeniable profits provided by a "large colored patronage," such displays voiced the anti-Black sentiments of their proprietors and reminded paying African Americans that they remained outsiders in White public space.

Even the democratized daydreaming of window shoppers was a privilege that some Whites attempted to deny African Americans. The height of such apprehension may have been reached in 1915, when *The Bee* reported that African Americans

> were walking quietly and ... slowly up and down Seventh street observing
> the displays in the several windows that presented such a beautiful appear-
> ance, and to their surprise and disgust the so-called guardians of the peace
> placed them under arrest, and carried them to the station-house. ("Seventh
> Street Raid," 1915)

Arresting African-American window shoppers was a rather brazen surveillance measure, but it certainly demonstrated that some Whites saw shoppers' daydreaming aspiration as a racially exclusive privilege (cf. similar example in Gaines 1996:53).

Public consumer space was a significant scene of such friction, and countless legislative codes restricted African-American rights in public space. Yet laws barring African-American entry to, and privilege in, consumer space were in many ways only the symptomatic veneer for deeply embedded, unwritten codes that structured and legitimized White supremacy in consumer space. Complicitious Whites shared a host of conscious and unrecognized surveillance practices that forged a tacitly White public space: Racist advertising caricatures, the presumption of racially exclusive material symbolism, the patrol of African-American window shoppers, and anti-Black violence were all part of an interlocking web of racist surveillance. Such mechanisms were used to deny African America symbolic, if not physical and material, access to consumer privileges, and to rationalize Whites' anti-Black hostilities.

This chapter outlines the many self-evident and subtle forms of racism that structured White consumer space, from violence to window displays. The chapter first surveys the Black caricatures constructed in advertising and suggests how they were part of dominant discourses legitimizing "authentic" White material meanings. I then examine the distinctive African-American construction of patent medicine consumption that reproduced, subverted, and adapted the dominant symbolism for medicinals such as mass-marketed mineral water. The chapter probes a particularly rich example of the African-American negotiation of dominant symbolism in an analysis of hair care services, hair styling products, and cosmetics. I then examine White Annapolitans' most overt forms of racism, including forced resettlement of African-American Annapolitans, Ku Klux Klan intimidation, and legal and physical violence. Any critical understanding of racialized consumption is compelled to confront how all these seemingly disparate mechanisms collectively constructed White supremacy in public consumer space.

BLACK SIMULACRA:
ADVERTISING RACIAL DIFFERENCE

Among the pantheon of consumer goods displayed at the Columbian Exposition was Nancy Green, an African-American domestic from Chicago (Strasser 1989:182–183). Once enslaved, Green was hired by the manufacturers of Aunt Jemima pancake flour to publicly portray the advertising icon by singing Black music, spinning yarns about plantation life, and making pancakes for prospective merchants. Stunned by over 50,000 Exposition orders, the manufacturers hired Green permanently, and she spent the remainder of her life parading around fairs and other venues singing the praises of Aunt Jemima pancakes.

Introduced in 1890, Aunt Jemima was a potent advertising icon that evoked White stereotypes of Blackness and soothed apprehensions of eroding racial liminality. Aunt Jemima placated White consumers with the fiction of a time and place when racial tension and ambiguity did not exist, a historical moment when African Americans understood and even relished their labor and social subordination. Nancy Green was in this sense what Jean Baudrillard (1983) calls a "simulacra"; that is, she materialized a Black caricature that never existed in reality, yet that caricature assumed the status of authenticity because of pervasive belief in it. Such caricatures are so widely recognized, even today, that a 1995 African-American cookbook envisioned a table "where Aunt Jemima takes off her kerchief and sits down at the table, where Uncle Ben bows his head and blesses the food, and Rastus, the Cream of Wheat man, tells tall tales over a 'taste' of whiskey" (Harris 1995:17–18).

Rather than reduce these figures to demeaning racist caricatures, the cookbook cleverly reclaims the humanity they have been denied in popular consumer discourse.

Like her counterparts Rastus and Uncle Ben, Aunt Jemima is typical of racialized advertising symbolism since the late nineteenth century. African Americans appeared in cigarette advertisements as early as 1859, when tobacco brands like Old Coon Cigars and Nigger Head Tobacco pioneered hateful, albeit simplistic, advertising appeals to consumer racism (Boskin 1986:138). These early advertisements echoed and amplified popular White animosity toward Blacks, and recognized the comforting appeal of Black caricatures to White consumers (Figure 9). Delighted African Americans rapidly became a stock advertising image, hawking a diverse range of goods designed to pleasure the White consumer, such as cigarettes, alcohol, and food.

Black advertising imagery did not really become widespread until the late nineteenth century (Boskin 1986:138), and it is not by chance that caricatures like Aunt Jemima were constructed at that time. Jim Crow racism's emergent legal foothold, the increasing White romanticization of antebellum plantation life, and the racialization of service labor placed race at the center of late-nineteenth century American life. More than merely a flat degradation of African Americans, Aunt Jemima was among a new assemblage of racialized images that established the appropriate labor, social, and emotional roles of African Americans in consumer culture. Advertisers attempted to capture transforming racial sentiments by constructing a harmonious code linking Black caricatures to racialized labor structure and White-exclusive public rights; that is, advertisers aspired to construct a comprehensive mode of symbolic organization which provided "correct" racialized interpretations of material culture (on codes, cf. Gottdiener 1997:10). Advertising's stock African-American depictions focused on content, servile Black laborers in both the past and present—cooks, domestics, waiters, porters, and the like—serving the needs of genteel White consumers. These images were attractive to many White consumers because they demonstrated a contrived historical basis for Black labor and social subordination. Ironically, advertisers presumed that a labor heritage ranging from enslavement to domestic service made African Americans material-consumption authorities. Consequently, many household goods were hawked by African-American service laborers, like Aunt Jemima, who authoritatively fortified claims to product quality (Edwards 1969: 214–215). However, African Americans never appeared in advertisements as consumers.

Not surprisingly, many African Americans resented how such

Figure 9. Constructing Black caricatures: These Naval Academy students posed in Blackface before the 1868 minstrel show (courtesy of the Maryland State Archives; Special Collections, Marion E. Warren Collection, MSA 1890-4003).

transparent caricatures rationalized racialized labor divisions, dehumanized Blacks, and delivered a resounding public reminder of White supremacy. In 1918, for example, *The Crusader* attacked Aunt Jemima, observing that

> One of the most widely advertised staple foods is given publicity through means that are decidedly insulting to the Negro. On its advertisements and on its containers it carries a most repulsive female face with thick red lips, coal black complexion, flat, face-straddling nose, deep ugly lines and other tricks of the "artist" intended to make the picture as hideous as possible. This picture stares at you from every subway car and elevated station. It is supposed to represent a Negro "aunt," yet neither in America nor in any part of the so-called "Dark Continent" is to be found any human being of such repulsive features as this caucasian-created "aunt." ("Insulting Advertisements," 1918:114–115)

The Crusader focused on how such advertisements aspired to dehumanize and disempower African America, observing that "You have seen them in the subway and 'L' and have burned red hot with impotent rage, no doubt. They are part of the white man's propaganda to demean, ridicule and insult the Race" ("Advertisements That Insult," 1918:9). Certainly such images must have been humiliating to African Americans, but advertisers were focused on securing a select class of White consumers and had no interest in (if awareness of) the effect of advertising on African Americans. In the advertising parlance that flourished between the world wars, African Americans were not qualified for "consumer citizenship" by virtue of Blackness, and they were not alone: Most European immigrants were not considered "modern," either, though a vague promise of consumer privileges was held out to some Europeans (Marchand 1985:193). Advertisers also extended their contempt to the WASP working classes and rural "rustics": Advertisers agreed that between one-third and as much as two-thirds of the population was socially, morally, economically, or racially "unqualified" for consumer citizenship (Marchand 1985:64).

Advertising originated very little racist imagery, but it contributed to a public consumer space that licensed its middling White audience to admit, believe, and perpetuate inherited caricatures. Advertising was what Michel Foucault (1984:108–113) refers to as a privileged discourse that exercised inordinate influence on the definition, circulation, and naturalization of racial subjectivities and White superiority. It is simplistic, though, to reduce it simply to an instrumentally oppressive anti-Black mechanism, because such a reduction risks ignoring advertising's effect on White consumers' racial subjectivity (as well as its unforeseen ability to mobilize resistance like that voiced by *The Crusader*). Aunt

Jemima sold White consumers an illusion of Blackness and White racial supremacy in lieu of genuine material and social self-determination. Aunt Jemima's power over White consumers cannot be separated from the contrasting impact of such imagery on African America.

Advertising was simply one of the most visible elements in a broad campaign to deny African America the material and symbolic privileges of consumption. That campaign reached into every facet of consumer space, including seemingly race-neutral venues. For instance, after the 1872 introduction of Aaron Montgomery Ward's mail-order catalog, virtually any mass-produced good could be purchased through the mail (Schlereth 1991:366). English traveler Katherine Busbey (1910) recognized that rural consumers were attracted to mail-order consumption because local stores offered relatively little selection, catalog sales terms were lenient, and prices were considerably better than those of most local merchants. She sensed the symbolic allure of mail order as well, suggesting that a rural consumer "feels himself a patron of a great establishment, and that he is given all the advantages of selection of any of the city dwellers" (Busbey 1910:162).

Busbey did not realize that the utilitarian and symbolic attractions of rural mail-order consumption were magnified for African-American customers. Mail order provided African Americans with a mechanism to avoid consumer spaces in which they were subject to personal humiliation and marketing inequality. Mail-order pricing likely was particularly attractive to African Americans, since mail firms used a one-price system, which eliminated the deceitful pricing merchants routinely inflicted on African Americans. Some African-American Annapolitans certainly purchased goods through mail houses, such as the Bellis Court resident who singled out "Montgomery Ward—we would get a lot of our dresses from there when we were younger" (Jopling 1991). It is impossible, though, to determine the archaeological share of goods purchased from mail-order firms, since they hawked mostly standard brands or goods bearing no identification of the mail-order supplier.

However, mail-order houses like Wards and Sears and Roebuck were uneasy to concede the volume or existence of African-American customers. Merchants in small communities recognized that mail-order consumption threatened their profits and influence on community relations, and they launched a frenzied critique of a mass market that loomed as everything "Americans" abhorred: It would be a locationless, impersonal, mass collective space, and racial ideologues stressed that it would not remain White. Southern general storekeepers, keen to wound mail-order sales, circulated the rumor that Sears and Roebuck was covertly managed by African Americans (Schlereth 1991:372). Horrified

Sears' officials felt compelled to include a picture of their White founder in the catalog, establishing that the firm was indeed run by (if not exclusively for) Whites. Confronted by similar gossip, Montgomery Ward offered a reward to anyone who could identify the source of a rumor that he was a Mulatto (Schlereth 1991:372). Such firms were keen to reproduce Whites' vision that their consumption was exclusive, bringing them commodities and implied rights that were not available to everyone.

Racial "Authenticity" and White Symbolism

The self-determination and momentary Reconstruction-era political sway of genteel African Americans endangered the antebellum illusion of a public space based on White supremacy (cf. Du Bois 1935). An increasingly visible post-Emancipation African-American community was utterly genteel, and many cities had quite aristocratic circles of well-educated and affluent African Americans. In large measure, Jim Crow was the post-Reconstruction South's answer to the emergence of this Black "middle class" (Gaines 1996:30). Yet completely barring African Americans from consumer space was infeasible: Consumption implicated African America in a racialized labor structure, and White consumption was dependent on Black work. Consequently, various ideologues attempted to reproduce the illusion of unique White racial and social capacity by denying African Americans symbolic comprehension of genteel material culture; that is, African Americans might possess genteel objects, but they inevitably were unable to "correctly" define and use them because material symbolism was itself racially exclusive.

White Victorians routinely reduced material goods' meaning to monolithic White symbolism. In 1880, for example, a *Harper's Weekly* writer noted that many African-American homes in Georgia were decorated with

> cheap prints of the Virgin MARY, of Catholic Saints, and of the Crucifixion—such as are favorites in shanties of New York.... I have often been much amused at their horror and indignation when I told them they were Roman Catholic pictures. "I ain't no Roman Catholic; I belong to Big Bethel, I do," was the usual answer, and that in a very resentful tone. ("Inside Southern Cabins: Georgia, Part I," 1880:733)

The correspondent's determination to demonstrate Black miscomprehension of "authentic" meanings exposed her inability to conceive of an African-American reconfiguration of "White" religious symbols. Part of her bemusement likely was African Americans' transplantation of Roman Catholic symbols that she associated with Irish "shanties." The

Irish were themselves not considered White, placing African-American Georgians two racial steps removed from Whiteness. These African-American pictures certainly borrowed dominant social symbols and retained a spiritual essence, though they were grafted onto a distinctive subjectivity and cultural connotation. Yet Whiteness depends on the assumption of a monolithic, racially exclusive social meaning for all symbols, and symbolic divergences are racialized by their distance from the ideal. Assuming that such images only could be interpreted in one "White" form, the *Harper's* correspondent evaded the distinctive meanings African Americans gave to a vast range of familiar material objects.

Jacob Riis (1971:118) racialized material symbolism in a similar way when he dismissed what he conceded to be materially genteel homes in African-American New York. Riis observed that African Americans'

> home surroundings, except when he is utterly depraved, reflect his blithesome temper.... The negro's great ambition is to rise in the social scale to which his color has made him a stranger and an outsider, and he is quite willing to accept the shadow for the substance where that is the best he can get.

Despite what he characterized as "very prosperous" parlors, Riis reduced African-American consumption to a "shadow" of Whiteness because Blackness denied African America the "substance" of genuine White gentility.

Some observers conceded that consumers determined a significant measure of objects' material symbolism. In 1927, for example, household writer Mary Hinman Abel (1927:43) suggested that a fundamental dimension of material symbolism was forged by the consumer who "contributes final or 'place value' to goods of all kinds by choosing and purchasing them and by establishing conditions in which they will be used." Social scientists, though, tend to invest objects with dominant *a priori* meanings. This maneuver tends to reduce consumer symbolism to an insubstantial facade, as opposed to having an objective, "authentic" meaning (Miller 1995:24–25). This symbolic reduction does not necessarily racialize material goods; however, it makes lapses into essential racial symbolism far more likely than an approach that views symbolism as meaning invested in objects by consumers (i.e., rather than emanating from the things themselves). Instead of assuming precoded material attributes and meaning as the point of interpretive departure, it makes more sense to approach consumer agency as the engine driving material symbolism. Every object is situated within a sociohistorical context in which consumers' positioning and decision-making circumscribe a range of possible social properties and material symbolism in objects. The African-American consumption of patent medicines provides archaeological evidence of the complexity of consumer agency and the struggle over its racial implications.

PATENT MEDICINES AND AFRICAN-AMERICAN BODY DISCIPLINE

In 1880, *Harper's Weekly* sent an anonymous correspondent South to document the Black caricature she and her readers "knew" from popular culture. She felt she had located such exoticism when she recounted African Americans' apparent rejection of mainstream medicine. In Georgia she noted that African-American women attributed "supernatural power" to "May water; that is, the first rain that falls in May. All of them bottle a large quantity of it.... They use it to make lotions, salves, tonics, etc" ("Inside Southern Cabins: Georgia, Part II," 1880:749). The correspondent's emphasis on the "supernatural" effects of water attempted to neutralize a distinctive, but enigmatic, African-American practice by stressing its divergence from a genteel norm. Archaeologists commonly approach these distinctions as African cultural continuities (e.g., Wilkie 1997), but they cannot be distilled to an alien African culture or covert spiritual tradition simply lurking within mass-produced goods. A century later, it is evident that African-American bodily care was far more complex than either a ringing endorsement of mainstream medicalization or a wholesale reproduction of African healthcare and religious practice.

The African-American favor of distinctive caregiving practices that resisted Western body disciplines struck the *Harper's* correspondent as an illogical obstinacy to mainstream medicine. She reported from Charleston, South Carolina that

> There is hardly anything the colored men and women dread so much as going to the hospital. Yet the Roper Hospital, a portion of which is open to them, is a beautiful building, admirably ordered, and scrupulously clean.... But the Negro is a born herbalist; his faith is in weeds and roots.... One man suffering from acute rheumatism begged me in the most impassioned manner to get him some rattlesnake oil to rub himself with, assuring me that it would cure him. ("Inside Southern Cabins: Charleston," 1880:765)

The *Harper's* writer reduced African-American caregiving to a racially coded inability to conform to medical disciplinary standards, unable to fathom alternative visions of White medicine.

The use of "May water" in African-American health care, and White observers' effort to neutralize what they did not understand, was a modest, albeit symptomatic, episode of cultural struggle; that is, it was a disruption of idealized White symbolism that was not readily interpretable in White terms. Water commonly was used in African-American caregiving, a practice descended from West African visions of water's symbolic significance as a barrier separating the realm of spirits and the living (cf. Ferguson 1992:115; Sobel 1988:71). There clearly may be a dimension of African cultural practice involved in late-nineteenth century African-American water consumption: Like much African health care, African-American treatments commonly came in the form of a variety of herbs, naturally occurring mediums such as water, and material charms that addressed the physical dilemma wreaked by mobile spirits (Genovese 1972:228). African-American health care retained a persistent belief that the body could not be separated from a spiritual realm, so African-American health care treated the corporeal body and spirit realm as a single entity.

The Maynard-Burgess assemblage is entirely composed of mass-produced and mass-marketed goods, so it would seem a problematic context to search for such cultural traditions. Yet cultures of resistance constantly reconfigure enduring cultural practices, subvert dominant symbolisms, reject some "traditions," and integrate elements of dominant practice. African-American material symbolism constantly mediates the contradictions between cultural traditions, structural relations, and innovation. Such mediations are evident in transforming material consumption practices and are not confined to any discrete body of objects (e.g., craft products).

Sometime after 1889, for example, the Maynard-Burgess household sealed an external entrance cellar with a dense deposit of late-nineteenth century household refuse. These discards do not contain any self-evident indications of African-American cultural distinction. The assemblage included 79 glass bottles, predominated by mass-produced patent medicines (25 vessels), and a range of potentially allied health-giving preparations, such as medicinal gins (Table 2) (Mullins 1996:167). Among these vessels were 6 bottles of mineral water bottled in the northeast. The northeast was a center of nineteenth century mineral water marketing, and it was home to some of the nation's most prominent water-care spas. Water-cure establishments throughout the country showered, sitz bathed, steamed, and sponged their guests with spring waters after the second quarter of the nineteenth century, though few entertained African Americans (exceptions are discussed in Hutton 1992:80). Four of the Maynard-Burgess vessels were from New York's well-known Saratoga Springs area, including Missisquoi Springs (two vessels), Highrock Congress Springs, and Congress-Empire Springs. In 1888, a Saratoga Springs tourism guide touted the Congress spring

Table 2. Maynard-Burgess Cellar Glass Minimum Vessel Count by Functional Type

Functional type	Quantity and percentage of assemblage minimum vessel count
Pharmaceutical	25 (28.73%)
Food	15 (17.24%)
Whiskey/liquor	15 (17.24%)
Fresh beverage	7 (8.04%)
Wine/champagne	5 (5.74%)
Preserving jars	2 (2.9%)
Unknown bottle	10 (11.49%)
Drinking glass	3 (3.44%)
Decanter	1 (1.14%)
Stemmed bowl	1 (1.14%)
Stemmed glass	1 (1.14%)
Unknown table vessel	1 (1.14%)
Unknown	1 (1.14%)
Total vessels	87

water with a relatively typical testimonial that its water was "slightly stimulating and tonic in its effects.... It is especially beneficial as a general preservative of the tone of the stomach and purity of the blood" (Cozzens 1888:24). Annapolis' own Maryland Hotel was among the establishments that championed its healthful waters, announcing in 1896 that it "will soon be watered from its artesian well, which is said to be from analysis, as pure as spring water" ("Capital Jottings," 1896).

Alongside these mineral water vessels in the Maynard-Burgess cellar was a greater number of patent medicines (25 vessels) than any other type of bottled good. An analysis of how rapidly the bottles' contents were consumed and the vessels discarded suggests quite rapid consumption of "cure-alls." This technique, known as a manufacture-deposition lag analysis, evaluates the span of time over which a bottle was manufactured and discarded (Hill 1982). First, a median production date was assigned to each individual vessel; that is, the date halfway between the vessel's earliest and latest manufacture. For instance, a bottle produced from 1850 to 1900 would be assigned a median production date of 1875. A mean manufacture date subsequently was calculated for each type of bottled good (e.g., patent medicines, wine, food) by averaging the median dates of each bottle of that particular type. More recent mean dates for a class of bottled goods indicate types of products that were manufactured, consumed, and discarded over the shortest span of time (Table 3). The complete assemblage had a mean production

Table 3. Maynard-Burgess Cellar Glass Manufacture–Deposition Lag

Functional type	Mean production date	Manufacture–deposition lag
Pharmaceutical	1885.47	34.53
Food	1886.60	33.40
Whiskey/liquor	1876.15	43.85
Fresh beverage	1878.35	41.65
Wine/champagne	1870.00	50.00
Preserving jar	1891.00	29.00
Unknown bottles	1880.83	39.17
Bottle assemblage	1882.10	37.90

date of 1882.10, and the patent medicines had the most recent mean production date in the assemblage (1885.47): This indicates that the household was consuming large quantities of mass-produced medicines, and those medicines were being produced, consumed, and discarded at a faster rate than other bottled products in the cellar refuse. The fresh beverage bottles had a mean production date of 1878.35 (including mineral water bottles and two vessels that contained either beer or soda). This older mean manufacture date is somewhat counter-intuitive: Fresh beverages generally were consumed more rapidly than other bottled products since they lose carbonation. The greater lag between the fresh beverage vessels' manufacture and discard suggests manufacturer recycling or household reuse. If the latter was the case, only liquids could have been stored in such vessels, since they were all small-mouthed bottles. The fresh beverage vessels are the only bottles in the assemblage whose dates suggest such recycling, so the household's water consumption may have been even greater than vessel quantities alone suggest.

The mineral water and patent medicine vessels illuminate the complexity of African-American health care. On the one hand, the Maynard-Burgess water bottles do suggest African traditions like those the *Harper's* correspondent reported concerning "May water." There is sound evidence of water's use in African-American medicinal care well into the twentieth century, strengthening that interpretation (e.g., Perdue et al. 1976:73–74). The source of the water, from spring rains or national producers, likely was consequential, but it may not have been absolutely decisive in determining water's symbolism. On the other hand, and seemingly diametrically opposed, is the possibility that the water was consumed as a genteel medicinal, which is how the many patent medicines in the assemblage were designed to be consumed.

Perhaps the household aspired to venture to tony water spas and reproduce dominant body discipline, harboring little or no tangible hearken-
ing to African-American heritage.

These interpretations are not mutually exclusive. Material symbolism of these goods inevitably was impacted by pervasive public discourses on mainstream health care, but the claims of patent medicine
manufacturers, the outcry for bodily discipline, and the emergence of
an institutionalized medical establishment did not determine their
consumed meaning. Instead, their symbolism was a provisional amalgam of consumer subjectivity and the dominant social inscription of
such goods. The *Harper's* correspondent suggested that African Americans were utterly self-distanced from mainstream medicalization, but
Annapolitan data instead suggests both an equivocal submission to
mainstream body discipline and the persistence of some independent,
culturally distinctive health care conventions. Rather than frame interpretation of the medicine consumption simply as either cultural tradition or consumer homogenization, an analysis that situates the vessels
within racialized power relations suggests their consumption secured a
degree of self-determination and cultural reproduction in defiance of
anti-Black medical ideologies. At the same time, the patent medicine
volume signalled some aspirations to maintain bodies disciplined within dominant societal standards.

African-American patent medicine consumption surely was shaped
by the social and structural realities of the White medical system. Annapolis had no mainstream hospital for any patients until 1902, when
the Emergency Hospital was constructed at Cathedral and Franklin
Streets, immediately across from the predominately African-American
Courthouse Site neighborhood (United States Department of Commerce 1913:290). Officially, it received African-American patients, but
the facility had only 12 beds and treated just 158 patients in 1910 (United
States Department of Commerce 1913:291). Many types of care were
denied to African Americans; for instance, African Americans were
refused maternity care, and an African-American maternity clinic was
not opened in Annapolis until 1946 (Brown 1994:44). In 1930, Maryland
still had only 100 African-American physicians in the whole state, so
many African Americans were compelled to treat themselves or to con-
sult White doctors (United States Department of Commerce 1969:305).

Commodifying Hair

The African-American consumption of mass-produced cure-alls in
household caregiving negotiated a White-dominated medical system
and Western body discipline, providing a measure of consumer control

over health care. Yet cure-all consumption posed a problematic empowerment. The tension between consumers' symbolic subversions and persistent structural domination yielded consumption patterns whose efficacy as either resistance or dominance often was ambiguous. Patent medicines offered African Americans typically paradoxical prospects: On the one hand, consuming mass-produced medicines evaded the institutional racism of mainstream White medicine and maintained a distinctive African-American cultural subjectivity; on the other, they implicated African Americans in a genteel body discipline that demanded commodity consumption structurally rooted in racialized labor space and mainstream medicine.

Like virtually all Americans, many African Americans saw their bodies as consumer sites that could be maintained, and even improved, by mass-produced commodities. Hair straightening treatments and skin whiteners provide the clearest testimony to the unsettling confluence of racialized body discipline, Whiteness, and commodity consumption in African-American bodies. The dominant social symbolism for Black hair and skin was forged most powerfully by eugenicists, who attempted to scientifically ground race in essential nature and biological attributes (cf. Gossett 1963). Various popular discourses appropriated scientific analyses of the physical, mental, and social capacities encoded in dark skin and "unruly" hair as a means to assess underlying Black character. Whites who lampooned African Americans' genteel material consumption often refuted the appearance of genteel African-American subjectivity by pointing to the "truths" of Black corporeality. On the eve of the Civil War, for instance, Samuel Mordecai's (1860:356–357) account of life in Richmond noted that

> Like their betters, the negroes of the present day have their mock-gentility, and like them, they sustain it chiefly in dress and pretension.... Dashing satin bonnets now cover woolly false curls, a handsome veil conceals a sooty face, which is protected from being sunburnt by a stylish parasol. A silk dress of gaudy colors sweeps the ground, concealing a splay foot with receding heel. The beau who struts beside this chamber-maid, is attired in a talma or shawl, pants whose checks or stripes exceed the circumference of his leg, and a vest in which every color vies for brilliancy. He twirls his watch-chain and his cane, and might also put a Broadway dandy to the blush.

Mordecai augured the future of anti-Black consumer discourses in his description of stigmatized Black body attributes that defused the genteel symbolism of accompanying White commodities.

Racial ideologues endeavored to show that African-American consumers' subversions of Black caricatures were contradicted by the undeniable reality of Black bodies, particularly hair and skin color. A coalition of scientific racists and Negrophobic popular commentators

forged a complex framework to analyze hair as an index to racial identity. Midcentury racists popularized the caricature of "wooly" textured
Black hair whose spiraling form distinguished it from straight White
hairs. Popular writers rapidly integrated the "wooly" adjective in their
expanding inventory of Black caricatures. Around 1850, for example,
English traveler Charles Olliffee noted that African-American womens'
"hair, or rather their 'wool' is usually longer than the men's" (Olliffee
1964:46). Hair was assumed in many quarters to be objective evidence to
gauge distance from Whiteness or even, in some formulations, differences between Black and White *species* (Gossett 1963:81).

Skin color was perhaps more thoroughly stigmatized than hair
because it presented Whites with the unsettling reality of fluid racial
divisions and miscegenation. Virtually all Americans assumed light-
complexioned African Americans were of mixed racial ancestry, which
was often true. The dilemma in making descent the origination of racial subjectivity was that visible heterogeneity muddied the fiction of
an unadulterated, "pure" White race (Harrison 1995:61). Confronted
with the troubling truth of racial mixedness, late-nineteenth century
ideologues constructed the "Mulatto" in an effort to stabilize racial
divisions by conceding degrees of Blackness that did not significantly
impact Whiteness. White observers sometimes extended distinctive
intellect to people classified as Mulatto, promoting widespread apprehension of Mulattos as organic revolutionaries; in contrast, others saw
racial hybrids as latent moral and sexual degenerates (Gaines 1996:73;
Gatewood 1990:150). White supremacy ultimately had no way to accommodate any "in-between" identity such as the Mulatto, and by the early
twentieth century, most Whites resolved that any person with African-
American blood was Black. This "one drop" Black/White racial polariza-
tion was inelegantly codified by Jim Crow laws, which classed people in
public space as legally either Black or White (Gatewood 1990:149).

Jim Crow never defused the lived class, gendered, and social complexities of the color line. Post-Emancipation African-American elite
overwhelmingly were light complexioned, intimating that skin color
privileges were extended over darker African Americans. Complexion
alone did not determine African-American status, because family heritage, education, and material wealth were all significant contributing
factors. Nevertheless, skin color was perceived by many African Americans as a preexisting reality that could variously bar admission to elite
status, erode Black unity, or endanger White supremacy. The African-
American politics of Blackness and "mixedness" was a shifting historical terrain: Blackness sometimes was cast as empowering solidarity
and Mulattos were reduced to evidence of White oppression; other

African Americans were less apprehensive of mixing and instead focused on race solidarity (Gaines 1996:125; Harrison 1995:61). Born free in neighboring Alexandria, *The Bee* editor Calvin Chase was himself of mixed ancestry, yet his paper was a vitriolic critic of color preferences in Washington's African-American community. *The Bee*'s editorials persistently hammered away at African-American elite's color-based prejudice, painting it as a source of dissension in a community demanding race unity (e.g., "The Lily Whites," 1907).

The Bee's exhortations against skin color prejudice stood in stark contrast to the advertising and beauty columns in the same newspaper. Like most turn-of-the-century African-American newspapers, *The Bee* was replete with advertisements for a profusion of cosmetic treatments that remedied various hair, skin, and bodily aesthetic dilemmas. Ladies' columns in *The Bee* and virtually every other African-American newspaper routinely discussed techniques and preparations to "manage" skin color and "unruly" hair. Products like skin whiteners extended therapeutic intervention to its most ominous extreme by suggesting that skin "inferiorities" could be masked, if not effaced, by a commodity. Chilling for its frank acknowledgement of the toll of Black skin but not at all atypical of such preparations, one absurdly unsettling 1898 skin whitener actually touted itself as a "Black Skin Remover" ("A Black Skin Remover," 1898). Mass-marketed straighteners and skin whiteners insidiously encouraged African Americans to acknowledge their bodies' stigmatization because that physical stigma could be effaced by commodities. Many of the producers of straighteners and whiteners argued that bodily racial attributes were the primary obstacles to African Americans' social ascendance; that is, if Black skin and hair could be minimized, masked, or effaced, African Americans' genteel discipline would provide the platform for social advance.

African Americans made or purchased hair care preparations long before mass-produced goods were marketed expressly to African Americans (Figure 10). In about 1850, a traveler in South Carolina noted that African-American

> women endeavor to make themselves irresistible by fashioning their coiffure.... They give the most burlesque appearance to their heads; after first making the indispensable part, they comb their hair up to the right and left, and, finally, fasten it in place with generous application of pomade. (Olliffee 1964:46)

Many different sorts of hair preparations were homemade; for example, a Gott's Court resident remembered that a neighbor "used to comb my mother's hair and she would take coffee grinds and make the waves in our hair" (Jopling 1992).

Figure 10. In the late nineteenth century, these Southern Maryland women posed while plaiting hair (courtesy of the Maryland State Archives; Special Collections, Teresa Avery Collection, MSA 3497-1).

A handful of mass-produced preparations were used in African-American hair care after the Civil War, most of which were general-purpose compounds, like Vaseline, which was first produced in the 1870s. Chesebrough Manufacturing Company began to manufacture a special Vaseline Hair Oil by the 1890s, and the ubiquitous Sears and Roebuck catalog was one of its sales outlets (Praetzellis and Praetzellis 1992:26–27). Comparable hair products soon began to be produced by other manufacturers: Armour's Meats, for example, produced hair creams from inedible animal wastes.

A bottle of Vaseline produced after 1908 was recovered from the Franklin Street privy, and another was recovered from inconclusively dated Bellis Court yard refuse. While no mass-produced African-American hair care preparations were included in Annapolitan archaeological assemblages, they were sold in local stores (Figure 11), and many African Americans likely had such preparations applied by their

Figure 11. This 1934 scene of the African-American-owned Leonard Pharmacy on Calvert Street showed a window display stocked with hair care products (courtesy of the Maryland State Archives; Special Collections, Annapolis, I Remember Collection, MSA 2140-666).

barber or hairdresser. Mary and Adrian Praetzellis (1992:26–27), for example, recovered 38 Vaseline jars, 1 Petrol petroleum jelly vessel, and an Armour's pomade or cream jar from a turn-of-the-century African-American barber's assemblage in Sacramento, California.

The Politicization of Hair Straightening

Straightening compounds and heating combs were marketed extensively in the late nineteenth and early twentieth centuries. In 1909, a typical commercial hair straightener promised to

> straighten the curliest head of hair [through the application of a] steel heating bar which irons the hair [after being] put into the flames of the alcohol or gas heater. The Aluminum Comb is easily detached from the heating bar, then after the bar is heated the comb goes back into place and is held by the turn of the handle. ("The Magic Shampoo Drier," 1909)

An African-American resident of Gott's Court remembered that members of her household "would put the hot comb on the stove and heat it, put some grease on our hair and straighten our hair. Make it shining and so that we could look pretty when we come out of Gott's Court" (Jopling 1992).

The Court's archaeological assemblage contained a steel hot comb like those described by its former residents. Uniquely entwined in a personal social practice ignored by most scholars, the comb illuminates the situational subversion of African-American symbolism, as well as the social production of archaeological knowledge. After it was excavated, the comb was a functional enigma outside the personal experience or material expertise of any archaeologist on the project, all of whom were White. Wide-ranging discussions between African-American Annapolitans and archaeologists had preceded the Gott's Court project, and beauty and hair conventions had been one of many topics discussed. However, we were slow to develop an archaeological sensibility that expanded on basic functional analysis and grasped the social consequence of hair care.

A *Washington Post* photographer came to the archaeology lab as part of a story on the African-American project and took a photograph of the comb among many other objects. An African-American housekeeper who worked in the building housing the lab had used such combs, and after seeing the picture she inspected the comb and explained the mechanics of hair straightening. Yet her resolution of the object's function provided no self-evident testimony of straightening's social significance. In retrospect, she quite clearly indicated that straightening was a significant cultural practice by recounting her use of such combs as a child, and she came to the lab expressly to see it. However, we did not comprehend that her memories were not of a material object or its mere function; instead, the comb evoked a complex range of related social settings. In hindsight, it is evident that complex material symbolism—particularly meaning that historically was enigmatic to, or concealed from, Whites—remains equally complex today and will not simply reveal itself to curious archaeologists. Practices like hair straightening are cultural legacies that African Americans may be reluctant or unwilling to share with Whites who are unable to probe their lived complexities, or disinclined to examine their continuity into the present.

We reduced the straightening comb to an African-American concession to White-controlled public space; that is, the comb reflected how racism compelled African Americans to conform to racist hair-care regulations to avoid surveillance and preserve their livelihoods. Hair straightening may well have tempered racism directed at African Americans by displaying an apparent measure of deference or promoting provisional material discipline. Yet this perspective frames African-American material symbolism simply as a response to a White supremacy that structured all possible forms of social meaning. We simply situated the comb's meaning within the forms of agency and symbolism proposed by a racist society, a maneuver that defined its symbolism in relation to an unspoken White backdrop. The power of conducting archaeology in public, placing African-American oral history at the project's heart, and discussing our analyses with African Americans is that we were compelled to confront the contradictions in that interpretation.

African Americans today often see the comb as a rich cultural symbol whose sociocultural significance was not structured by racism. The appearance and meaning of straightened Black hair in White space assumes far less significance in African-American memory than the social context of hair care in living rooms and salons, as the prelude to important life events, and as an activity shared by family and friends. African Americans consistently evoke a heritage of cultural solidarity and distinction through the comb. To many contemporary African Americans, hair straightening only made African Americans *appear* integrated: They believe that archaeologists were taken in with the appearance of deferential assimilation much as Whites always have been taken in by African-American appearances. African Americans stress that hair care embodies culturally unique symbolism that cannot be understood by reference to White consumer ideology.

The Political Economy of Hair and Beauty

The marketing and consumption of African-American cosmetics reflects the complicated interchange of racial ideology, African-American entrepreneurial aspiration, and deep-seated African-American hair and beauty conventions. The significance of African-American hair care and bodily presentation was boosted by its construction of a self-empowered African-American labor and social space. Unlike almost every other enterprise, hair care and beauty counsel were the province of African Americans serving themselves both before and after Emancipation. Entrepreneurs who catered to African-American bodily presentation (e.g., barbers, salons, undertakers) virtually never faced White competition for African-American customers (Cohen 1990:149; Frazier 1924:293). Consequently, during the early twentieth century, African-American consumers' demand for hair styling, skin care, and beauty services supported a thriving personal service and cosmetics market managed by African-American entrepreneurs.

Barbers were typical of the entrepreneurs who emerged in late-nineteenth century African-American consumer space. W.E.B. Du Bois noted that in many post-Civil War Southern cities "the master's valet set up his barber-shop in town and soon had a lucrative trade" (Du Bois 1899:9). In the wake of Emancipation, some of these barbers faced WASP and European immigrant competition for White consumers. In 1899, Du Bois (1899:10) observed that "nearly all barbers are Negroes" in Philadelphia, but he speculated they were on the decline because of anti-Black unions and European immigrant competition (Du Bois 1996:116). In 1907, though, he admitted that African-American barbers were more numerous than ever; they simply had shifted their business to other African Americans, rather than an exclusively White clientele (Meier 1964:145).

The shift Du Bois identified from White to African-American clients apparently happened in Annapolis as well. In Annapolis, 27 African-American barbers have been identified from the period 1870–1930. It is not possible to conclusively identify the ethnicity of their patrons, but there are strong suggestive clues. Some were employed by the Naval Academy, where they certainly barbered primarily for White students and faculty. In 1870, John and Maria Spencer Maynard's sons John Henry and Lewis both appeared in the census as barbers, likely at the Academy. John Henry's daughter married a Naval Academy barber, and an Academy barber boarded at their home in 1910, suggesting established links between Academy barbers. Other barbers had their own shops in predominately African-American neighborhoods, indicating that they almost certainly focused their trade on African Americans: George W. Brown, for instance, conducted his business in the living room of his 22 Washington Street house (Brown 1994:41).

The socioeconomic viability of African-American barbers and hairdressers was a national phenomenon. In 1890, one source identified 17,480 African-American barbers in the United States, numbering among the most prosperous African-American entrepreneurs (Praetzellis and Praetzellis 1992:110). In New York City, George Edmund Haynes (1968:99) found that the most common African-American business in 1909 was the barber shop. In 1923, Charles Johnson identified 515 African-American barbers, hairdressers, and manicurists in Baltimore alone (Johnson 1923:13). Scattered throughout every African-American community, these barbers' and hairdressers' spaces were materially viable enterprises that provided exclusively African-American social spaces and business venues. Not simply market venues in which consumers obtained a service, barber shops and hairdressing salons were community social spaces removed from the direct gaze of White surveillance.

By the turn of the century, many African-American women likely conducted hairdressing and beauty care enterprises in their Annapolis homes, when beauty salons became common throughout the country (Schlereth 1991:166). In 1890, *The Bee* contained a typical notice for an early "Hair Artist" who "will open a hair salon for the beautifying and straightening of the hair.... No one need despair; for no head is too difficult for her to straighten" ("Hair Artist," 1890). On the eve of World War I, *The Bee* regularly contained a photograph of Madam Agnes Smith's "electrical hair, face and skin culturist" shop, an enterprise typical of early twentieth-century salons maintaining whole bodies ("Madam Agnes Smith's," 1916). Unfortunately, census keepers generally ignored such enterprises, just as they evaded virtually all Black women's labor. These businesses also were "advertised" primarily by word of mouth, posing documentary dilemmas that make even the most prosperous women's enterprises difficult to identify. None can be conclusively pinpointed in Annapolis until 1920, when Sarah Duke and Annie McPherson each appeared in the census as hairdressers. Roger Williams' wife Alevis was recorded in the same census as a "hairworker," probably in her husband's Cornhill Street barber shop (cf. Brown 1994:46).

Buoyed by the communal significance of hair and bodily presentation, and deterred by other capital-intensive enterprises, African-American entrepreneurs rapidly embraced the cosmetics and hair care market. African-American-owned cosmetics companies, like the Madame C.J. Walker Company, the Nile Queen Company, the Poro Company, and Marcus Garvey's Black Star Line, profitably sold a diverse range of skin and hair care goods, including Black-No-More Cream, Cocotone Skin Whitener, and Madame C.J. Walker's hair straightening system (Cohen 1990:149; Frazier 1924:294). African-American newspapers extensively marketed such skin and hair preparations. In 1925, the quantity of these advertisements and the social implications of their products attracted the critical attention of the National Urban League's journal *Opportunity* ("Race Pride and Cosmetics," 1925). *Opportunity* examined a study that reviewed advertisements for "skin and hair adjustors" in five African-American newspapers. Chicago's *Defender* and Marcus Garvey's *The Negro World*, the "most race conscious papers" in *Opportunity*'s study, respectively had 79.8% and 79.6% of their advertisements devoted to beauty preparations ("Race Pride and Cosmetics" 1925:293). (In contrast to *Opportunity*'s analysis, Lawrence Levine [1993:132] notes that skin lightener and hair straightening advertisements were banned by Garvey himself, who was in prison when the *Opportunity* article was published.) The journal recognized the profound contradiction: The newspapers most associated with Black racial pride were themselves "giving greatest emphasis to the mechanism for obliterating racial characteristics."

Cosmetics and hair product consumption reflect neither an utter belief in racialized body caricatures nor a complete capacity (or willingness) to step outside of them. African Americans viewed Black stereotypes with a complex fusion of credibility, ambivalence, enigma, and outright disbelief that did not provide a clear distinction between caricature and reality. Somewhat ironically, racial stigmatization bolstered the business of African-American cosmetic manufacturers dedicated to minimizing or evading such stigmatization. Yet African Americans' adaptation of dominant bodily beauty ideologies, even when they illuminated the fallacy of Black caricatures, could not be the basis of a radical critique without interrogating the notion of race itself. At the turn of the century, though, it was difficult for any Americans to utterly dismantle race and frame subjectivity in other terms.

The dilemmas of borrowing from racial body ideologies are illuminated by a complex 1910 editorial on hair straightening in *The Bee*. *The Bee* associated straight hair and genteel body disciplines with "civilization," noting that the "first evidence of civilization was noted when the aborigines began to put rings in their noses and ears, and decorate their bodies with paint and feathers, and by tatooing [sic]. This was their show of [a]esthetic taste" ("Straighten the Hair," 1910). The paragon of such aesthetic taste was reached by Whites, and "now 'melady' in white runs the whole gamut of the art beautiful." The modern White woman, according to *The Bee*, "corsets her form until it is wasp-shap[ed] ... arranges her hair to suit gorgeous headgear ... and massages her face and body to preserve, if possible, the show of youth and vigor." *The Bee* contrasted this commodity-sustained beauty with that of African-American women and concluded that African-American womens' hair was impeding their undefined contribution to the race. The paper argued:

> For some unaccountable and unjustifiable reason an All-Wise Providence retarded the growth of the hair on the heads of most Negro women until its a struggle for it to emerge from what might be termed the embryotic [sic] state. Who ever put it into the Great Master's head to thus discriminate against our dear women whose color runs from a saffron hue to a chocalate [sic] brown we are unable to say. But who ever, back in the Genesis days, did suggest this damnable idea have had, have now, and ever will have the just condemnation of the women with the rich, tantalizing brown color. With women's bonnets designed each year especially for women who have wealth of long flowing tresses, can you blame the lady of color if she coaxes out her kinks into long tresses of raven black? Can you blame her if she does her best to add to what God has given her, and does her best to supply what God overlooked? If "melady" of creamy white, touched with a bit of delicate pink, complexion may blondine [sic] her tresses, may curl, frizzle and puff her hair, why may not the chocolate brown or saffron hue lady straighten her hair? We say straighten your hair, ladies, beautify yourselves, make those aggravating, reclusive, elusive, shrinking kinks long flowing tresses that may be coiled or puffed to suit Dame Fashion's latest millinery creations, even if it takes every ounce of hair straightening preparation that can be manufactured. ("Straighten the Hair," 1910)

The Bee editorial went still further when it brazenly concluded that "we are for the beauty in our women, and even God, who discriminates against our women on this hair proposition, knows that straight hair beautifies a woman." *The Bee*'s commentary illuminated some African Americans' disturbing appropriation of dominant beauty ideals (e.g., straight hair), the commitment to commodifying beauty, and the profound effort to impress body discipline on African-American women. Like Chase's *Bee* editorial directed to "our dear women," by the early twentieth century African-American cosmetic and straightening advertisements almost exclusively directed their appeals to women. In the 1880s, advertisements for straighteners illustrated African-American men as well as women, but most body aesthetics counsel was directed expressly to women by the turn of the century. The focus on women consumers began by 1895, when Pratiau hair straightener drew attention to its advertisement with the prominent heading "ATTENTION! LADIES!" ("Pratiau Hair Straightener," 1895:1). In 1909, an advertisement for the "Magic Shampoo Drier and Hair Straightener" contained a similarly exclusive gendered appeal, proclaiming "Ladies Look! Every lady can have a beautiful and luxuriant head of hair if she uses MAGIC" ("The Magic Shampoo Drier," 1909).

Even among radical African-American voices, there was considerable support for the bodily discipline of women. In 1919, the socialist-leaning *The Crusader* joined the chorus advocating womens' consumption of cosmetics, arguing that "It is most amusing to hear someone railing against the use of cosmetics, especially when it is a sourced and pitilessly unattractive female or a loud mouthed whiskey soaked male" ("The Use of Cosmetics," 1919). The launch pad for African-American consumer boycotts and collective political action among domestics, *The Crusader* seemed an unexpected champion of womens' cosmetics consumption.

Some African Americans publicly questioned the implications of hair straightening. A 1900 "Woman's Column" in *The Bee*, for instance, lamented that "if some of us would spend half the time we use in trying to get white and make our hair straight we would be far better off" ("Our Woman's Column," 1900). In 1905, the *Afro American Ledger's* "Midnight's Musings" column pondered the ramifications of anxiety about racial appearance and identity. Author of a weekly column, the anonymous "Midnight" described a woman in St. Louis

> who was busy washing her head, saying that she was going to have it ironed. "You see Mr. Midnight, I have made up my mind to get married, and these men here don't go with kinks, so if you want to shine in St. Louis you must do away with kinks and get straight. I wash and iron my hair every week just as I wash and iron my linen, and I am just having all the proposals I can answer. I have a preparation for making my face white by degrees. It will not be long before it will be impossible to see a dark woman in St. Louis." ("Midnight's Musings," 1905:1, 5)

Midnight suggested that hair straightening reflected how racial stigmatization had produced baseless, yet deep-seated, shame about Black identity. He appreciated that hair straighteners and skin whiteners fanned Black shame and alienated African Americans to common interests, concluding "I don't understand why so many of my race are ashamed of their race and hair. I am of the opinion that character and worth will win in this country." That conclusion betrayed relatively typical bourgeois moralizing: Despite his critique of the stigmatization of racialized bodies, Midnight submitted the nebulous, ostensibly race-neutral genteel values of "character" and "worth" to assuage African America's social and material discomfit.

In their 1925 analysis of African-American beauty advertising, *Opportunity* recognized that the consumption of straighteners and skin whiteners "reflects the tragic dual life of the Negro in this country.... There are no special Negro styles, and the penalty of non-conformity here as elsewhere bears down with even greater severity than the bitter ridicule directed at an incongruous attempt at conformity" ("Race Pride and Cosmetics" 1925:293). The journal's editors were sympathetic to African-American cosmetic consumers, because "if crinkly hair and shiny black features are the butt of Nordic ridicule, it can be understood why the commonality of Negroes will seek to change these features, and thus contribute to their chances for success in a country in which circumstances force them to live." But rather than see such consumption as an effort to assimilate, the journal concluded that "it is all an unconscious protest against an inferior status." *Opportunity* incisively likened hair straightening to the beauty standards thrust upon women, arguing that women who followed such standards were protesting "against the inferior status assigned to them by man.... Woman does not want to be man—but she wants his freedom. The analogy, one may reasonably argue, carries with the Negro." Such a conclusion clearly grasped the multivalence of material culture, cut to the contradictions embodied in cosmetics, and opened beauty standards and commodities to situational interpretations.

"I LEFT THERE AN INNOCENT MAN": RACISM AND WHITE PUBLIC SPACE

In April 1921, Robert Robinson was executed on Annapolis' gallows as the penalty for a 1919 murder conviction. An *Evening Capital* headline trumpeted that over a hundred people gathered to witness the Calvert Street execution "at dawn this morning, and while rain, intermingled with hail, beat down upon his black kinky head, Robert Robinson ... ascended the gallows and gave his life in expiation of the crime" ("Robinson Calmly Goes to His Death," 1921:1). The headline sensationally proclaimed that Robinson's "neck [was] not broken by fall so life ebbed by slow strangulation." Eager to illuminate Black criminality, the editors printed "Robinson's Illiterate Note to Public before Execution," an allegedly verbatim letter by the accused. The note soberly lamented that

> From the time I been in Annapolis Jail I been knock round and doy round by all kind of Farmer they think they was doging round the right man but the wont and they will all see that I left there an innocent man.... best port of the people know I dident kill him two they knew I am an innocent man but what can they do no notheing. ("Robinson's Illiterate Note," 1921)

White Annapolitans pride themselves on what is commonly taken as a history of racial tranquility. In 1957, for example, Clarence Marbury White and his wife Evangeline Kaiser White surveyed the first half of the twentieth century in Annapolis and romantically noted that

> At the present, wild talk and agitation about segregation and desegregation are passing by us .... Annapolis has always had desegregation, and nothing was ever thought about it. I cannot remember when there was not several families of colored people on every street in town. (White and White 1957:86)

Such a memory of an "integrated" Annapolis was, at best, a fanciful recollection that ignored the systemic and often violent racism that was unavoidably part of African-American Annapolitans' lives, despite its invisibility to (or evasion by) White Annapolitans.

African-American Annapolitans had genuine reason to distrust a White justice system that was openly sympathetic to racist violence and enjoyed the complicitious public support of the local press. In 1875, for instance, an African American attempting to vote was murdered in an "election riot" by a White assailant in front of a large crowd of witnesses. Yet because the witnesses were all African Americans "the jury doubtless considered the testimony of too contradictory a nature to fasten the killing upon any particular person," and the murderer was released ("Inquest," 1875). Two months later, an African-American Annapolitan was accused of raping a White woman, and the *Maryland Republican and State Capital Advertiser* frenzied anxious Whites by warning "our authorities to keep a close guard and strict watch upon the prisoner. Better have an enraged lion and tiger loose in a community than such a beast. It is important that he be made to serve an example of, as a warning to others" ("The Black Fiend," 1875). The next day, the prisoner was taken from the Calvert Street jail and lynched. Ten years later, the *Maryland Republican* reported the same justice by "the Mob Method" when "Townshed Cook, the negro, who assaulted Mrs. Knott ... was taken out of jail this morning by a mob and hanged to a tree a short distance from here. Pinned to the body was a paper bearing the words: 'This man confessed his crime'" ("Let Out and Lynched," 1885).

The *Evening Capital* flippantly acknowledged in 1886 that "Judge Lynch is having a busy time of it," painting lynching as an accepted element of the regional justice system ("Judge Lynch," 1886). In this atmosphere publicly condoning violence, Anne Arundel County courts were notoriously lenient on accused lynchers. For instance, in 1907 a Circuit Court Judge instructed a grand jury that they were compelled to charge lynchers "if information could be found to convict the guilty" ("Circuit Court Meets," 1907). However, he was hesitant to convict White men who lynched accused Black rapists, because "it was not remarkable that persons should take the law in their hands when a woman was robbed of that which was far dearer than any mere property." In 1896, *The Bee* lamented the racist Maryland justice system when it observed that "some Negro in Maryland must hang. That is a settled question. The unwritten law of Maryland is that if a white person is killed and the murderer cannot be found, some Negro must hang for it" ("A Negro to Die," 1896). The last documented lynching in Annapolis came in 1906, when a mob gathered at St. John's College chapel, donned disguises, and stormed the jail for an unconvicted African American in custody. The prisoner was lynched when sympathetic jail guards admitted the crowd ("A Disgrace," 1906).

In one of the city's most controversial cases, John Snowden was hanged in February, 1919 after 18 months of imprisonment and torture at the hands of Annapolis police. Maintaining his innocence until his death, Snowden was convicted of the rape and murder of a White woman. This sort of charge against African-American men was commonplace, but 11 members of the jury that convicted Snowden signed a petition requesting his death sentence be commuted. This alone was astounding, and another 67 Whites signed a petition to the Governor pleading for a more lenient sentence ("The Colored Citizen's Part," 1919). Despite such sentiment, Snowden was hanged in the Calvert Street jail yard on February 28, 1919 ("Big Funeral," 1919).

A stunned *Evening Capital* recognized the unsettling alliance of Whites and African Americans against the Snowden sentence and condemned the "serious dissension of feeling ... between intermingled whites and blacks" ("The Colored Citizen's Part," 1919). The paper observed that

> The death of John Snowden points a moral to the colored people of Annapolis which it is well they should heed.... Colored people who are honestly convinced of the innocence of Snowden or who have even the slightest feeling that their race has been persecuted must accept the judgement of the courts as good citizens. They must do more. They must so conduct themselves that racial prejudice will be dismissed even if it cannot be eliminated, and thus make less likely the possibility of injustice being done to them as a race. They must seek to gain the respect of the white people by a course of conduct equal to that of the best of whites.

Yet on March 3 of that year, the paper printed an anonymous letter from the victim's jilted lover, which admitted "I am sorry you killed Snowden today. He is not the guilty man. I am the man" ("Anonymous Letter," 1919).

The racism of the legal system and police was amplified by a variety

of Whites who aggressively attempted to police public space. The Ku
Klux Klan was the most radical voice of racism in the wake of World
War I, but its basic sentiments enjoyed far more following than most
Whites admitted. Formed in 1867, the Klan lay dormant until 1915,
when immigration hysteria, anti-Bolshevik frenzy, and the ascendance
of eugenics provided a fertile ground for its reemergence (Gossett
1963:371). Despite its reputation for strategic terror and secretive violence, the Klan articulated deep-seated White apprehensions that were
explored by numerous postbellum organizations cut from similar cloth.

The reborn Klan literally paraded into Annapolis and southern
Maryland in the 1920s. In October 1922, a phalanx of "Two Thousand
Men, In White Robes" proceeded to a Klan cross-burning on the city's
outskirts. The *Evening Capital* loftily described the parade through
African-American neighborhoods along Duke of Gloucester and West
Streets as a "Spectacular Pageant Saturday":

> Members of the Ku Klux Klan came into the wide open Saturday night.
> Marching behind a huge emblazoned cross, symbol of the organization, the
> illumination being by acetylene gas, and clad in the full regalia of the order of
> white robes and hoods, except that the face-caps of the hoods were thrown
> back, to comply with legal requirements, about 2,000 Klansmen—from var-
> ious parts of the state ... participated in a spectacular parade through the
> principal streets of Annapolis.... The visiting K.K.'s were the guests of those
> of Annapolis and Anne Arundel County, of whom there are reported to be in
> the neighborhood of 1,000, and street parade had its finale in an oyster roast
> and feast at Horn Point.... Hundreds of residents of the city, who had never
> before seen a parade of the secret organization, gathered along the principal
> streets covered by the line of march—Gloucester, West and Main.... Floods of
> dodgers were scattered about like confetti, all of them inscribed as follows:
> Member ship [sic] in the KU KLUX KLAN is systematically against and
> regularly opposed to any and everything contrary to PURE AMERICAN-
> ISM. It works within the law legally and morally and welcomes honest
> criticism. It is an active Protestant organization, with strong backing, insist-
> ing upon the unhampered maintenance of all American institutions, and
> continues to advance and will go ahead notwithstanding all opposition from
> any quarter whatsoever because of its determination for right and its belief
> in PURE AMERICANISM. Membership open to all American gentlemen.
> Your name, address and telephone number will be held sacred when placed
> on the reverse side hereof ("Ku Klux Klan in Full Garb" 1922:1,5)

The Klan articulated the most aggressive coordinated campaign to
racially "purify" America and refine the construction of Anglo-Saxon
subjectivity, and the pamphlets distributed in Annapolis reflect its central interests. The Klan assertively established a relationship between
"Americanism" and Whiteness, a current of nationalist racism that had
simmered in racial thought since the Civil War. They exploited the
erosion of White religiosity in the early twentieth century by asserting

a racial basis for Christian identity and targeting Jews, Catholics, and Blacks as inverses to Northern European Protestantism. The Klan also manipulated White mens' deepest fears about the dangers to White "manhood" that were posed by Blacks and Europeans. By clothing all these anxieties within the secrecy of shrouds and personal anonymity, the Klan developed a particularly ominous forum for many Whites to brazenly express, inflate, and in some cases maliciously act out their apprehensions. The Annapolis press fanned popular curiosity in the Klan with frequent sensational coverage of the Klan's seemingly respectable public face. For instance, the *Evening Capital Maryland Gazette* reported in 1924 that the Klan held

> a demonstration at Patuxent last night. It was a "naturalization" meeting, and nearly 30 new members were initiated. Between 200 and 300 Ku Kluxers, in their white robes, but without hoods, participated, and there were 600 or more onlookers.... An illuminated cross was set up in a field near the station. ("Grand Dragon 'Lost' on Road," 1924)

Not all White Annapolitans sympathized with the Klan, recognizing that it threatened to amplify restrained local racism with a more violent public hatred. A few days after the October 1922 Klan parade through Annapolis' streets, a reader responded that the organization

> which is masquerading under the name of the Ku Klux Klan is no more the original Ku Klux Klan than the Americanism which they profess is true Americanism. It is racial prejudice, bigotry, religious jealousy, hatred, superstition which no amount of flag-waving, ballyhoo and mouthing of the name of GOD can disguise.... Aside from the fact that the Ku Klux Klan is anti-Catholic, anti-Jewish, and anti-Negro, the mob-intention of the thing is intolerable.... Take Annapolis, with its small suburbs and little country districts where people have lived together, done business, inter-married, lived, worked, died together in neighborliness for years, with amiable toleration and no actually bitter differences—but with the spread of the Ku Klux Klan this is going to be broken up. ("Recent Parade of Ku Klux Klan," 1922)

The state-sanctioned anti-Black legal system and the covert popular front of organizations like the Klan provided legal and extra-legal mechanisms to patrol White public space. The legal system amplified a tenacious White illusion that Blacks were inherently criminal and must be subject to codes and penalties unlike those applicable to White citizens. Violence and coercive threats like those of the Klan were integral to legally coded White racism because they demonstrated the profound reach of White sanctions. Most racialized codes were more subtle than lynchings and an anti-Black justice system, yet everyday racial regulations were dependent on the apprehension engendered by lynchings, Klan hyperbole, and White mob justice.

This racist web spread to all facets of everyday African-American life. For instance, even though it was supported by an immense African-American labor staff, the Naval Academy Superintendent brazenly restricted academy access to Whites in 1890 ("The Naval Academy," 1890). The Secretary of the Navy was forced to rescind the Superintendent's order, which attempted to eject African Americans who picnicked at the Academy and banish the many African-American nurses and housekeepers who brought their White charges to the grounds. Mount Moriah Pastor I.F. Aldridge applauded the Secretary's order in the *Evening Capital*, concluding that "I have always believed (from the signs of actions, conditions, and prejudice,) that [Academy Superintendent] Captain Simpson would not have issued such an order against anybody but colored people" ("The Naval Academy," 1890). It was indeed a rather bold gesture to racially restrict what Annapolitans considered a public space, the city's closest approximation of a park. Such gestures were made possible by a racial climate that legitimized increasingly oppressive legal regulations on African-American rights and tacitly condoned the violent sentiments eventually enforced by the Klan. This atmosphere gave Whites some contorted rationalization to usurp labor rights as well. In the 1930s, for instance, Academy officials uprooted some African-American staff in hopes of securing a "less undesirable" Filipino minority (Brown 1994:35). Racist violence and anti-Black jurisprudence did not create such ventures, but they enabled the routine racism that made the notion of marginalizing an indispensable workforce seem like a reasonable possibility.

The Politics of Racial Resettlement in Annapolis

Perhaps the most forceful strategy to restrict African-American civil rights was persistent city, county, and Naval Academy schemes to resettle African Americans. Relocation plans were driven by a complex amalgam of interests, which included disbanding African-American voting blocks, eliminating Black neighborhoods, and securing room for Academy and state and local government expansion. Some resettlement plans were directed at White neighborhoods, but African-American communities clearly received disproportionate attention. Why certain neighborhoods were chosen for Academy expansion, government buildings, or public parking lots was for the most part unspoken, a situation much like that in many other communities. In 1889, for example, *The Bee* noted that any African American who doubted the presence of racism in Washington should try to rent a house from any of the leading real estate agents and you will discover your mistake. We do not say that they will not rent houses under their control to tenants, but we do say that they will not rent a colored man a house in a desirable and central location. They have plenty of death and disease breeding traps in the alleys ... in the disreputable quarters which colored persons can, if they so will, rent. ("Prejudice," 1889)

The paper revisited the subject in 1918 and painted it as a longstanding, albeit strategically unspoken, anti-Black socioeconomic strategy. The owners of Washington's many alley homes "do not come out flatly and state their real attitude. Just now they would not be so frank as was a certain agent who a few years ago said at a private meeting, 'We want to keep the niggers in the alleys.' These people are influential" ("The Alley Law," 1918). Much like in neighboring Washington, there is no unequivocal evidence that resettlement forces in Annapolis intentionally sought out African-American neighborhoods. Nevertheless, given the persistent resettlement of African-American neighborhoods and evidence of the city's racist climate, it certainly seems probable that some White Annapolitans saw government and Academy expansion as an opportunity to displace African Americans and other "undesirable" communities.

Six years after the Naval Academy was established in 1845, it had already begun the forced resettlement of African-American Annapolitans. In 1851, the Academy's Board of Examiners advocated the purchase of a row of free African-American homes for Academy expansion (Todorich 1984:93). In June 1853, the Academy purchased these homes as part of three tracts covering 33 acres (Sweetman 1979:45). The homes were leveled along with the entire acquisition, and soil and debris from the lots was pushed to the edge of the Academy's seawall, where it was used as fill in the Severn River and Annapolis Harbor.

In 1873, a four-acre, predominately African-American neighborhood known as Lockwoodsville was selected for Academy expansion (Sweetman 1979:102). Lying along the northwest edge of the Academy's holdings, the community was described by the city paper as "about fifteen acres, more or less, and is mostly inhabited by colored people.... The houses are mostly of an humble character" ("Enlargement of the Naval Academy," 1873). In June 1873, the *Maryland Republican and State Capital Advertiser* reported haggling over the tract, which resulted in the neighborhood being "declined by the government, owing it is said, to the high price asked by the owners" ("Not Sold," 1873). But in January 1874, the paper reported that the dispute had been resolved, because

Government agents have instituted a jury of inquisition ... to settle the price of all property the government desires to obtain possession of. By the sale of this property a large number of families will be compelled to procure residences in other portions of the city. ("The Lockwoodsville Property," 1874)

City officials had a particularly uneasy relationship with the Academy. Periodically, the Academy threatened to leave Annapolis in order to secure new parcels and maintain leverage over city officials. Reluctant to deny Academy demands and reliant on Navy income, Annapolis officials and merchants at the very least tolerated annexation of the marginalized neighborhoods around the Academy.

Such expansion continued relatively unabated until about 1950. After World War II, the Academy brazenly pressed the city to turn over the St. John's College campus for Academy annexation, which had been undisturbed since 1697 (White and White 1957:148–149). Eager to ensure the flow of Academy dollars into the local economy, the Chamber of Commerce sided with the Academy and sparked a grass-roots movement to save the campus. Defeated at St. John's, the Academy continued to prod the city to turn over and raze several of the city's most prominent colonial homes, and Annapolis preservationists gained an energy and influence that they have never lost. Unlike the annexation of African-American neighborhoods, losing Annapolis' colonial landscape posed a significant threat to the city's tourist economy and imagined genteel past (Potter 1994). A patriotic White history provided a mechanism to mask the city's social, class, and racial unrest in the past and present, so the Academy's attempts to remove the material symbols of that history were met with articulate and powerful resistance. In contrast, African-American neighborhoods complicated optimistic Cold War tourist histories.

The city's deference to the Academy was distinctive, but the city government's pattern of tacitly sanctioning destruction of African-American neighborhoods reached throughout the community. A handful of state and local government buildings were built in African-American neighborhoods after the 1920s, including the state government complex around Bladen Street, a county government building at Calvert and Northwest, and the county courthouse expansion between South and Franklin Streets. Like Gott's Court and the lot across from the Court on Calvert Street, the Courthouse neighborhood's homes were razed simply to clear parking lots for government employees and tourists. In 1957, Clarence Marbury White and Evangeline Kaiser White wrote that the Bellis Court neighborhood along

South Street has completely changed from a street of small frame residences in very good condition, occupied by our best colored citizens. All of these

> homes except about three at the corner of South and Cathedral were razed, and many families were bereft of their homes before adequate substitutes had been built for them to move to. (White and White 1957:42)

Historian Philip Brown (1994:19) concludes that by the 1930s Annapolitan realtors systematically refused to sell or rent to African Americans in White neighborhoods, so displaced African Americans had increasingly fewer housing options. The expansion of the Academy and city and state government dovetailed with the decline in housing options and stimulated African-American movement to the city's West Street outskirts. Some displaced African Americans settled in a series of public housing projects. The first of these, College Creek Terrace, contained 100 households and was opened on Clay Street in 1940 (Brown 1994:27). Other uprooted African Americans moved into the largely unsettled Parole area, which lay along West Street outside the city limits. In doing so, these Annapolitans followed a trail blazed by dislodged African Americans in the early twentieth century. In 1906, the *Afro-American Ledger*'s Annapolis news column reported that

> The Afro-Americans of Camp Parole and Germantown, two growing villages near this city, have commenced to purchase lots for the purpose of building.... These people are beginning to realize that the Academy will need more ground in the near future, taking in another colored settlement as it did before and smoking them out before they could buy elsewhere. ("Afro-Americans Building Towns," 1906)

One man who grew up on South Street remembered that after African Americans were uprooted "most of them went to Parole. There are quite a number who are living, who are descendants of those people, who live in the Parole area. Well, actually that was the only place that they could get any more land" (Warner and Ford 1990). One African American described the community that emerged in Parole as "a black paradise.... They had some of the cutest little cottages and houses and farms" (Warren 1990). Parole today is developed with a mix of shopping and residential areas, of which one African American said "ninety percent of that was owned by black people" prior to development beginning in the 1950s. Working-class Whites began to move to the Parole area by the Depression, and several Parole neighborhoods established covenants in the 1930s that barred Black residency. In the late 1950s, a shopping center was built in the neighborhood, once again swallowing up many former African-American neighborhoods.

Forced resettlement clearly was intended to break up African-American voting blocks. One African American acknowledged the impact of dissolving a voting population like the one around Clay Street and Washington Street.... that was really a thriving, a rather thriving community.... There were politics, because it was a concentrated site. And so to break up the vote, those things happened, and so now it's that much separated all over the place, so there's no concentrated vote. (Warner and Ford 1990)

Another man commented that "what is interpreted as urban renewal ... was a displacement of people, certain types of people, that some people felt they were undesirable" (Warren 1990). He believed that "urban renewal" was stimulated by White apprehension of African-American communities who "really had what we would call a voter block.... we had those types of neighborhoods. And one of the things that government, whether it be state, county or city, did not appreciate was to have so much power in that one particular [group], you see" (Warren 1990).

RACE AND RACISM
AS CONSTRAINING AND ENABLING

None of these interests of anti-Black racists existed separately; instead, they were all part of a densely interwoven web that was so common that it was beyond question. Certainly many archaeologists recognize that racism has considerable power to construct divisions between groups. However, only a handful explicitly define racism as a social and material process more complex than separate public rights and barriers to economic opportunity (e.g., Babson 1990; Epperson 1990; Paynter 1988). Generally, archaeologists simply assume the presence of racism without any consideration of its complexity or precise constitution in a particular time and place. Others think we have overestimated its influence: Lu Ann De Cunzo (1998:52), for instance, voices the concern that archaeologists have painted racism as an overwhelming material and social structure that fails to concede African-American agency. For thinkers like De Cunzo, race and racism have been portrayed only as disabling structures of totalizing might in the form of plantation domination and Jim Crow. Reducing racism to its most coercive conditions or exaggerating their sway could indeed produce analyses that insinuate African-American powerlessness. It is shortsighted to fixate upon racism's limitations of agency, because race is a variously routine, discursive, historical, and coercive symbolic and material phenomenon that is both constraining and enabling. It is perhaps even more shortsighted, though, to simply dispense with race as an element of African-American subjectivity. Racist codes, Whiteness, and racialization were coeval with, rather than separable from, subjectivity; that is, it is infeasible to approach racism simply as a system of transparent coercion that self-conscious agents escaped to forge culture, ethnicity, or other identities. Racialization was the fundamental framework for defining and contesting social subjectivities; race even contributed to subjectivities in defiance of racial caricatures. Certainly many African Americans were unable to define race as a sociohistorical construct, rather than a natural identity, so it would be reckless to argue that African-American consumers used commodities to defy the existence of race itself. However, increasingly more African Americans advocated sociopolitical unity based upon some articulation of Blackness during the early twentieth century, ranging from entrepreneurial champions like Calvin Chase, to separatists like Marcus Garvey, to Alain Locke and the thinkers involved in the New Negro movement and Harlem Renaissance (cf. Gilroy 1987:245–246).

African-American material meaning was both circumscribed and empowered by a network of racist codes and racialization. To appreciate the force of racism, it is critical to understand that all forms of anti-Black regulation and enforcement were interdependent, from window displays to hair straightening to Academy resettlement to Klan parades. These racist discourses constrained African-American privileges, yet alongside consumer goods they provided a launching pad for an utterly politicized African-American material symbolism.

"Producers as Well as Consumers"

Market Space in African-American Annapolis

4

In 1902, the *Afro-American Ledger* succinctly outlined perhaps the most optimistic vision of African-American entrepreneurship. The paper captured a widespread commitment to constructing an African-American business space when it argued that "when we get to be in a business community, producers as well as consumers, the race question will in great measure disappear as we more and more increase in wealth and business capacity" ("A Question of Business," 1902). The hope invested in African-American business often was this profound. In 1890, for example, *The Bee* soberly surveyed African-American social and material prospects in the face of withered Reconstruction-era African-American political influence. The paper concluded that there "is nothing to be made out of politics, but broken bones and empty pockets. . . . What we must do is to establish stores of our own and hire our own boys and girls, men and women" ("Co-Operation," 1890:2). Two years later, the paper again emphasized that marketing likely harbored African America's most critical transformative potential: Calvin Chase's *The Bee* went so far as to argue that *"The Bee* is of the opinion that there is a race problem and there is but one way to solve it and that way is co operation in business" ("The Race Problem," 1892). Eventually these calls for mercantile organization were expanded to embrace production as well. In 1909, for instance, *The Bee* concluded that "The Negro must be able to stand upon his own bottom and when he can produce as well as consume he will be a factor and not until them [sic] should he crow" ("The Negro in Business," 1909). By 1919, Marcus Garvey's Negro Factories Corporation proposed to establish African-American factories "to manufacture every marketable commodity" throughout the Western Hemisphere and Africa (Levine 1993:127). Garvey's ambitious goals were never realized, but in the early 1920s his United Negro Improvement Association did enjoy the support of many African Americans who

hoped to establish increasingly self-determining African-American production and marketing spaces.

By the turn of the century, racist regulation in politics, housing, and
White consumer space disheartened many African Americans once en-
ergized by the possibilities of freedom and Reconstruction. A vast range
of conservative and radical African-American thinkers believed that
marketing could transform racism, economic inequality, and even
African-American collective psychology. For many African Americans,
an African-American market space emerged as one of the most likely
venues to fashion material, social, and civil self-determination. As suggested by the *Afro-American Ledger*'s suggestion in 1902 that African-
American business could make race "disappear," the hope invested in
business was often unreasonable, naive, or rhetorical. In 1904, for instance, the normally cynical *The Bee* observed that "when the negro has
his own places [of business] he will forget his color, and will be less
dependent on places controlled by white people" ("Oppress Him," 1904).
This may have been a rhetorical gesture by editor Calvin Chase, but for
some observers a self-determining African-American market space
could at least evade, if not erode, racism.

A complex tangle of social, moral, and self interests converged in
African-American business discourses, yet most of these thinkers
shared an acknowledgement that African-American consumption could
empower the collective community. Always an energetic champion of
African-American business cooperativism, *The Bee* attributed its support for an African-American market space to anti-Black racism in
White consumer space and the social cohesion—what some scribes
termed "race pride"—that cooperative businesses would foster. In 1891,
for example, the paper lamented the

> restrictions and discriminations which certain business houses practice
> against us…. At a low estimate, the colored people spend $5,000,000 each
> year in the stores of this city…. At least two thousand persons are employed
> in various capacities to manage this trade, and to share in the proceeds. But
> of this vast number there are very few of our own race and blood. We are thus
> supporting, seemingly, willingly, the very oppressions of which we com-
> plain. We are giving to the caucasian a golden cane to crack our own heads
> with. ("The People Aroused," 1891)

Numerous local consumer marketplaces developed in turn-of-the-
century African America, and Annapolis mirrored many of the national
trends in African-American marketing and business. In Annapolis,
African-American entrepreneurs operating storefront businesses stabi-
lized around the turn of the century by focusing on an African-American
clientele, and entrepreneurs enjoyed social status in the community,
yet the city's African-American consumer marketplace never assumed

grand proportions. Instead, African Americans always were compelled to purchase a considerable amount of goods from White marketers. Ideologues like Chase prophesied significant potential in African-American entrepreneurship, but a truly sovereign African-American consumer space never emerged anywhere. Clearly the objective control of production and capital by a White manufacturing elite made the fabrication of an autonomous market space infeasible, but it was not an inconceivable possibility to many African Americans. Certainly the story of African-American entrepreneurship includes many failed ventures, and is to some extent an account of the objective control of one class over the masses. Yet these African-American businesses were not inconsequential in their material impact, since many provided essential goods and services, and they structured African-American social space in many communities. Perhaps more significantly, businesses served as a pivotal focus for African-American material discourse, a way to ponder the relationship between African-American consumers and White marketers, African-American class structure, and shared African-American social and material aspirations.

"WHAT CAN BE DONE BY THE NEGRO": AFRICAN-AMERICAN ENTREPRENEURSHIP

Always eager to promote successful African-American businesses throughout the region, in 1898 Baltimore's *Afro-American Ledger* hailed the Annapolis grocery of Wiley Bates (Figure 12). The paper observed that "Mr. W.H. Bates, our enterprising grocer is showing to the world what can be done by the Negro from a business standpoint, and should receive the praise and cooperation of the race" ("Annapolis Notes," 1898). Bates' grocery at the corner of Cathedral and South Streets in the Courthouse neighborhood was home to Annapolis' best-known African-American merchant. In many ways, Bates' story was quite comparable to that of many African-American entrepreneurs. Born enslaved in North Carolina in 1859, Bates came to Annapolis when he was 15 and shucked oysters for a livelihood. A fellow shucker helped Bates secure work as a waiter at a Point Comfort, Virginia, resort, and in 1878 he worked for a season at the stylish Bryn Mawr Hotel in Pennsylvania. A White contributor to Bates' 1928 autobiography, George Shearman, believed the Pennsylvania employment was a critical formative experience for Bates. Shearman noted that

> being a close observer, he listened with wide-opened ears to his and his associates' discussions, which gave him more inspiration to keep going to that high reward which he had often pictured in his mind. As he listened to

Figure 12. Around 1919, Wiley Bates sat for this photograph with wife Annie (right) and May Ella Watkins (left) (courtesy of the Maryland State Archives; Special Collections, Banneker-Douglass Collection, MSA SC 2010-25).

the eloquence of those assembled around the table, a thought came to him
that he had five senses as well as they and, says he, "I am going to use them."
(Bates 1928:24)

Bates began to peddle oysters and crabs in Annapolis in 1879. In
1884, he used his crab profits to rent a one-room store on Cathedral
Street ("W.H. Bates, Grocer," 1897). He expanded his business to include
wood sales, but Shearman observed that "so many of his customers
would come in asking for starch, soap, and other articles that Bates
deemed it wise to invest something in groceries" (Bates 1928:25). Bates
stocked a small grocery store with $25.00 worth of staple goods, includ-
ing 10 pounds of ginger snaps, 1 pound each of chewing tobacco, salt,
and yeast, and one-half barrel each of two different brands of flour.

Bates' grocery was one of many African-American market spaces
in turn-of-the-century Annapolis. As in most communities, African-
American marketing in Annapolis was relatively modest and geared to
staple needs (e.g., grocers) or an exclusively African-American clientele
(e.g., hairdressers). In the wake of the Civil War, African-American
enterprises generally had very little stability. When the *Afro-American
Ledger* championed Wiley Bates' grocery in 1898, Annapolis' African-
American market venues remained economically precarious, short-
term ventures. The transience of early African-American businesses
reflects a host of dilemmas, including lack of investment capital, an
inability to compete with financially stable consumer venues, and the
stigma attached to Black businesses by most White, and some African-
American, consumers. The seeds of the most stable African-American
enterprises were planted by Reconstruction, and likely far earlier, when
a handful of relatively unnoticed barbers, peddlers, seamstresses, and
other small-scale entrepreneurs managed businesses geared primarily
to African Americans. By the early twentieth century, many of these
sorts of operations were among the city's most prosperous African-
American enterprises.

Free African Americans had managed a few poorly documented
storefront enterprises prior to the Civil War. Thomas Folks, for instance, owned a retail store in Annapolis early in the nineteenth century; John Smith opened an oyster house in the city after the War of
1812; and Charles Hanson opened a second oyster house in the 1820s
(Calderhead 1977:16). By the 1820s, African Americans also ran an ice
cream parlor and a bakery and managed two stalls at the market house
(Calderhead 1977:15). In 1844, 18 Blacks held carting licenses in Annapolis, hauling merchandise and supplies throughout the city and the
region (Calderhead 1977:16). An untold number of African Americans

sold goods in the street, and municipal jobs, such as street cleaning
and maintenance, often went to African Americans.
The first significant wave of African-American entrepreneurship in
Annapolis apparently came in the 1890s. This timing reflects a range of
factors; chief among these was eroding African-American roles in partisan politics, vigorous efforts to disfranchise African Americans, and the
promotion of racialized public laws (e.g., segregated rail and streetcar
laws) that were codified in the early 1900s (Mullins 1996:237–244). In
the midst of this upheaval of African-American public privileges, African Americans vested more hope in marketing. In January 1897, *The
Bee* featured a full front-page biography of Wiley Bates and reviewed
Annapolis' embryonic African-American marketplace. *The Bee* noted
that Bates' grocery

> takes rank among the leading grocery houses of the city. The premises are
> large and commodious. Mr. Bates deals in dry goods, groceries and provi-
> sions, and always has on hand a splendid stock, which is sold at reasonable
> rates.... His trade embraces many of the leading families of the city and
> surrounding districts. ("W.H. Bates, Grocer," 1897)

The paper observed that Bates' "large wholesale and retail grocery store
on Cathedral street ... has a large patronage from both races" ("What the
Colored People of Annapolis, Md. are Doing," 1897).
Bates was the archetypal self-made African-American businessman who saved his money and managed a modest yet stable business for
most of his life. Unlike Bates, though, most of Annapolis' pre-1900
African-American merchants either ran quite modest enterprises or
struggled to remain viable. In 1880, most of the city's African-American
businesses probably were managed from the home. That year's census
indicates that seamstresses, shoemakers, barbers, and a florist all apparently were conducting their trades from their parlors, and many
more enterprises of the same scale probably evaded the census enumerator's attention (Mullins 1996:560–567). However, by 1900 virtually
all of these 1880 enterprises had disappeared. Thomas Queen's florist
shop in his Market Street home was the lone exception, with Queen still
in business in 1925.
More African Americans launched businesses in the 1890s but,
like the 1880s enterprises, they were relatively short-lived ventures.
The Bee identified 10 African-American merchants in their 1897 review.
John Carroll, for instance, ran "a nice grocery and confectionery store
on Main street, and is doing a fair business"; W.S. Stepney "runs the
leading hotel in the city ... [and] has a first class barber shop"; John
Lain had "a first-class bootblack establishment on Main street"; Charles

Harris was "proprietor of the Market Restaurant"; Hall Brothers was called "the leading undertakers of Annapolis"; and Stephen Smothers had "a nice little grocery store on Cathedral street, and is doing a good business" a few doors away from Wiley Bates ("What the Colored People of Annapolis, Md. are Doing," 1897). Yet none of these men appeared three years later in the 1900 census; only 2 of *The Bee's* 10 entrepreneurs appeared in any subsequent record. Official record keepers may well have ignored some African-American businesses, but the complete absence of these marketers in any subsequent census, directory, or other record argues that the enterprises identified by *The Bee* in 1897 were very short-lived. Beside Bates, the lone long-term business survivor among the 10 men in *The Bee* article apparently was Henry Hebron, who in 1897 was "the president of the Union Oyster Packing Company" ("What the Colored People of Annapolis, Md. are Doing," 1897). In 1925 *The First Colored Directory of Baltimore City* included among its Annapolis business entries Henry Hebron, a "Dealer in Fish and Crabs" who was likely the same man or a son of the man in *The Bee's* 1897 story (Coleman 1925:128).

The high collapse rate among Annapolis' African-American businesses was a familiar national pattern. African-American merchants usually had modest capital to invest in their ventures, compelling entrepreneurs to secure marginal sales spaces, purchase smaller quantities of goods, and market their goods at higher prices. In 1916, the *Afro-American Ledger* reported on a group of African-American entrepreneurs in Philadelphia that had banded together "to establish co-operative stores of their own. Here was the rub, the capital with which to begin. One man only, and he 'a saloonkeeper' had as much as one thousand dollars to invest in the new enterprise" ("On Money," 1916). Even the most prescient marketers were compelled to generate objective capital, a significant obstacle for African Americans. Many marginalized entrepreneurs were forced to parcel their scarce capital to cover rent, store stock and supplies, and then hope that the venture turned a reasonably rapid profit. This was a dilemma that plagued African-American marketers well into the twentieth century. In 1932, Paul Edwards (1969:137) noted that

> the inability to obtain capital from within the group and the extreme slowness of the accumulation of individual savings at least partially explain the fact that the great majority of Negro retailers in the urban South begin operations with wholly inadequate fixed and working capital.

An African-American Annapolitan noted the effect of inadequate capital, remembering that during the 1930s

> We did have a few black people who had stores, but they were smaller.... they
> were mostly, well, a few canned goods like beans and sugar and, maybe, a
> small amount of meat, pork chops, maybe bologna and cheese, a few eggs
> and stuff like that. Their volume was very small. (Warren 1990)

Aspiring African-American merchants had very few banks from which they could borrow money, and the failures and deceits of White bankers did nothing to increase African-American faith in such repositories. In 1908, the *Afro-American Ledger* reported that the country had only 35 African-American banks ("Colored Men in Business," 1908). The number of African-American banks and their security did not increase much by the late 1920s. In 1928, only 34 of the nation's 26,227 banks were African-American-owned, and 5 of those 34 banks failed in 1929 (Edwards 1969:143). The absence of an African-American bank in Annapolis undoubtedly made it difficult for African-American entrepreneurs to mount significant initial funds, afford to advance credit, or survive the losses of a new enterprise. Wiley Bates probably was not the only African American to raise his or her initial capital by working as a huckster or waiter. But African Americans often had few other sources of income or credit that would support their business while it established itself.

African-American fraternal organizations, such as the Masons, had capital reserves that may have been loaned to aspiring entrepreneurs. Annapolis' African-American Elks Club, Prince Hall Freemasons, and social organizations, such as the Royal Flush Club, all purchased meeting houses, so they clearly had tangible club coffers. Many African Americans were members of one or more fraternals, with the *Maryland Republican and State Capital Advertiser* noting in 1875 that "Nearly every colored man in the South belongs to at least one secret society" ("A Negro Funeral," 1875). Fraternals collected dues that funded a rich range of social activities, as well as essential services such as medical care, burials, loans, and support for deceased members' widows (cf. Brackett 1890:48).

Such groups were a common mechanism for sharing experience and resources among African-American merchants (Meier 1964:137). Wiley Bates, for example, was among Annapolis' African-American Masons, achieving 33rd degree in the labyrinthine Masonic degree system and serving as the local grand master ("Marylanders Who Have Made Good," 1921). The Masons accumulated significant assets, but it is unclear how widely such resources were lent to struggling marketers. Before the turn of the century, the Masons were conspicuous elitists who only included among their number a small circle of prosperous, well-educated men (Gatewood 1990:212). Another African-American social organization, Elks Lodge No. 175, was formed in Annapolis in December 1910 by undertaker and liquor dealer J. Albert Adams (Brown 1994:110). The presence of these and many other African-American businessmen in Annapolitan fraternals suggests that they certainly shared business acumen, but the likelihood or extent of financial loans is unclear.

Most of Annapolis' African-American merchants knew each other through fraternals, churches, or social and cultural organizations. In 1900, for example, a collective of genteel African-American entrepreneurs, including Wiley Bates, physician William Bishop, teacher William H. Butler, caterer Henry Valentine, and grocer Robert M. Davis, formed the Bamuke Literary and Musical Association ("Colored Literary Association," 1900; "Officers Elected," 1900). Designed to "develop a taste for classical literature," the relationship between genteel status and education was clear in the group's membership: their number included graduates of Howard University, Morgan College, Lincoln University, Arcon College, and Boston University ("Colored Literary Association," 1900). A 1910 *Evening Capital* article hinted at the long-standing relations among the city's African-American entrepreneurs, relations that are concealed by censuses and directories. The paper noted that

> the colored business men of the city tendered a stag party to Dr. R.P. Keese.... Among the subscribers were Henry Valentine, Henry Hebron, N.O. Cully, J. Harvey, J.R. Adams, Benjamin Stevens, A. Murray, John Cornish, N. Harris, R. Fletcher, and Perry Dobson. ("A Stag Tendered," 1910)

The newlywed Robert Peyton "Keese" (Keesee) was a physician who lived in Annapolis from 1906 to 1910 (Brown 1994:41), and the attendance at his party indicates that he knew many of the city's African-American entrepreneurs. Valentine, Hebron, and Adams still had Annapolis businesses 15 years after the party (as a caterer, fish and crab dealer, and pool hall owner, respectively). "R. Fletcher" likely was William R. Fletcher, a waiter who supervised over 100 African-American waiters at the Naval Academy's Bancroft Hall and was the grand master of the local Masons chapter in 1925 ("Waiters at the Adjunct," 1918). J.B. Harvey was the head waiter at Carvel Hall Hotel in 1905 and a Mason ("Masonic Emblem Presented," 1905). In 1910, Norman O. Cully was a barber living at 140 Market Street, the home of pool-hall proprietor John R. Adams. Aaron Murray was also a barber living at 110 Market Street, near Adams' home and Norman Cully's barber shop. Party attendee Benjamin Stevens was a barber living a few blocks away at 41 Calvert Street, which was still a shop in 1925 (when it was run by Benjamin Holt).

Some African-American entrepreneurs shrewdly moved from one venture to another, either trying a different trade or cutting their losses in one enterprise as they began another. J. Albert Adams, for instance, was operating a blacksmithing and horseshoeing business at 34 Calvert Street in 1901. In 1903, a map identified the business of "J.A. Adams, Undertaker" at 22 Calvert Street, suggesting a distinctive entrepreneurial shift (Sanborn Insurance Company 1903). The Elks Lodge Exalted Ruler, Adams was listed in the 1910 city directory as a "liquor dealer and funeral director," managing the liquor store with Jewish businessman Morris Legum (Gould and Halleron 1910:5). In 1925, Adams was still running his funeral and embalming business on Calvert Street, and his wife was managing it in 1932 (Chesapeake and Potomac Telephone Company 1932:11). Adams also served as an alderman on the Annapolis City Council from 1907 to 1909 and again from 1915 to 1921.

Many African-American entrepreneurs operated small ventures alongside their primary business or other labor. Ellen Parker, for instance, was running an undertaker's parlor from about 1910 into the 1930s, while in 1910 she was also a music teacher. Single households also tended to diversify their enterprises. John R. Adams ran a Clay Street pool parlor from about 1910 to 1925. His wife Beulah was a chiropodist from their Market Street home, and in 1925 their 24-year-old son, Adam, was living with them and working from home as a violin instructor (Coleman 1925).

AFRICAN-AMERICAN MARKETING IN JIM CROW ANNAPOLIS

African-American businesses in Baltimore and Washington began to stabilize around the turn of the century. In 1890, Jeffrey Brackett acknowledged that Baltimore had some African-American business successes. Yet he concluded that "the greater number of stores, however, are small, and deal mostly with the colored people and the poorer whites. In these are sold china and glass-ware, groceries, produce, oysters, 'notions,' &c., as the case may be" (Brackett 1890:29). In 1902, in contrast, the *Afro-American Ledger* more optimistically observed that in one area of Baltimore

> There are over fifty business enterprises carried on by our people. In this number is included business as well as professional people, barber shops as well as a few saloons; dress makers as well as furniture movers, and laundries. ("In the Matter of Business," 1902)

In 1908, the paper reported that Baltimore had "fully five hundred men and women engaged in business, and though, in some instances, conducted on a small scale, and with small capital, yet a fair living is made" ("Colored Men in Business," 1908).

Much like their Baltimore neighbors, African-American entrepreneurs in Annapolis carved a viable niche between 1900 and 1925. The increasing stability of Annapolis' African-American marketers is reflected in a comparison of the 1910 city directory and a 1925 directory of the city's African-American businesses. The two directories reflect a general national pattern in which African-American businesses grew more stable by concentrating their trade on African-American consumers. Of the 1111 entries for African Americans in Annapolis' 3777-entry 1910 city directory, positions as laborers (295), oystermen (138), servants (122), and waiters and waitresses (102) dominated the Black entries. These occupations almost universally would have placed African Americans in the employ of Whites, although some of these laborers probably worked for themselves or for other African Americans. Businesses owned and managed by African Americans were not identified in the directory, but barbers (18), doctors (4), undertakers (3), attorneys (2), a dressmaker (1), and a hairdresser (1) were the sorts of positions that primarily, if not exclusively, catered to African Americans.

In 1925, *The First Colored Directory of Baltimore City* included 37 businesses in its Annapolis section (Coleman 1925). Of those 37, 26 proprietors either had been doing the same work or living in Annapolis in 1910. In 1925 13 African Americans were still managing the same businesses at their 1910 addresses. Robert M. Davis, for instance, managed a Clay Street grocery from 1910 to at least 1925. In 1925, just as 15 years earlier, Thomas Queen was still running his Market Street florist shop; John Hall still had a barber shop at 42 Washington Street (which son Charles would be running by 1928); and Benjamin Holt still was a barber on Calvert Street, where he would remain until at least 1939. Five 1910 entrepreneurs were in the same business in 1925, but had changed addresses to business locations in the heart of the predominately African-American West Street neighborhood. Many African-American women certainly managed viable enterprises, but they were ignored by compilers of the 1910 directory, who simply recorded their husbands as the head of household.

In 1899, W.E.B. Du Bois identified the emergence of venues catering to African Americans and saw this as the basis for future African-American marketing. Du Bois found 83 caterers, 23 barber shops, 23 restaurants, 13 grocery stores, and 4 undertaking parlors among the African-American enterprises in Philadelphia's Seventh Ward (Du Bois

90

Chapter 4

1996:117–119). Du Bois noted that the 13 grocery stores were "mostly new ventures, eight being less than a year old.... most of them will soon go to the wall and their places taken by others" (Du Bois 1996:117). Despite what he saw as the imminent failure of most of these early African-American groceries, he believed that the "ambition of the middle class of Negroes lies in this direction.... the number of Negro groceries will undoubtedly grow considerably in the next decade" (Du Bois 1996:117).

Du Bois' conclusion that groceries would be the focus of African-American entrepreneurship certainly was correct in Annapolis. Most of Annapolis' corner stores solely or predominately marketed grocery staples and catered to neighborhood trade. These included African-American groceries like those of Wiley Bates (Cathedral Street), Sarah Boston (Northwest Street), George W. Brown (West Street), James Chapman (South Street), Robert M. Davis (Clay Street), John Gross (College Avenue), Benjamin Holt (Calvert Street), Carrol Hynson (Acton Lane), Philip Langford (South Street), William Russell (Calvert Street), William Sharps (probably Calvert Street), Stephen Smothers (Cathedral Street), Sarah Watkins (Acton Lane and Washington Street), and Ethel Weems (Washington Street).

The corner grocery merchants left specialized commodity sales to stores along West Street and elsewhere in the city, virtually all of which were White owned. In May 1908, Annapolis' *Evening Capital* included a summary of the city's businesses. The paper included 117 entries, excluding all African-American merchants, and several Jewish merchants as well. Despite its selective lapses, the inventory provides a sense of the makeup of the city's overall marketplace. The most numerous entries were for taverns and saloons (11), followed by groceries (8), and coal/wood/feed dealers and banks (5 each). Some of these businesses probably included African Americans among their clients: Louis Baer's Washington and Clay Street liquor store, for instance, was located in the heart of an almost completely African-American neighborhood, which Baer represented in the City Council. It is unclear, though, exactly what products or services African Americans could purchase only from White merchants, or what the pricing differences were between White and African-American stores. Of 117 White businesses identified in the 1908 inventory, 27 sold specialized goods, including 5 coal and fuel dealers, 4 druggists, 3 stationery stores, 3 clothiers, and solitary examples of an antique store, hatter, screen store, and jeweler ("Historical and Industrial Edition," 1908). A few African-American stores sold a specialized range or type of goods, such as James Bishop's 1880 tobacco shop or Charles Butler's 1904 novelty store ("Novelty

Store," 1904). However, the paucity of these African-American specialty stores and the fleeting amount of time most operated suggests that they were not particularly profitable.

The most common specialized enterprise in Annapolis was the saloon, with 11 saloons in the city's 1908 inventory. At least one African American, James Albert Adams, ran a liquor store, but no African-American saloon owners could be identified in the city. It is unclear if Annapolis' absence of African-American saloons reflects national trends, but there appear to have been few African-American-owned saloons in the 20 years before Prohibition. In 1897, for example, Du Bois noted only 2 saloons among 118 African-American businesses in Philadelphia's Seventh Ward (Du Bois 1996:118). The *Afro-American Ledger* reported in 1902 that Baltimore's African-American business district had over 50 African-American enterprises, but these only included "a few saloons" ("In the Matter of Business," 1902). In 1912, New York's 309 African-American merchants included just 5 saloons and cafes (Haynes 1968:99), and on the 1919 eve of Prohibition, Baltimore had only 5 saloon keepers among 929 African-American entrepreneurs (Johnson 1923:13). African-American consumers frequented White-managed saloons, but African-American entrepreneurs apparently did not focus their aspirations on the saloon trade.

The growth and stabilization of African-American business in Annapolis at the turn of the century was typical of African-American marketing throughout the country. The Negro Business League conservatively reported that the 20,000 African-American businesses in the country in 1900 mushroomed to 40,000 in 1914 (Meier 1964:140). The federal census noted a similar rate of growth, but recognized an even larger number of African-American businesses, identifying 40,445 in 1900 and 74,424 in 1920 (Oak 1949:48). Despite this growth, in most cities African-American merchants never significantly threatened White marketers' business, and most African-American Annapolitans shopped at neighborhood stores owned by African Americans, Jews, and Whites, as well as at downtown White specialty stores. Despite the vitality of racism, African Americans were virtually always accepted customers in White Annapolis stores. One woman even admitted that "I never knew that there were stores you couldn't go into and you could, until I began going to Baltimore to shop.... And then I found out there's May Company and different stores that you couldn't go to" (Warren 1990). At some Annapolis stores African Americans could not try on clothes, and some White restaurants would sell food to African Americans but not permit them to eat inside; despite such obstacles, most Annapolis stores were frequented by African Americans.

AFRICAN-AMERICAN CONSUMERS
AND JEWISH MERCHANTS

African-American consumers may have had a closer relationship with Jewish marketers than any other group of non-African-American local merchants. In the predominately African-American neighborhoods off West Street, a handful of Jewish residents conducted small businesses catering to African-American consumers, including groceries, shoe stores, clothiers, and tailor shops. Annapolis' earliest Jewish merchants were German immigrants who came to the region beginning in the mid-nineteenth century. Many likely began their careers as peddlers in the counties around Annapolis. In that form of countryside marketing, they certainly traded with African Americans, and their familiarity with African Americans, the low cost of property in African-American neighborhoods, and the opportunity to cater to a largely neglected consumer community swayed a few Jewish peddlers to open businesses in the city (cf. Goldstein 1991).

Facing weakened eastern and southern European economies and Russian persecution after the 1880s, many Jews came to the United States in a second more voluminous migration (Heinze 1990:34; United States Bureau of the Census 1900:60–62). Like the earlier wave of Jewish immigrants, many late-nineteenth century Jewish arrivals peddled goods. By 1906, a New York City government report estimated that 61% of the city's 5,000 peddlers were Jewish (Heinze 1990:195-196). Many of these New York peddlers used their profits to establish businesses within five or six years (Heinze 1990:195), and some Jewish Annapolitans followed that basic pattern. Jews opened several businesses along West Street in the 1880s and 1890s, and from these shops they marketed to local African Americans and people coming into the city from outlying areas. Morris Legum, for instance, came from Russia in 1884 and worked as a laborer at the Naval Academy before operating a series of liquor stores, corner groceries, and a hotel in African-American Annapolis for over 50 years (Goldstein 1991:7). Legum also rented numerous houses to African Americans and owned the African-American alley community Legum's Court, off Monument Street. Michael Baer, another Jew, was born in Poland in 1850 and came to the United States in 1861. He opened his first saloon at Calvert and Clay Streets in 1889, eventually moving it a block to Clay and Washington Streets (Goldstein 1991:8). Edward Weiss, a German Jew, opened a liquor store on West Street in the early 1890s (Goldstein 1991:8).

Eric Goldstein (1991:9) estimates that in 1900 about half of Annapolis' Jewish population of approximately 80 people lived at the edge of African-American neighborhoods in which the Jewish business community expanded and diversified in the early twentieth century. For instance, Samuel Copland opened a general merchandise store on Calvert Street in 1909, and Sara Finklestein opened a grocery on Washington Street in 1915. In 1910, over half of the city's 55 Jews in the city directory were merchants selling goods, including liquor (6), groceries or clothing (4 each), and general merchandise (3) (Goldstein 1991; Gould and Halleron 1910). With the expansion of these businesses and the growth of the Jewish community, Jewish marketers began to be recognized as a distinct body of merchants in the Annapolitan marketplace. In 1905, for example, the *Anne Arundel Examiner* noted that "Annapolis Hebrews" had formed a local chapter of "the Baltimore committee for the relief of the Jewish sufferers of the Russian massacres" ("Annapolis Hebrews Help," 1905). The group collected $85 from a variety of Jewish Annapolitan businessmen, which included three saloon keepers, two department store owners, two liquor dealers, two clothiers, and solitary examples of a shoe merchant, cigar and tobacco merchant, dry good merchant, junk dealer, shoe repairman, and a paper and paint merchant.

Some Jewish-owned businesses in Annapolis were large ventures located outside African-American neighborhoods. Annapolis' first grand department store, for instance, was a Main Street venture opened in 1899 by Russian-born Leon Gottlieb (Goldstein 1991:7). Aaron Goodman immigrated from Germany in 1885 and opened the city's premier clothing store at Main and Market Space in 1909 (Goldstein 1991:7). According to the 1900 census, Isaac Silver immigrated from "Poland/ Russia" in 1889, and he was managing a Main Street clothing store by the turn of the century (United States Census Population Schedules 1900). The Lyric, the city's first movie theater, was opened by Samuel Rosenberg in 1908 (Goldstein 1991:7). These venues primarily catered to White consumers, but African Americans frequented most of them.

By the mid-1920s, Jewish merchants were quite common in the African-American neighborhoods off West Street. Jews owned several groceries, liquor stores, and tailor shops, as well as the two most significant African-American entertainment venues in the city, the Star Theatre and the Washington Hotel. Opened in 1921 at the corner of Calvert and Northwest Streets, the Star billed itself as "the Only Up-To-Date Colored theatre in Annapolis" ("Star Theatre Advertisement," 1922). Morris Legum unveiled the Washington Hotel in the mid-1920s, and the hotel was among the city's most important scene of African-American live entertainment into the 1940s. African Americans worked in these establishments alongside Jewish owners, just as they did in many other Jewish-owned neighborhood businesses.

An African American mystified by the concentration of Jewish merchants in West Annapolis remembered that "I used to ask the Jews, I would ask them because, you know, 'Why do you open your store here?' 'Black people are better to deal with. It doesn't take too much to make them happy'" (Warren 1990). The appearance of satisfaction was of course not always genuine. In 1932, a White Southern shoe merchant brazenly told Paul Edwards (1969:97) that "'I'd rather have Negro than white customers, they are so much easier satisfied. But if one of them ever gets fresh with me, I'll crack him over the head with a chair.'" African-American consumers routinely were treated this unscrupulously, so they were quick to at least appear satisfied, and they were model customers when extended anything approaching equity. In 1875, Edward King observed that Jewish merchants in the South recognized and capitalized on that African-American desire for marketing fairness. King observed that

> The shrewd Hebrew ... understands the freedman very well, and manages him in trade. The negro likes to be treated with consideration when he visits the 'store,' and he finds something refreshing and friendly in the profuse European manner and enthusiastic lingo of Messrs. Moses and Abraham. (King 1875:274)

Annapolis' 1900 *Negro Appeal* included an advertisement by Jewish merchant Isaac Silver that contained a rhyme proclaiming that "all my customers I treat alike, And all who wish to buy a Suit may a Bargain strike" ("Silver's Advertisement," 1900). The verse may seem like an innocuous advertising inducement, but it reflected Silver's critical realization that African Americans desired to be treated "alike"; that is, with the same conditions extended to White consumers.

Some African Americans saw Jewish merchants as models for African-American businessmen to follow. Booker T. Washington, for instance, believed that African Americans should emulate Jews' social and marketing unity (Meier 1964:105). The Bookerite *Negro Appeal* agreed in 1900 that "the Jews are great financiers. They have great business interests and so we must get the same" ("Some Sound Sense," 1900). Yet African America's contemplation of Jewish business success harbored a complex fusion of admiration, frustration, and resentment. In 1912, for instance, *The Bee* reprimanded struggling African-American entrepreneurs by comparing themselves to self-made Jewish successes. *The Bee* argued that

> For a number of years the Jews were the most despised race in the United States. Today the Jews are the most potent factor in political as well as in commercial body politic. Take the Jew out of business in this city and the city will put on a garb of holiday.... There is too much selfishness among colored Americans to enable them to accomplish very much, which is a race weakness. Follow the Jews. Their examples make monuments. ("Our Weakness," 1912)

The Bee's commentary reflected African America's ambiguous admiration for Jewish marketers and paradoxical resentment that their eradication would prompt a "garb of holiday." Clearly the success of Jewish merchants fostered a frustrated bitterness that Jews had risen to positions of mercantile dominance from low social stations; indeed, many Americans had once considered Jews to be Black (cf. Sacks 1994). Some African Americans (and Whites) both admired and resented that success: On the one hand, it apparently demonstrated that great socioeconomic advancement was possible for subordinated races with appropriate solidarity; on the other, though, it seemed to illuminate the failure of African-American entrepreneurial and consumer cooperation, and loss of power to another marginalized race.

Some African Americans believed that Jewish marketers prospered because they willingly marginalized African-American consumers and strategically undermined competing African-American businesses. Consequently, Jewish merchants catering to African-American consumers were often viewed warily. In 1911, for example, *The Bee* criticized businesses in African-American communities that were managed by allied Jews and African Americans, arguing that a "majority of the moving picture theatres that are claimed to be owned by colored men are under the control of the Jews. The Jews are united ... while the Negro takes his time in being used by the Jew" ("Owned by Jews," 1911). In Annapolis, African-American and Jewish entrepreneurs were affiliated in at least one business, a liquor store opened by Morris Legum and James Albert Adams in 1910. Adams purchased a Calvert Street lot from liquor store owner Edward Weiss in 1902, indicating that Adams had longstanding interaction with Jewish merchants. It is unclear, though, if Adams' case was an isolated example of African-American and Jewish business relations in Annapolis.

The social and economic inequality between Jews and African Americans probably was most evident in landlord–tenant relations. An African-American woman born in Annapolis in 1917 noted that "very few Negroes in Annapolis bought homes. They rented. Because most Jews had the neighborhoods, and you had to rent" (Warren 1990). Discrimination against African Americans certainly was not restricted to Jewish landlords or limited to African-American tenants: A 1938 Annapolis Housing Authority analysis indicated that 1,042 of 2,703 families in Annapolis lived in substandard housing, including 812 African-American households (Goldstein 1991:27). Jews began purchasing property in Annapolis by the turn of the century, and some of the least expensive property in the city was in or at the margins of African-American neighborhoods. In 1906, for instance, Isaac Hohberger and Max Kotzin purchased lots in Acton Lane and Block Court, which were exclusively African-American neighborhoods on West Street and the dockside Hell Point, respectively (Goldstein 1991:25). Several alley communities were managed by Jewish landlords, including Bear's Court and Bloom's Court. Saloon keeper and grocer Morris Legum eventually accumulated about 65 houses along with his eponymous Legum's Court, most of them in African-American neighborhoods (Goldstein 1991:25–26; Warren 1990).

CHAIN AND CORNER STORES

The corner store marketing on the West Street corridor and in the Courthouse neighborhood changed relatively little before the late 1930s. At the turn of the century, though, the seeds of a stunning national marketing transformation were being planted by chain stores. The most famous of the chains was the Great Atlantic and Pacific Tea Company, a Civil-War-era firm that had nearly 200 stores by 1900 and added its first Annapolis branches in the first decade of the century (Longstreth 1997:71; Strasser 1989:222). Unlike the gargantuan A&P, most chains remained regional operations with relatively few branches until the 1920s. Early chains operated more or less like neighboring corner stores in their delivery services, telephone ordering, and extension of credit (Strasser 1989:224). On the eve of World War I, though, stores led by A&P popularized "cash and carry" terms: Consumers came in, purchased their goods with cash, and took their purchases with them, eliminating the overhead of peddlers' routes, delivery boys, and large clerking staffs. In 1908, for instance, Annapolis' Sanitary Meat Market already was trumpeting its cash-only policy, noting that because of such efficiency the store "can afford to make prices to suit a Workingman" ("Sanitary Meat Market Advertisement," 1908).

After World War I, chain sales were intensified by mergers of small stores and capital consolidation, a streamlining that led to the establishment of several enormously profitable national chains. In 1918, Asa Philip Randolph (1918:14) recognized that chain-store consolidation posed a significant threat to independent marketers. He suggested that

> In this country, all big business is carried on through the chained store system.... The isolated, individual business man has no place in the present order of things. Colored nor white can withstand the onward march of corporate capital, centralized management and direction in the hands of business experts—specialists.

As Randolph intimated, these national chain stores were considerably larger, carried a higher volume of standardized commodities, and priced goods about 10% cheaper than corner stores (Cohen 1990:109; Long-streth 1997:72).

Prior to these transformations, most chains operated much like surrounding corner stores. This was the case in Annapolis, where the Department of Commerce's 1930 census of retail trade reported that the city had 220 retail stores with an annual business of $7,877,785 (United States Department of Commerce 1933). Of those 220 stores, 192 were single store independents; 20 were regional or local chains with as few as 2 stores; and only 8 were considered part of a national chain. Chains may have weakened the business of Annapolis' neighborhood stores by the Depression, but they did not eliminate the city's corner stores: Annapolis' 28 chain stores in 1930 were responsible for only 15% of the city's total merchant profits. In contrast, chains accounted for 22% of the country's gross retail sales in 1929, including an impressive 40% of grocery sales (Longstreth 1997:71–72).

In most cities, chain stores emerged in genteel and wealthy neighborhoods, rather than marginalized communities (Cohen 1990:109). In Annapolis, chain stores were focused along Main and West Streets. In 1924, for instance, A&P had three branches in the city, including one on Main and one on West Street; the grocery chain American stores had a branch on West Street; United Cigar Stores had a Main Street outlet; and F.W. Woolworth had a five and ten cent store on Main Street (Polk 1924:231, 239, 241).

African Americans shopped in all these stores, but corner stores along the West Street corridor and in the Courthouse neighborhood held their own until at least the late 1930s. The tenacity of Annapolis corner stores was typical of most American marketplaces. In 1926, for instance, Kelsey Gardner and Lawrence Adams (1926:35) found that about one-half of all consumers bought their meats in a store within two blocks of their home. In a survey of 4,466 housewives in 16 cities, Gardner and Adams (1926:19) found that, regardless of ethnicity, consumers usually shopped in their immediate neighborhood: About one-half of poor consumers and one-third of the "middle and well to do classes" traded at the nearest meat market. Of 362 African Americans who recorded the type of market patronized, 198 (54.69%) shopped at a single-unit store marketing groceries and meats. Quite comparably, 51.9% of White consumers (i.e., excluding European immigrants) shopped in the same type of venue. Chains were patronized by only 5.24% of African-American meat consumers. Foodways likely were particularly resistant to consumption change, but inexpensive mass-marketed meats certainly were available at A&P and comparable chains to consumers motivated primarily by economy.

In the wake of World War II, many African-American consumers were dislodged by neighborhood "renewal." These programs targeted African-American neighborhoods for government and Naval Academy expansion and aimed at constructing a "historic" Annapolis to cater to the tourist trade. The main land entrance into Annapolis since the eighteenth century, West Street remains a busy artery into the city even today, but the 1950s construction of the new Rowe Boulevard entrance into the city significantly decreased the traffic flow along West Street. This dispersal of consumer communities and the construction of a shopping mall at Parole in the 1950s likely delivered a lethal blow to remaining corner marketers throughout the city.

AFRICAN-AMERICAN CONSUMER DISCIPLINE

African-American marketing discourses were central to the critique of racism in consumer space because they attempted to accept, evade, minimize, or resist economic and civil injustices inflicted by White merchants. African-American entrepreneurs probed how to appropriately construct African America's relationship to White consumer culture, a discourse that inevitably pondered the relationship between African America and White America. The result was a broad range of economic organizations ranging from acquiescent accommodation to sovereign Black business communities. Practically, most African-American marketers were unable to utterly circumvent White elite control of dominant labor structure, production, and capital distribution. Nevertheless, a host of small merchants marketed a wide range of essential goods and services to African Americans and helped African Americans articulate their shared desire for material and social self-empowerment denied in White consumer space. Laden with sociopolitical implications, African-American marketing confronted White consumer space's racist boundaries and envisioned how African America could secure increasing influence over consumer space.

Moralizing Work and Materialism

5

The Morals of African-American Labor and Consumption

Between World War I and the mid-1920s, African-American Annapolitan Wiley Bates penned a collection of essays and poems that were published as his autobiography in 1928. Fashioned in the mold of Booker T. Washington, Bates equated African-American character with stern self-discipline, genteel performance, and, perhaps most significantly, labor. Bates (1928:19) rhapsodized that the African-American laborer

> is the backbone and sinew in agricultural sections of our great country. He produces three-quarters of the cotton raised in this country. He is the most reliable laborer in America; he is not given to strikes; he is not an anarchist; he is patient and forbearing under the most exasperating circumstances.

Like his Tuskegee model, Bates romanticized the independent laborer who transformed nature through manual labor and produced an essential good, unfettered by the intervention of bureaucrats, union bosses, or Bolsheviks. He sounded a familiar Washingtonian celebration of the morality of manual labor, envisioning an African-American laborer whose work forged material providence and social discipline. Bates' vision of the African-American laborer implied that hard work, even under the most "exasperating" circumstance, provided a disciplined morality that was clear testimony to African America's worthiness for citizenship.

For thinkers like Wiley Bates, African America's capacity to perform socially essential labor was undermined by individual material desire. Much like Bates, an African-American lawyer addressing the 1888 Maryland Colored Industrial Fair fashioned a clear separation between production and consumption, celebrating the former and denigrating the moral symbolism of the latter. Nearly a half-century before Bates, this anonymous lawyer observed that "we propose to show the people of our city, State and country, that we are a producing as well a consuming class; that the idlers and vagrants among us are but the cast off clothing of the race" (Brackett 1890:35). For this attorney, as for Bates, it was labor, and not material consumption, that forged African-American character and staked African America's claim to citizenship. The notion that individual identity was defined by labor persisted among African-American and WASP thinkers of conservative and radical sentiments alike. These pundits shared a wariness of consumer culture's burgeoning materialism, increasing mass leisure, and apparent muddying of dominant values. The effort to moralize labor and materialism was not a new phenomenon, but in the late-nineteenth century that moralism aggressively focused on consumption and revolved around racial difference. Genteel labor morality was not a particularly stable or explicit code of behavior or ethics; instead, much like Whiteness, it was an ambiguous discipline that was tacitly defined by illuminating the inverse of genteel labor and consumption morality. The post-Emancipation flourish of moral discourses on African-American work and materialism reflected their authors' struggles to reformulate racial distance and class deference in labor space. In the wake of the Civil War, many Whites hoped to relegate African America to subservient work, providing a necessary, but subordinated, labor source structured along racial lines. For many of these moralizing Whites, African-American consumption implied that Blacks could hope to be full citizens with equal labor privileges, so it inspired singular apprehension. For genteel African Americans like Wiley Bates, consumption forebode the erosion of communal moral standards, a focus on individual desires over group needs, and the decline of their own personal influence. Consequently, the genteel White and African-American denunciation of consumption harbored an apprehensive appreciation of African-American consumers' politicization.

This chapter examines the effort to moralize African-American work, probing the underlying material interests of regional producers, African Americans' negotiation of labor relations, and racial subjectivity. I focus on African Americans' experience in Chesapeake Bay seafood production, the only labor enterprise in southern Maryland that could lay claim to the status of industry. Genteel moralists thoroughly racialized seafood production, marketing, labor, and consumption, and forged an idealized, racially based labor structure, genteel acquisition pattern, and White consumer symbolism for Bay commodities. These commodities were produced by a legion of African Americans who were the backbone of the Bay seafood industry. Some African Americans evaded a measure of White producer domination through relatively independent labor roles as oyster tongers or street and market hucksters, but many were mired in low-paying and physically arduous seasonal labor. Despite the racist symbolism projected onto Bay labors and goods, archaeology suggests that African-American Annapolitans at least provisionally adopted many genteel seafood consumption patterns. Material culture argues that African Americans decreased non-genteel consumption forms, such as household acquisition, purchase from street hucksters, and public marketing, while they attempted to evade the racist inequalities sponsored by genteel moralists.

As with all material transformations, the shifts in Chesapeake Bay labor relations, production, marketing, and household consumption were interwoven changes. Popular commentators used transparent moralism and racist caricatures to reduce complex social and material transformations to reflections of racial identity. It is tempting to simply ignore these racialized moral discourses and focus on clearly influential factors, such as labor relations or economic organization. However, it would be shortsighted to dismiss moral discourses as hollow racist and producer class deceptions having no tangible influence on how seemingly objective factors were perceived, articulated, and transformed. Like labor structure and market economics, moral discourses on work and materialism were a significant factor shaping African-American consumption, the public meanings of that materialism, and White constructions of consumption.

THE WORK ETHIC
AND AFRICAN-AMERICAN SUBJECTIVITY

A staple of genteel sentiment, the work ethic had deep roots in puritanical pre-industrial thought (Rodgers 1974). Most visions of a labor ethic cast work and morality as inseparable phenomena, and such thinking persisted well into the twentieth century, when it was wielded as a mechanism to degrade Black labor. In 1927, for example, a White commentator on African-American laborers in central Virginia opined that "An education to raise the standard of Negro labor, must embrace not only strictly industrial training but also a training which will improve his moral character" (Brown 1927:109). Such associations of virtue with work were complicated profoundly by industrialization, particularly factory labor, and many wage laborers clearly did not believe their moral subjectivity was produced through the chimera of "hard work" (Ewen 1988:79–82). Yet the easy association of labor and morality remained at the heart of discourses on African-American materialism well into the twentieth century.

Public depictions of a stark contrast between labor and consumption exaggerated the distinction between the "reality" of work and the "illusion" of consumption, a rhetorical caricature many genteel thinkers employed. Wiley Bates' (1928:14) essays were typical examples of such hyperbole, arguing that with regard to consumer frugality

> The Negro must learn the secret of the application of wealth; he acquires it, but he does not know how to apply it to advantage. The Negro is a spend-thrift; he is reckless and also a hypocrite. He tries to make people believe what he is not, by the imitation of the shadow and not the real substance.

Bates sounded a relatively conventional genteel critique of consumption by casting it as a hollow compensation for "real substance." For Bates, that moral "substance" was a race-neutral standard accessible to any appropriately disciplined individual. These sorts of African-American critiques championed the morality of "honest labor," disparaged consumption of non-utilitarian goods, and evaded the impact of racism on labor and consumer opportunities alike.

Asa Philip Randolph (1919:12) confronted the idealistic notion of "honest labor" when he pleaded

> Workingmen and women of my race don't allow Republican and Democratic leaders to deceive you. They are paid by Rockefeller, Morgan, Armour, Carnegie, owners of Southern railroads, coal mines, turpentine stills, cotton-plantations, etc., who makes [sic] millions out of your labor. Don't be deceived by the small increase in wages which you are receiving; the capitalists are taking it back by increasing the cost of food, fuel, clothing and rent.

Randolph's penetrating analysis of labor and consumption appreciated the material interests of politicians, the dubious consumer gains brought by wage increases, and the anti-Black obstacles to labor organization. Yet African Americans confronting profound labor inequality clearly were frustrated by their inability to transform racist labor relations. Randolph was promoting working class, interracial unionization, but many African-American workers apparently viewed labor as Marx said all working classes do—an ungratifying task that did not fulfill need and was instead a vehicle to satisfy other needs (Marx 1959:85). For any marginalized worker, perceiving one's fundamental identity in labor often was disheartening; the bleak opportunities for African-American workers seemed to hold relatively tenuous hope for the revolutionary interracial unionization Randolph championed.

By the early twentieth century, African Americans clearly were disillusioned by thinkers like Bates who championed manual labor and assumed that White Americans would at some point willingly concede African-American laborers modest civil rights. Rather than entertain such fantasy, increasingly more African Americans sought social possibilities outside work space. However, as Randolph implied, to focus political goals on consumption or to ignore the relationship between labor and materialism was an imprudent strategy. Such fetishism might be avoided in this analysis by examining African-American labor in Chesapeake Bay industries and probing its relationship to the popular discourses that racialized and moralized that work and its products. In that way, we can examine how consumption patterns negotiated both labor structure and popular genteel discourse and confronted race and racism in both.

WAGE SLAVERY: LABOR AND MATERIAL OPPORTUNITY IN ANNAPOLIS

The Bee dryly assessed the economic impact of a racialized work-force in 1906, suggesting that to "make a dollar a day off of each of 100 employees means $100 a day profit. That is more than any chattel slave owner ever made off of 100 black slaves. Wage slavery is better for the masters than chattel slavery" ("Wage Slavery," 1906). Emancipation momentarily muddied the racial contours of work and posed a host of new laboring alternatives for African Americans, but "free labor" was rapidly exposed as a hollow status (Roediger 1991:85–87). Retrenched racism in workplaces and social space rendered African-American labor less than "free" in critical ways that hindered prospects of long-term material and social self-determination.

Annapolis had no substantial industrial enterprises outside Chesa-peake Bay fishing and oystering, which encompassed a wide range of semi-skilled and unskilled tasks (e.g., oyster dredging) and supporting industries (e.g., canning) that never were highly mechanized. The scale of these industries was insignificant by northeastern standards. Com-pared to the utterly non-industrialized post-war South, Maryland was at least a marginal industrial success (Fields 1985:200). Yet intensive industrialization almost completely bypassed southern Maryland, where manual and semi-skilled labor dominated African-American employ-ment well into the twentieth century.

The oyster industry was dominated by African-American labor. Federal researcher Ernest Ingersoll (1882:169) estimated that of the 6,179 men he identified in Maryland's packing and shucking employ-ment in 1879–1880 "about three-fourths are negroes." In contrast to the highly centralized northeastern industrial workforces, the oyster industry did not have significant concentrations of laborers. Many la-borers worked in small groups in scattered oyster houses or on boats, with the greatest concentration of laborers in packing houses, where they shucked oysters and placed them on ice or in cans for transport to markets. Oyster shuckers removed oysters from the shell for canning, packing in ice, or immediate consumption, and they were usually paid a piece wage determined by the amount of oysters shucked. In Ingersoll's (1882:168) 1879–80 study, Maryland had 98 oyster-packing houses with a total of 8,639 laborers; that average of 88.15 workers per packing house was a far cry from the concentrations of laborers in northeastern factories. Baltimore was always the epicenter of Bay resource preparation and shipping: 45 of the Maryland packing houses and 6,627 of the state's packing laborers were located in Baltimore (76.71% of the state's packing-house workforce). The Baltimore operations were considerably larger than the oyster houses scattered along numerous Bay inlets and shorelines: Baltimore's packing houses had an average of 147.26 laborers per oyster house, compared to 37.96 outside Baltimore.

Annapolis' local oyster houses were relatively typical of operations outside Baltimore. In 1873, the *Maryland Republican and State Capital Advertiser* reported 11 packing houses in Annapolis ("Our Oyster Trade," 1873). Nine years later, Ingersoll's study reported that Annapolis had 8 packing houses and 315 laborers (Ingersoll 1882:168). One of the late-nineteenth century Annapolis operations was managed by African American William H. Stepney, who in 1897 had an "oyster house near the Navy wharf, and employs about 10 shuckers, and fills large orders daily to Washington and Baltimore" ("What the Colored People of Annapolis, Md. are Doing," 1897). Stepney's workforce clearly was rather small by industry standards. His enterprise apparently was short-lived, as well, since no other record of it has been found outside *The Bee*'s 1897 notice.

Regional canneries shipped the Bay's shellfish and fish catch throughout the country, and equally voluminous quantities of canned vegetables and fruits were marketed from Chesapeake canneries. Canneries included a handful of massive factories in Baltimore that employed up to a thousand laborers, and a few Baltimore packing houses canned fruits during the summer using the same workforce that packed oysters in winter. However, like oyster houses, most canneries outside Baltimore were comparatively modest in scale. In 1918, for instance, an "up-to-date" Annapolis tomato cannery planned to include as its labor force "48 colored women for skinners," but this was an insignificant number of laborers in comparison to those in Baltimore or northeastern industrial workplaces. Some shuckers in rural Bay communities lived in employers' housing for the season and then migrated to fruit and vegetable packing work during the summer, but roughly half the canneries and shucking enterprises were makeshift seasonal operations scattered along the edges of rural fields (Warren and Warren 1984:55–58). Oystering offered some unassuming but important opportunities for self-employment, and independent oystermen were an integral element of the shellfish industry into the 1930s. The only obligatory tools to an oyster tonger were a small boat and oyster tongs, a pair of coupled 15- to 30-feet long rakes. Tongers boated out over relatively shallow oyster beds and then raked their tongs over the bed, gathering sufficiently large oysters and returning smaller "culls" (usually less than three inches) for subsequent growth (Thom 1901b:1121–1125). Tongers typically sold their catch to "runners," ships that anchored in a tongers' ground, were filled with purchased oysters, and then transported their catches to regional packing houses or northeastern ports (Ingersoll 1882:164; Thom 1901b:1121). Other tongers hawked their catches on the streets or in public markets. In Baltimore, for instance, there was "a large number of men who sell oysters around the streets; others who rent a cellar room and sell from there" (Ingersoll 1882:170). In some rural areas, oysters were even a form of currency in local barter exchange (Ingersoll 1882:170).

As budget researcher William Taylor Thom recognized in 1901, tonging was attractive to African Americans because the "oyster tonger is his own master.... If he has good luck he may, especially if he owns his boat, make enough money in the open weather, in the fall months practically, to carry him through the season, possibly the year" (Thom 1901b:1125–1126). Ingersoll's (1882:157) earlier report concurred that "A tongman can, at any time, take his canoe or skiff and catch from the natural rocks a few bushels of oysters, for which there is always a market." Even under quite difficult conditions, African Americans favored such independent labor. The tonger's life was a prime example: Tonging was primarily a winter activity, so it often was physically harsh, and it was materially risky because freezes could significantly reduce profit. Nevertheless, African-American tongers were limited primarily by nature itself, not by an employer.

The Bay's ecological decline was hastened by oyster dredging technologies introduced on a widespread scale in the 1870s. Dredge boats, Thom (1901b:1122) observed, let "down a kind of grating onto the bottom of the river, setting sails, and thus making the dredge scrape along the bottom. ... The oyster bed is thus soon destroyed for years to come, sometimes for good and all" (cf. Bayliff 1971:297). Dredging was a capital and labor-intensive operation that removed massive quantities of oysters of all sizes and did not return immature oysters. The short-term profit of dredging massive volumes of shellfish was immense: "at the close of the [Civil] war the demand for oysters was very great, and high prices were paid, and many who had been reduced from wealth to poverty were glad to avail themselves of the chance to make a support by oystering" (Ingersoll 1882:180–181). Increasingly firm regulation of oystering during the 1870s limited the oyster season, regulated the size of oysters that could be removed, and required licenses for tongers and dredgers, but these laws did not significantly curb the ecological impact of dredging. That impact was made even worse by the pollution of industries that dumped vast quantities of waste into the Bay and its tributaries (Works Projects Administration 1940:311).

In addition to their profound ecological impact, dredgers' increased catch periodically drove down shellfish prices, much as their fishing counterparts deflated fish prices (cf. "Extensive Fish Packing," 1885; "Glut of Herring," 1885; "Utilizing the Herring," 1885). This compelled industrial fishing and oyster merchants to seek new Western markets in the 1880s, and it made independent oyster tongers' livelihood even more precarious. After World War I, independent tongers were peripheralized further by companies that leased oyster beds for exclusive exploitation, driving tongers to marginal public oyster beds (Works Projects Administration 1940:311). Corporate fishing "combines" likewise leased tracts of Bay waters and threatened the profitability of self-employed fishermen. Moses Shepard, an African-American fisherman in Newport News, Virginia observed in 1940 that "De whole bay used to be fishing ground. Now dey got it staked off so choice spots belong to de combine.... Lucky if you ketch a dog-fish nowadays, cause de nets ketch de fish as fast as dey come up de river" (Works Projects Administration 1940:312).

"Sufficient force of character": Morals, Race, and Chesapeake Labor

Bay resources were generally plentiful and easily harvested by self-employed tongers and fishermen, providing an independence and profit potential that inspired apprehension among many genteel White observers. This apprehension was fanned by Bay laborers' irregular work schedules, occasionally substantial profits, and often-unsupervised labor. This was a labor organization that was the direct opposite of the dominant vision of a disciplined wage laborer working under genteel supervision, so some observers concluded that tongers and fishermen inevitably had debased morality. Among Litwalton, Virginia's oystermen, Thom (1901b:1166–1167) suggested that

In spite of so many of them owning their homes and of being able to earn the greater part of their living within two-thirds of the year, their economic condition is not good. The opportunity for economic success is too great, the means of obtaining it too easy, hence the lack of success. Except in the case of a very few individuals, there seems not to be sufficient force of character to rise above the mere provision for present needs.

The suggestion that Bay labor was "too easy" was a common delusion of observers analyzing independent African-American work. Along similar lines, Ingersoll's (1882:157) report on Chesapeake labor observed that the

Oyster-trade of the Chesapeake bay is of vast extent, giving employment to thousands of workmen and millions of invested capital; and yet there are many intelligent men who believe that the blessings so lavishly bestowed by nature upon the tidewater counties of Maryland and Virginia, in the abundant supply of oysters and fish, are in reality productive of more harm than good. This belief is based upon the non-progressive character of the oystermen, who, as a class, are illiterate, indolent, and improvident. As the great natural productiveness of the soil in the tropical countries has tended to retard man's improvement, by taking from him the necessity for constant labor, so has the abundant supply of oysters in the Chesapeake tended to make the oysterman unwilling to engage in any steady occupation.

Such moral critiques routinely concluded that African-American Bay laborers made substantial earnings that were instantly spent on alcohol. The caricature of the drunken Black oysterman was often wielded by regional temperance advocates intent on fanning support for local prohibition. In Litwalton, for example, Thom (1901b:1169) argued that a "local option" prohibition law was necessary because the oystermens' "habit of congregating at the barrooms was a form of social life in itself. It was a kind of rude club life in which the Negro men wasted the money that should have gone to home and family." Thom (1901b:1169) argued that "the group life of Litwalton seemed to be of a very unorganized kind. This aspect of Litwalton is probably typical of the semi-predatory life of the oyster-tonger." Ingersoll (1882:157) likewise lamented that after selling oysters a tonger invariably

stops work until that [profit] is used up, often a large part of it being spent for strong drink. When his money is all gone he can repeat the same course. Unless spent in the indulgence of intemperate habits, a small amount of money will enable an oysterman to live in comparative comfort.

The concern for African-American laborers' temperance was a facade for White apprehension of a swelling workforce that entertained aspirations for modest social and material self-determination. Many White employers yearned to replace African-American laborers with

Whites or European immigrants, and some African Americans in the Chesapeake fishing and oystering industries actually were supplanted by European immigrants and their children after the late 1870s (Fields 1985:201–202). Ingersoll's (1882:169) report noted that the 2,460 women employed in packing houses were "almost without exception of foreign birth or parentage, the largest proportion being of Bohemian origin, with Irish probably coming next." By 1907 a commentator characterized the 20,000-person workforce in Maryland's canneries as "in racial complexion ... a composite of Bohemian, English, German, Ethiopian, and, in lesser degree, many other nationalities" (Warren and Warren 1984: 55). In general, though, particular facets of regional industries became racially exclusive, with the more arduous manual labor remaining predominately African American. Workplaces tended to have a relatively uniform racial workforce, even though the complete production process involved laborers of many different backgrounds.

Various cities and regions tended to have distinctive racialized labor structures. For instance, the large oyster dredging boats based in the Baltimore port primarily hired European immigrants, men who Ingersoll (1882:160) hyperbolically characterized as

> one of the most depraved bodies of workmen to be found in the country. They are gathered from jails, penitentiaries, work-houses, and the lowest and vilest dens of the city. They are principally whites, many of whom are foreigners (almost every European country being represented), unable to speak more than a few words of English.

In contrast, Ingersoll (1882:169) noted that three-quarters of the men in oyster-packing employment were African Americans, and he characterized them as "comparatively steady workmen, while the whites are more generally disposed to be idle and intemperate. The few whites in the business are generally of a very low class of society." He observed that Virginia's oyster-tonging workforce included far fewer Europeans than that in Maryland, and "in certain parts of the state [i.e., Virginia] it is almost monopolized by negroes" (Ingersoll 1882:181). Competition between European immigrants and African-American laborers certainly was more marked in Baltimore and Washington than Annapolis. In 1890, Jeffrey Brackett observed that in Baltimore "foreign labor came in, especially after the [Civil] war. German women could shuck oysters cheaper than colored men" (Brackett 1890:29–30). Such wholesale replacement of African Americans with competing immigrant laborers was not common in Annapolis. In the 1930s, though, some of the African Americans in the Naval Academy mess halls were replaced by Filipinos, who the Academy expressly hired to replace African Americans (Brown 1994:35).

Ingersoll (1882:157) spoke for many Marylanders committed to restoring the state's agrarian economy—and revealed perhaps the central White interest behind the discipline of Black Bay labor—when he concluded that "So long as they are able to live in this manner, it is almost impossible to get them to do any steady farm-work." The cry for "steady farm-work" was a familiar lament in the post-Emancipation South. The post-Civil War South saw itself as a White agrarian society whose socioeconomic recovery hinged on the reestablishment of agricultural production. The dilemma was how to position African-American laborers in that society and maintain the domination that antebellum White Southerners enjoyed.

In predominately agricultural regions of Maryland, like most of the South, many formerly enslaved farm laborers eagerly abandoned farm labor and left the countryside for towns. In 1875, newspaperman Edward King (1875:740) observed that in Maryland "Eighty-five thousand slaves were emancipated as the result of the war, and these persons constituted the main agricultural laboring population of the State. As elsewhere throughout the South, they have left the country in swarms and flocked to the towns." Migration to Baltimore and Washington was indeed quite voluminous during Reconstruction (Borchert 1982:6). In contrast, there was a steady African-American migration to Annapolis, rather than an instantaneous "swarm." The African-American percentage of Annapolis' population rose slightly after Emancipation, from 28.72% of the town's total population in 1860 to 32.41% a decade later to 37.21% in 1910 (United States Department of Commerce 1915: 37). The increase from 1860 to 1910 suggests a steady half century of African-American migration into Annapolis, not simply one Reconstruction-era flood of newly freed slaves. Censuses do not reveal where new Annapolitans came from by county within Maryland, but most African-American Annapolitans were born in Maryland. In 1910, for example, Gott's Court had 23 households with 98 residents, all African American: only 1 was born outside Maryland, and 96 of the 98 residents had both parents born in Maryland as well.

In Maryland, post-Emancipation migration had a less dramatic impact than in the plantation South. Antebellum Maryland was decreasingly dependent on enslaved labor in the half century leading up to Emancipation, and the absence of Reconstruction administration or extensive post-war physical damage allowed Marylanders to rebound more rapidly than they admitted (Fields 1985:171). White Marylanders, much like their Southern neighbors, suggested that Emancipation was actually a welcome opportunity to install WASP and (in their absence) European immigrant laborers in the fields. In 1870, for instance, the

Maryland Republican and State Capital Advertiser resolved that "it must be our duty to make the best use of this influx of industrial material [i.e., European immigrants]. We find that the negro, upon whom the south depended prior to his becoming free, fails to meet the ends required as an operative" ("Immigration," 1870; cf. "Immigration, Labor, Etc." 1870). Three years later, the paper triumphantly reported that "several of our farmers, being unable to procure sufficient colored labor, have succeeded in getting from Baltimore a number of Germans who ... seem willing to work and are easily managed" ("Eighth District Items," 1873).

White Marylanders were unwilling to acknowledge their dependence on African-American agricultural labor, and the futile hunt for "easily managed" labor never disappeared (cf. Foner 1988:419). In 1878, for example, the *Maryland Republican and State Capital Advertiser* championed "a general movement among the colored people of the Southern States to organize colonies of emigrants to settle on government or railway lands in the West" ("Movement Among Southern Colored People," 1878). The paper enthused that "the places left by the negroes may in time be filled up with thrifty white people." In 1899, Annapolis' *Anne Arundel Examiner* clung to the self-deluded search for a White agricultural labor force, reporting that "the secretary of the Maryland State Bureau of Immigration ... is traveling through the Netherlands drumming up immigrants for Maryland" ("The Dutch to Invade Maryland," 1899). Scientifically inclined racists joined the refrain criticizing the capacity of African-American laborers. A typically convoluted empirical study of the comparative yield of African-American and Italian field laborers in 1910 determined that the Italians were far more productive, concluding that "it is now very clear that the negro is not an essential factor in any single sphere of the life of the South" (Weathorford 1910:56–58).

Stigmatizing Fish

In 1957, 71-year-old Evangeline Kaiser White (White and White 1957:57–58) remembered being awakened as a little girl by the familiar fish hucksters' cry of

"Herroin feesh, her-ro-in feesh." ... That cry—what did it mean? Is it not hard to imagine that few remain who have heard it or who can conceive what it meant? How did the little girl know that spring was here? The old Negro fish vendor, Kimball, with his fish cart full of wriggling fish, herring predominating, was a sure harbinger of spring for all of Annapolis. The cry as mentioned meant herring and other fish, still wriggling, right at your door in time for breakfast. Mother would go out to bargain for the fish she wished, which would be scaled and cleaned right from the cart in a bucket hanging underneath. Then by 7:30 A.M. when the cook arrived, the fish were ready for her to fry for breakfast.

White romanticized the morning call of Thomas Kimball, a South Street fish and oyster huckster who was among the many African-American Annapolitans who made their livelihood off Bay resources (Gould and Halleron 1910:67; Johnson 1896:39). White described a common pattern for turn-of-the-century Annapolitan seafood production and consumption, a pattern made possible by a procession of African-American laborers—from fishermen to hucksters to cooks (Figure 13).

Hucksters like Thomas Kimball, enterprises like oyster houses, and the many African-American cooks who prepared Bay resources placed African Americans at the heart of every phase of Chesapeake Bay food production, marketing, and consumption in White and African-American households alike. Bay foods and associated culinary tech-

Figure 13. Sometime around 1890, these young men posed on the Annapolis docks with a string of freshly caught fish (courtesy of the Maryland State Archives; Special Collections, Mame Warren Collection, MSA SC 985-234).

niques had considerable importance in African-American culture, but their symbolism was shaped significantly by African Americans' labor and dominant White visions of such food and labor. Inevitably, the social symbolism of fish, shellfish, and Bay resources was shaped by both African-American culture and racist oppression in African-American Bay labors, from the water to the kitchen.

The Chesapeake Bay and its numerous inlets contained a vast range of sealife that could be taken from the shoreline or from a modest boat, and household-caught fish and shellfish were a staple in the diet of many regional residents. In 1899, for instance, a comparison of "dietary protein" among African Americans in Tidewater, Virginia and Tuskegee, Alabama found that the Virginians' diet had considerably more protein because of

> the close proximity of salt water, which made fish an important article of diet. Among the families studied near Franklin [Virginia], salt herring were used to a large extent. In the families near Hampton [Virginia] large amounts of various fresh fish were used.... As shown by the average results for the 19 [Virginia] families, over one-fifth of the total protein of the food came from this source. (Frissell and Bevier 1899:40)

Like most household-based consumption, the Tidewater households consumed diverse seafoods, predominantly herring and bluefish, but also eel, turtle, and frogs. Although the households obtained some foods from markets and community producers, the study indicated that the majority of the household's fish was obtained by family members fishing in area waterways.

This consumption of a diverse range of fish caught by the household or purchased from hucksters likely was standard throughout the region until the final quarter of the nineteenth century (for earlier periods, cf. Yentsch 1994:252). The earliest Maynard-Burgess deposit indicates that fish accounted for a significant portion of the household's diet, and it is likely that much of this fish was caught by household members. The construction of the home's rear addition between 1874 and 1877 preserved layers of household refuse that had been scattered around the back door since the 1850s. This debris included 3885 bones (excluding 209 fish bones and 1322 fish scales recovered in wet screening and 229 trowel-recovered scales) (Warner 1998). Mark Warner (1998) analyzed this and a series of African-American assemblages recovered throughout the Chesapeake and concluded that the Maynard-Burgess rear addition suggests extensive household-based fishing into the 1870s. Warner identified 678 fish elements in his number of individual specimens count (NISP), which is a literal count of the bones in the archaeological assemblage (fish accounted for 17.45% of the rear assemblage

NISP, excluding all fish scales and wet-screen recovered bones) (Table 4). Warner also generated a minimum number of individuals count (MNI) using all bones that could be identified to species. An MNI identifies the minimum number of individual animals represented in an archaeological assemblage; 44 individual fish were recovered from the rear assemblage (47.31% of assemblage MNI) (Table 5). Warner argues that household-based fishing is suggested by species diversity and the almost exclusive presence of species that could be caught at or near the Annapolitan shoreline. The assemblage contained 18 different species,

Table 4. Maynard-Burgess Number of Individual Specimens Fish Counts

Fish	1874 *TAQ* rear addition	1889 *TPQ* cellar	1905 *TPQ* privy
White perch	19	3	6
Striped bass	16	7	3
Croaker	13	2	2
Genus catfish	13	0	1
Pike	9	0	0
Yellow perch	9	2	1
White catfish	7	0	1
Menhaden	7	0	1
Black sea bass	6	2	1
Brown bullhead	6	0	1
Shad	6	0	0
Herring	5	0	0
Genus bass	4	1	0
Genus crappie	4	0	0
Drum	4	1	0
Spot	2	0	0
Bluegill	1	0	3
Pumpkinseed	1	0	0
White crappie	1	0	0
Mullet	1	0	0
Weakfish	1	1	1
Unidentified	543	43	54
Scales	229	1	0
Blueback herring	0	2	1
Shark/dogfish	0	1	0
Unidentified panfish	0	2	0
Total	907	68	79

Note: Only elements from dry screen recovery are included in this count (Source: Warner 1998).

Table 5. Maynard-Burgess Minimum Number of
Individual Fish Counts

Fish	1874 *TAQ* rear addition	1889 *TPQ* cellar	1905 *TPQ* privy
White perch	4	2	2
Striped bass	3	2	2
Croaker	3	1	1
Pike	2	0	0
Yellow perch	5	1	1
White catfish	2	0	1
Menhaden	4	0	1
Black sea bass	3	2	1
Brown bullhead	2	0	1
Shad	3	0	0
Herring	3	0	0
Drum	4	1	0
Spot	1	0	0
Bluegill	1	0	2
Pumpkinseed	1	0	0
White crappie	1	0	0
Mullet	1	0	0
Weakfish	1	1	1
Blueback herring	0	1	1
Shark/dogfish	0	1	0
Unidentified panfish	0	1	0
Total	44	13	14

Note: Only elements from dry screen recovery identifiable to species are
included in this count (Source: Warner 1998).

but only 1 species (represented by a single sea bass element) was exclusively available from a deep salt-water context.

Fish species distribution and scale quantities bolster Warner's argument that much of this fish was caught by household members.
Determining exactly what share of the fish was household-caught, purchased from hucksters, or obtained in markets is impossible, but evidence suggests that household fishing was a central element of the
family's fish acquisition pattern. The diversity of shoreline species, for
instance, argues for generalized household fishing focused on no particular species. In contrast, fish sold in Annapolis markets focused on a
few species, particularly herring, shad, and perch. The rear assemblage
MNI of 44 did include 3 herring, 3 shad, 4 white perch, and 5 yellow
perch, all of which may have been acquired in the market house or from
street hucksters (Warner 1998). A suggestion of what regional fish

markets offered at the turn of the century is provided by a 1906 *terminus post quem* privy in Wilmington, Delaware, which contained a staggering 25,561 fish elements (Beidleman et al. 1986:314). The privy neighbored a fish market that contained most of the same Chesapeake Bay species available in Maryland fish markets after the Civil War. The Wilmington assemblage was dominated by sea trout (18.1%) and sea bass (13.9%) (Beidleman et al. 1986:317). In contrast, the Maynard-Burgess rear assemblage contained just 1 sea bass element and no sea trout. The Wilmington assemblage did include significant quantities of yellow and white perch, both of which are represented at Maynard-Burgess, so the rear assemblage likely reflects a combination of household and huckster or market consumption.

Scale quantities in the Maynard-Burgess rear addition suggest household acquisition predominated. Fish marketed by hucksters, open-air marketers, or retailers were more likely to be fully or partially cleaned than fish caught by a household member or neighbor. For instance, White (White and White 1957:58) remembered that Thomas Kimball's fish were scaled "right from the cart in a bucket hanging underneath," a preparation technique that would result in few archaeological scales. The consistency of such preparation among hucksters is unclear, and partial cleaning could also have removed particular bones as well, both of which would effect archaeological analysis. In any case, a significant quantity of fish clearly was being cleaned around the Maynard-Burgess back door: Trowel and wet screen excavation recovered 1780 fish scales in the rear assemblage, indicating preparation of a considerable amount of freshly caught fish.

The rear addition assemblage also included 53 turtle bones. This "mud turtle" likely was recovered wild by household members; a survey of 1630 single editions of 13 regional newspapers published between 1850 and 1930 included no notices of turtle sales (Mullins 1996:120). It may well have been sold in regional markets, though; the Wilmington fish market assemblage included 259 turtle elements, slightly less than 1% of the assemblage's total bone count (Beidleman et al. 1986:317). The percentage of turtle in the Maynard-Burgess rear assemblage NISP is quite low (1.36%), so it certainly was not a staple element of the household's diet. Nevertheless, as Warner argues, percentages alone belie the symbolic significance of culturally meaningful foods. Even though the assemblage contained a relatively low quantity of turtle, distinctive African-American acquisition, preparation, and consumption of turtle likely had cultural significance that is not reflected in gross quantities alone.

The acquisition of Bay resources by the Maynard-Burgess household or from local marketers apparently underwent significant changes in the final quarter of the nineteenth century. Regional seafood production was undergoing significant structural and symbolic shifts while the Maynard-Burgess household discarded fish remains into the rear addition space, and the shifts in Bay production and subsequent Maynard-Burgess fish consumption are likely closely related. The central structural transformation in Bay production was the rapid growth and subsequent decline of the Chesapeake fisheries and Bay industries. After the Civil War, the Chesapeake industries expanded swiftly and flooded the local and national market with prodigious quantities of Bay seafood (Bayliff 1971). In 1865, dramatically efficient "purse" nets were introduced to Bay fishing, with the catch reaching an 1890 peak of 36,000,000 pounds of edible fish (Bayliff 1971:297). By the 1880s, Annapolis markets hawked codfish, shad, white perch, herring, and pike in vast quantities, and the glut of herring compelled many regional fish dealers to pickle and can herrings and cure codfish for sale in national markets.

The rapid growth of Bay seafood production had significant ecological and economic repercussions. In 1885, the *Evening Capital* acknowledged that overfishing had dramatically driven down prices, observing that

> Those who like codfish needn't go hungry this winter.... The catch of codfish has been enormous. In fact such a huge quantity was brought home from the banks that it proved disastrous to the fishermen and owners of fishing vessels. On every quintal of fish (112 pounds) coming to Boston as the central market of the U.S. the curer loses on the average $1. ("Codfish Catch," 1885)

Fifteen years later, the ecological consequence of such fishing was evident when the *Evening Capital* reported that "fishermen are complaining of the scarcity of fish in these waters. Fish were never known to be so scarce as at the present season" ("Scarcity of Fish," 1900). The Bay's fish catch decreased every year after 1890 (Bayliff 1971:294). In 1956, a commentator still painted a bleak ecological picture of the results of overfishing when he noted that "most of the fresh fish now sold in the chain stores of Annapolis are caught off New England or the West Coast" (Bayliff 1971:297).

Archaeological material culture reflects a significant decrease in African-American fish consumption after the 1870s (Table 6). For instance, the Bellis Court privy (1920 *terminus post quem*) contained a relatively small NISP of 355 bones, but it did not include any fish (Aiello and Seidel 1995:1:226–228). The somewhat larger Gott's Court assemblage (1907 *terminus post quem*) contained 678 bones, yet only 18 fish elements were in the assemblage (Warner 1992). Only 1 fish element was recovered from sheet refuse in backyards of Cathedral Street homes

Table 6. Percentage of Fish in Maynard-Burgess Deposits

Deposit	NISP (% of deposit NISP)	MNI (% of deposit MNI)
1874 *TAQ* rear addition	970 (17.45%)	44 (47.31%)
1889 *TPQ* cellar	68 (7.11%)	14 (38.46%)
1905 *TPQ* privy	79 (7.61%)	14 (34.14%)

in the Courthouse Site block (NISP 742). At Maynard-Burgess, the 1889 *terminus post quem* cellar had a fish NISP of 68 (7.11% of assemblage NISP), and the fish NISP for the 1905 *terminus post quem* privy was 79 (7.61%), both significantly lower than that from the 1877 *terminus ante quem* rear assemblage. Formation processes (e.g., sheet refuse, differential preservation) likely impacted archaeological quantities in various deposits, particularly with bone elements as fragile as fish. However, it is unlikely that this variation accounts for such a significant paucity of fish from all the deposits post-dating the Maynard-Burgess rear assemblage, which otherwise have good faunal preservation. Turtle shell, which is more durable than fish elements, reflects an even more striking decline: Although it was only found in modest quantities in the rear addition assemblage, not a single turtle element was recovered from any other African-American site in Annapolis.

Diminished African-American consumption of fish among these Annapolitan households certainly is related to the impact of industrial fishing on market availability and fluctuating prices. Nevertheless, there always was fresh fish and shellfish available in Annapolis markets, and even today Annapolitans fish from bridges and shorelines around the city. Periodic overproduction often drove down prices and made fish particularly inexpensive, which would make it cost-attractive to frugal consumers. If consumption was simply economically determined, we would expect to see considerable fish consumption among African Americans at Gott's Court and Bellis Court well into the twentieth century, since both sites were homes to economically marginalized consumers. Instead, very little fish was recovered from Gott's Court and absolutely none came from Bellis Court. There is also the thorny inconsistency that African Americans in other regions on the Bay continued to consume fish, yet it is virtually nonexistent in Annapolitan assemblages (cf. Frissell and Bevier 1899; McDaniel 1982). Consequently, a supply-side analysis alone provides a suggestive, albeit only partial, explanation of decreased fish consumption in Annapolis. A more thorough explanation of declining Annapolitan fish consumption requires an examination of the social transformation in fish and seafood labor and consumption that influenced African-American demand.

CONSTRUCTING GENTEEL CONSUMERS

In the final quarter of the nineteenth century, African-American culinary symbolism was transformed by the racial and social stigmatization of non-genteel household consumption techniques like fishing and oystering. On its surface, much of the moral critique of African-American fishing was simply standard anti-Black racism. Racist ideologues moralized African-American consumption in an effort to induce White consumers to see themselves as racial subjects who should internalize White-exclusive genteel consumer behaviors. Caricatures of Black consumption certainly were not intended to lure African Americans into genteel materialism; etiquette books, traveler's accounts, and similar discourses did not even recognize African Americans as an audience. Yet many African Americans wished to stake a claim to genteel subjectivity and already were well-schooled in genteel behavior as a consequence of slavery's heritage, service labor (e.g., waiters and domestics), and everyday racist negotiation. Ultimately the racialized moral critique of consumption patterns such as household fishing and street huckster sales dampened African Americans' commitment to those patterns. Aspiring to be genteel Americans with the privileges of that status, many African Americans embraced genteel materialism that demonstrated their suitability to civil and consumer citizenship.

Among the most stigmatized of household-based consumption patterns was fishing. Many White writers reduced fishing to the archetypal diversion of lazy and content Black people. In New Orleans, Julian Ralph (1896:376) unleashed a particularly hateful depiction of African Americans who fished

> wherever they and any piece of water, no matter how small, are thrown together. One would scarcely expect to find the New Orleans darkies given to fishing, yet it is a constant delight to them. They do not merely dangle their legs over the sides of the luggers and steamers to sit in meditative repose above a line thrown into the yellow Mississippi, but they fish in the canals and open sewers in the streets that lie just beyond the heart of the city.... when at every few hundred feet a calm and placid negro man, or a "mammy" with a brood of moon-faced pickaninnies sprawling beside her, is seen bent over the edges, pole in hand, the scenery becomes picturesque, and the sewers turned poetical.

That "picturesque" labor of men and women fishing in sewers likely was essential to the subsistence of some African Americans as well as

Whites. Yet by caricaturing it as a leisurely distraction of placid Blacks, Ralph infused fishing with Black stereotypes, reducing it to a racial behavior rather than a sound material tactic. Even African-American observers sometimes stigmatized fishing. In 1898, for instance, W.E.B. Du Bois (1898:23) concluded that Farmville, Virginia's African-American community had "the usual substratum of loafers and semicriminals who will not work.... There are also able-bodied men who gamble, fish, and drink."

Many African Americans saw fishing as a marketing strategy as well as a household subsistence tactic. For instance, H.B. Frissell and Isabel Bevier (1899:33) found one particularly enterprising African-American household in which "The boys worked at the fisheries and took their pay in fish, a part of which they afterwards sold. They earned about 15 cents a day, besides sufficient fish for the family." Much as they critiqued oystermen, White observers were apprehensive of African Americans who were able to make even a marginal living—and evade wage labor discipline—hawking seafood. In 1913, a White observer in South Carolina suggested that African America's "temptation is to 'live in the creek,' where the fish, crab, oyster, and terrapin afford an abundance of food supply and the source of a small money revenue" (Christensen 1969:65). Through contorted racist reasoning, this commentator reduced African Americans' consumption and marketing of fish to an essential racial "temptation" to avoid the social discipline of wage work.

Such discourses constructed "respectable" genteel consumption by displaying contrasting material patterns. Hucksters, for instance, were the target of material discourses that encouraged retail marketplace consumption by contrasting non-genteel materialism (Figure 14). In 1867, Thomas de Voe (1867:25) noted that

> Many respectable purchasers, not having the time to go the public markets, will sometimes purchase of the 'cheap shops,' or s[t]reet-ped[d]lers.... The fish, fruit, vegetables, etc., which are usually peddled about the streets in carts and wagons, are seldom found so good as those offered for sale in the public markets, they being either the refuse of the markets, unfit to be offered by the respectable dealer, or it happens to be a glut.

An 1875 household manual likewise noted that "the first rule of marketing is to purchase from respectable tradespeople, who have to support the character of their shops." (Southgate 1875:17)

A potent thread of genteel moralizing ran through critiques of non-genteel marketing spaces such as streets and, to a lesser extent, public markets. After Emancipation, a stream of commentators ventured into the South to probe the social and economic life of the freshly vanquished Confederacy, where street sales and open-air markets remained com-

Figure 14. This African-American huckster was selling strawberries on Annapolis' streets in 1893 when photographer Francis Benjamin Johnson took this picture (courtesy of the Maryland State Archives; Special Collections, Robert G. Merrick Collection, MSA SC 1477-3589).

monplace. Many of the visitors emphasized the challenges of restructuring Southern socioeconomics by probing how Southern exchange systems hindered the reconstructed nation's march into modernity. In 1866, for instance, John Trowbridge (1866:179) characterized traders in Richmond's market as impoverished Blacks and Whites exchanging inferior goods through arcane barter, noting that

> Many come to the market with what they can carry on their backs or in their hands. Yonder is an old negro with a turkey, which he has walked five miles to dispose of here. That woman with a basket of eggs, whose rage 3 and sallow complexion show her to be one of the poor whites whom respe :table colored people look down upon, has travelled, it may be, quite as fa : Here comes a mulatto boy with a string of rock-fish caught in the James... People of all colors and classes surround the sheds or press in throngs thr(ugh the passages between the stalls.... There is little money to be seen anywhere.

Trowbridge's analysis of Richmond's market reflected that the construction of a genteel consumer was not a simple Black/White opposition: Trowbridge belittled rural Whites as well as African Americans in a persistent anti-Southern tone that betrayed his Republican Reconstruction sentiments. His observation that money was rarely an exchange medium in Southern markets was true of many public markets and informal exchange after the Civil War, as it would remain in numerous rural settings well into the twentieth century. An 1886 grocer's handbook contrasted such archaic barter to the genteel cash economy, observing that a consumer who barters "does not know the price at which the goods will sell in the city and is often and easily lead to pay more than he can realize after all the charges are paid" (Ward 1886:22). The denunciation of barter and its association with inferior quality goods contrasted it to the fixed price cash exchange of genteel urban marketing. Critics of barter aspired to draw consumers into cash exchange and, by extension, wage labor, by dismissing the influence consumers had to define exchange terms in barter.

These critiques never eliminated Southern open-air markets (or, for that matter, Northern public markets); instead, such venues assumed a position alongside retail storefront venues offering different sorts of goods. Unlike streets, where hucksters sold their goods unsupervised, public markets and stores were circumscribed spaces that were regulated to varying extents by city fathers and merchant associations. Nevertheless, some observers disparaged public markets as well as street hucksters by stressing the moral erosion such undisciplined exchange spaces produced. In 1897, for instance, C.R. Henderson extended this moral critique to its most absurd extreme when he concluded that poor homes were stocked with

> burnt and spoiled food, bought in markets where no one buys unless his money is low, where deception is rife, where adulteration is unchecked. Is it any great wonder that men take to alcoholic drinks when such meals leave them with indefinable cravings and demonic gnawings? (Henderson 1897:26)

However hyperbolic its conclusion, this commentary reflected the relationship many Americans drew between marketing space and consumers' moral subjectivity. Despite such sentiments, many public markets remained economically vital consumer spaces until after the Depression because they were cheap and convenient and specialized in produce and fresh foods that did not compete with most retailers' mass-produced goods.

African Americans were marketers and consumers in virtually all Southern public markets, but they were racially, spatially, and materially marginalized transactors who were considered "outside" White consumer space despite their routine participation in those markets. English traveler Katherine Busbey recognized this on a 1910 tour of Washington's market, when she observed that an African-American "semi-rural element" would "appear outside the big market in the city's heart on market-days, offering the products of their tiny garden patch" (Busbey 1910:217). Seven years later, *The Boston Cooking-School Magazine* columnist Jeanette Young Norton toured the Washington market and perceived the same social and spatial marginalization, noting that a "real air of 'down South' is given to the market by a fringe of colored farmers' wagons that line the curb" (Norton 1917:510).

A significant volume of staple perishables was traded by these curb-side African-American marketers, but Busbey and Norton both reduced them to innocuous racial ornamentation. Busbey (1910:217) observed that in the winter, when African-American marketers could be found outside the market "squatting about their little charcoal fires in the midst of their wares, the flickering light playing over their shining black faces and glistening the whites of their up-turned eyes, they make, to me, one of the most picturesque details of Washington life." Norton (1917:510) also considered Black marketers quaint scenery, concluding that their "wagons, harnesses, and horses of all sorts and descriptions … furnish a novel and amusing spectacle." As in 1910, African-American marketers were exiled to the physical and social boundaries of the Washington marketplace and their trade was disparaged by racial caricature.

Public markets generally were an accepted element of community marketing, but many observers resisted according hucksters a recognized place in public consumer space. In 1888, for example, Juliet Corson (1888:17) championed public markets over hucksters, noting that "As a rule, it is not a good practice to buy from street peddlers in cities: their stock is generally that left on the large dealers' hands at the close of market demand, and in danger of spoiling, if not already spoiled." Yet Corson conceded that a consumer still could obtain "quite fresh fruits and vegetables" from known local hucksters whose products often were "better than those which have been exposed to the sun and dust at the green-grocer's, notably if the vendor has a little market garden in the suburbs, as many Germans and negroes have near New York, Cleveland, Washington, and other large cities."

Corson's guarded promotion of consumption from European and African-American hucksters was a somewhat uncommon counsel, because considerable racial animosity was directed at European and African-American hucksters. In the Northeast, hucksters were overwhelmingly European immigrants: In 1906, 97% of New York's approximately 5,000 peddlers were foreign-born (Heinze 1990:196). The racist sentiments directed at hucksters reached back into the 1830s, when many German Jews began to peddle goods, and caricatures of peddlers as conniving drifters preying on gullibility were projected onto all Jews (Lears 1989:79). Like their Jewish counterparts, African-American hucksters were targets of racist caricature. The stereotype of the foolish, humorous Black peddler with a rickety cart, old donkey, and modest wagon of mediocre vegetables cast African-American marketing as a quaint racial vignette, rather than a thriving mode of consumption. For instance, a *Harper's Weekly* correspondent in South Carolina wrote in 1880 that:

> The most picturesque and interesting class of Charleston negroes are, I think, the licensed venders [sic]. Some of them, both men and women, are very handsome, and all of them seem to be endowed with most amusing eloquence. If the vender was of a religious turn of mind, he mixed up Scripture and vegetables, fish and fruit, in a style which could hardly fail to attract attention. I have heard them with an intense solemnity inform the inhabitants of a street that this was their last chance to buy vegetables, the last time they were going through the street that day, and that no more beans or potatoes were to be bought, though perhaps a stout handsome negress, with large gold hoops and bright turban, and a great flat basket on her head, was crying 'Beans and potatoes' a block behind him. ("Inside Southern Cabins: Charleston," 1880:765)

Such commentaries reduced African-American hucksters to an innocuous and comic element of public consumer space. In 1932, a contributor to a Maryland cookbook reminisced that his fondest memory of Baltimore was "on a warm morning to hear the coons going up and down the back alleys shouting, 'Strawbe'ey—Strawbe'ey!'" (Stieff 1932:18). Despite such caricatures, huckstering offered a reliable income and some measure of self-determination. Whites' reduction of huckstering to benign marketing ultimately protected the livelihood of African Americans like Thomas Kimball, and ensured a steady supply of goods to White consumers.

MORALIZING DISCOURSES AND SOCIAL STRUGGLE

Daniel Horowitz (1985) argues that consumer ideologues commonly used moral overtones to mediate the contradictions in assorted perceived and genuine threats to prevailing social relations. Consequently, moralism was a complex public articulation of a host of unspoken apprehensions, a mechanism that obliquely probed social and structural tensions that could not be squarely confronted. Clearly the moralism surrounding African-American labor fits this analysis: The appearance of moral overtones in post-Emancipation work discourses was an effort to legitimize a racialized restructuring of the nation's workforce in the face of African-American freedom and burgeoning European immigration.

This moralism was not simply empty ideological artifice; it had a concrete impact on African-American visions of both work and material consumption. The construction of fishing as a non-genteel, if not morally suspect, activity likely was one of several key elements in the gradual decline of African-American household fish consumption. Certainly the racialization of the regional labor force had a material impact on African-American consumers, at the very least in terms of concrete buying power, but that buying power alone cannot explain shifting consumption patterns. If markets simply were peopled by economically rational consumers, we would expect to find marginalized assemblages dominated by inexpensive foods like fish. Annapolitan archaeology, though, suggests African-American consumption was fueled by something more complicated than cost. Indeed, virtually every consumption transformation was the product of a group of related, convergent processes: It is not the case that we can simply look at a change like that in Annapolitan fish consumption and point to one circumscribed social or material process as the engine of transformation.

Social change is shaped by networks of processes that structure the conditions in a particular time and space. Consequently, we expect some similar shifts throughout the region and country because of dominant structuring processes, but some areas certainly should evince different consumption shifts than those identified among African-American fish consumers in Annapolis. For instance, suggestive evidence indicates that African Americans in rural Southern Maryland remained devoted fish consumers long into the twentieth century, posing the possibility of fundamental urban and rural differences (McDaniel 1982:118–119). Moralizing discourses, though, attempted to deny the distinctiveness of local contexts and consumer agency, instead projecting a monolithic racialized explanation of material differences and White privilege.

Moralizing discourses should not be dismissed as artifice concealing an objective material reality, nor should we assume they had universal effects. Instead, they mark a struggle directly linked to broader social and material processes, but it was an oblique struggle that did not always acknowledge or necessarily comprehend the processes various groups were negotiating. Social struggle can take many forms, but it typically is enigmatic, as people in various social positions attempt to articulate their relationship to dominant mechanisms and variously reproduce, modify, or resist those mechanisms. The shifts in fish consumption, like most of the material tactics in this study, indicate that material consumption often became one way to articulate struggle. Like many marginalized politicized statements, it typically was a circuitous articulation.

Modes of Consumption | 6
African-American Consumption Tactics

In 1881, the Maryland and City Hotels were refurbished by owner W.H. Gorman in anticipation of the approaching 1882 legislative session. The *Maryland Republican and State Capital Advertiser* hailed the hotels' new African-American kitchen staffs:

> For a century past has Annapolis been famous for the famousness of her negro cooks. They know more about the transmogrification of raw oysters and ungainly looking terrapins into utmost toothsomeness than is known unto any other race of men and women now residing upon this variable globe. And Messrs. Gorman & Co., have retained a very respectable and highly colored corps of these "old mammies" in the Maryland hotel kitchen. What they don't know about the cooking of oysters and terrapins, and canvass back ducks, is not worth knowing by anybody. ("The Maryland Hotel," 1881)

This confession of African-American culinary distinctiveness risked conceding that regional cuisine was rooted in African-American culture. Yet Whites dodged the insinuation of African-American culture—and the troubling potential of hybridization with White subjectivity—by construing practices like cooking as Black racial attributes. The *Republican*'s analysis was typical of racialized discourses that negotiated the tension between labor inclusion and social exclusion and refused to concede sociocultural syncretism: The paper indirectly acknowledged African-American culture by recognizing distinctive African-American preparation of turtle, oysters, and duck, but its editors racialized those cooking skills by constructing African Americans as a "race" of cooks disciplined by a productive White labor and consumption space. In effect, the *Republican* editors constructed African-American cooks and cuisine as commodities produced by and for a White consumer space. That maneuver inelegantly rationalized the White consumption of terrapins, laundry, other African-American labor products, and Black laborers themselves, reducing all to the status of White commodities.

The *Republican*'s facile dismissal of African Americans' impression on White subjectivity skirted its editors' apprehension of racial syncretism. Such discourses conceded material transmissions in practices

127

such as African-American cooking, but their authors stubbornly refused to acknowledge the impression of that transmission on White subjectivity. Genteel ideologues championed an ideal mode of consumption, a strategic means of acquiring and representing goods that reproduced consumer culture's racial differences and White privilege. Yet the sociocultural hybridization in the Maryland Hotel's kitchen illuminated the illusion of that White ideal and demonstrated the transparency of racial autonomy, clear material distinction, and a tangible White "mainstream."

The paradoxical power and instability of the White consumer ideal is reflected in the myriad consumer tactics that were conceived within, against, and oblivious to that ideal. The social and material implications of the cuisine and labor relations in the Maryland Hotel, for instance, are enigmatic if we assume they were products of an instrumental dominator/dominated relationship. Marginalized people can be notoriously difficult to analyze, as such groups negotiate domination in many different forms and generally lack a conscious, clearly defined articulation of common interests. Consequently, social scientists sometimes minimize or discount everyday agency in the absence of a collective strategy or a clear cause-and-effect relationship between the actions of subordinated people and ensuing social change. Rather than frame agency as decision-making with no relation to power, this chapter borrows from Michel de Certeau's (1984:35–36) distinction between forms of agency that he calls strategies and tactics. Strategies are forms of willful agency based on power over other groups and spaces. Strategies are conceived to unfold in time, identifying articulate goals and formulating a calculated action towards which a self-conscious collective works. Tactics, on the other hand, are pragmatic actions conceived in the moment, seizing unexpected opportunities that manipulate the conditions of domination. Tactical agency does not necessarily forge a clear goal, and subordinated people often conceive of their actions individually because they cannot clearly define the social collective that shares their interests. Nevertheless, the repetition of tactics in defiance of dominant strategies can destabilize the power structure in many unforseen, yet meaningful, ways.

A distinctive element of African-American consumer tactics is the oblique critique of White privilege and "unfree" African-American labor and social conditions. Unfree labor certainly had its most extreme dimension in literal chattel slavery, but African Americans outside and after slavery were "unfree" in their capacity to determine the most elemental conditions of their economic, laboring, and social lives (cf. Gilroy 1987:200). A heritage of negotiating White surveillance and assuming the deceptions of White discourse provided African America an ironic insight into the contradictions of White public space. Certain work spaces with powerful racialized implications, such as domestic labor, witnessed a particularly novel range of material tactics that secured consumer abundance while they provisionally circumvented the anti-Black labor racism that made abundance possible. Domestics were among the many African Americans who directed White consumption, social interaction, and child care from the heart of White homes and social spaces, even though they were racial outsiders. African Americans honed a distinctive proficiency negotiating White consumer space, a skill that encouraged the growth of acquisition tactics that transformed African-American subjectivity and subverted the ideal consumption mode.

In this chapter I examine the relationship between African-American consumption, labor structure, and race by focusing on a series of tactics that were cultivated by, albeit not unique to, African-American domestic laborers. Domestic labor was a highly contested scene of struggle in which racist ideologues attempted to reproduce and elaborate Black caricatures; simultaneously, African Americans thwarted those caricatures, provided their families a livelihood, negotiated the vagaries of gender inequality, and secured a footing in an American society profoundly influenced by African America. African-American domestics fashioned a particularly broad range of material consumption tactics that had a significant impact on African-American consumption, quietly shaped the White South, and variously embraced and subverted dominant social and material interests. African-American consumer tactics like those detailed in this chapter forged African-American distinctions, undermined anti-Black racism, and quietly fueled an often-ignored material and social hybridization.

"WHAT A RACE THEY ARE!": RACIALIZING DOMESTIC LABOR

Antebellum racists often legitimized enslaved labor by demonstrating its basis in essential Black nature, a line of thought that persisted in domestic labor discourse well into the twentieth century. In a malicious, albeit typical, 1860 legitimization of the racial structure of Southern plantation labor, dime novelist J.H. Ingraham (1860:117–118) proclaimed

> What a race they are! How naturally they fall into the dependence of bondage! How familiarily they dwell in Southern Households!... How necessary

> to the happiness and comfort of the beautiful daughter or aristocratic lady of the planter, is the constant presence of an Africaness, black, thick-lipped, and speaking broken English,—a black daughter of Kedar—whose grandmother may have danced the Fetish by the fires of human bones, and whose father sacrificed to idols more hideous than themselves!... Yet these descendants of barbaric and Afric [sic] tribes are docile, gentle, affectionate, grateful, submissive, and faithful! In a word, they possess every quality that should constitute a good servant. No race of the earth makes such excellent domestics. It is not in the training! They seem to be born to it!

On the eve of the Civil War, Ingraham's effort to legitimize servitude by reference to racial nature was a strained defense of an already-doomed institution. Yet subsequent observers would postulate, much as Ingraham had, that African Americans had essential racial attributes that could only be disciplined within domestic and manual labor.

Domestic labor was stigmatized racially throughout the country, even though European immigrants composed the bulk of the Northeastern domestic labor force and African Americans dominated Southern domestic service. Orra Langhorne (1901:170) saw the problems of African-American domestics as a universal shortcoming of all non-White laborers, suggesting that "The faults of which we complain are to a great degree the faults of the servant class the world over, and not alone those of the race once subject to us." Yet White observers were willing to consider and eventually extend some White privileges to European immigrants, privileges which would be forever denied African Americans. In 1871, for instance, an etiquette book already wondered how long Whites could oppress European-born domestics, admitting that

> The servant has her future in America as well as others. We can not always calculate upon the present supply of the raw material of Germany and Ireland, which requires only to be kept in working order by an abundance of beef, potatoes, and wages. Employers will be forced, sooner or later ... to compensate them not only by a fair day's pay for a fair day's work, but by treatment which will recognize to its fullest extent their human dignity. (Harper and Brothers 1871:233)

The notion of extending service laborers full "human dignity" was potentially quite radical. Europeans could hope to secure some measure of this White "dignity," but such privilege was never willingly extended to African Americans.

The association of domestic labor with Blackness and slavery had a profound influence on domestic service's social symbolism throughout the country. An 1875 household manual recognized that

> Domestic service is obnoxious to the native American laborer.... While negro slavery was permitted, and the service of the house was generally

executed by the subject race, the two became so closely associated, that the servile dependence of the one was regarded as inseparable from the other. It is not unnatural, therefore, that men and women, however depressed by the circumstances of life, if elevated with the consciousness of freedom, should turn away from a labor which was so often seen in fetters. This has undoubtedly been one of the causes that the natives of the United States are so averse to all forms of domestic service. (Harper and Brothers 1875:119–120)

A 1933 study of a community outside Charlottesville, Virginia noted that there still "are undoubtedly certain types of work which are relegated to the negroes and which no white person, not even the lowest of the economic groups, would ever consider doing" (Leap 1933:46). As a White member of the neighborhood observed, "'Why the poor white girls would rather do nothing or go to work in a packing house than do house work of even the lightest kind. It is impossible to get a white servant. They just will not do it'" (Leap 1933:46).

Even in the North, domestic labor bore the stigmatization of chattel slavery and Blackness, so domestics were almost universally European immigrants and African Americans. In 1908, English traveler Sir Alfred Maurice Low (1974:138) noted that the domestic service workforce was thoroughly racialized and its labor socially stigmatized, observing that "The native American girl does not take kindly to domestic service, and would rather work in a shop or a factory than cook or make beds, so that most servants in America are Irish, German, Scandinavian or negroes." The stigmatization of Blackness, as well as Europeans' attainment of White privileges, eventually drove many Europeans from Northern domestic service. By 1926, a household manual was reduced to lamenting that European immigrants could no longer be coaxed into domestic service:

> Why should it be true, that with our thousands of immigrants anxious to make their way in the new land, that these women object so decidedly to taking service in families, where good homes await them and no demand upon their earnings is made but to clothe themselves?... They flock to the factories, the sweatshops and the stores, and seem to prefer to huddle in dirty tenements and unclean surroundings instead of placing themselves in the comfortable homes in which they might be employed. (Cushing 1926: 230–231)

Without the structural domination of slavery, post-Emancipation White scribes stressed the necessity for disciplined White surveillance to regulate Black laborers. Many of these writers brazenly yearned for the days of servitude and resolved that White mistresses must recreate a similar working environment in its absence. An 1884 housekeeping manual, for instance, suggested that

> As for Southern housekeeping, it is simply *self-evident* that nothing short of
> the solid organization of housekeepers among themselves in Co-operative
> Housekeeping can possibly bring again the untruthful, dishonest, sensual,
> half-civilized negresses with whom Southern house-mistresses have to deal,
> within anything like the bounds of domestic law and order. For the slavery of
> a master the slavery of an organization must be substituted before such low-
> grade moral natures as those of the African can possibly be trained, disci-
> plined, or controlled. Experience is proving every day that there was far more
> *raison de être* for the absolute subjection of the colored masses to the white
> masses of the South than we of the North for years were willing to admit.
> (Peirce 1884:173; italics in original)

Such romanticization of servitude was amazingly persistent. Over
a half-century after Emancipation, Ethel Frey Cushing (1926:234) still
suggested that

> Probably the servant that has best understood and thrown himself into the
> complicated household life peculiar to America is the old-type Southern
> negro, who is a product of our own land. This class is passing into the new
> fields of enterprise open to all. But if managed with the gentle firmness
> that we use with children, these servants rose to heights of efficiency and
> loyalty that could not be surpassed.

African Americans clearly recognized these desires for "old-type" and
"childlike" African-American laborers as a racist illusion. In 1912, the
White-edited Baltimore *Sun* praised "A church in memory of the faithful 'black mammies' of the South," a project the *Sun* characterized as
"A noble and worthy monument!" ("Black Mammies," 1912). But the
city's *Afro-American Ledger* acidly replied that "We would suggest
that it be built out of the skulls of the sons of those 'black mammies' who
have been lynched in the South during the past forty years" ("Black
Mammies," 1912).

In Southern domestic labor, race relations were characterized by
a paradoxical intimacy and invisibility that amplified longstanding
tendencies of Southern racial structure (Figure 15). In his uniformly
vicious 1860 portrayal of African Americans, Ingraham (1860:117) allowed, without self-consciousness, that African-American domestic laborers were "necessary to the happiness and comfort of the beautiful
daughter or aristocratic lady of the planter." Yet he concluded that
"these familiar looking negroes, which we see about us, are indelibly
foreigners!... no alien in America is as much a foreigner as the negro!"
This incongruous familiarity and enigma between Whites and African
Americans did not end with Emancipation. White Southerners viewed
the post-Emancipation Black workforce with an ambiguous tangle of
contempt and ease. In 1901, Langhorne (1901:169) observed that

Figure 15. Around 1915, African-American domestic Blanche Butler posed with her youthful charges Virginia and Raymond Rayhart in their Annapolis yard (courtesy of Maryland State Archives; Special Collections, Annapolis, I Remember Collection, MSA SC 2140-381).

When a Southerner speaks of servants, negroes are always understood.
Irish Biddy, English Mary Ann, German Gretchen, and Scandinavian maids
are as yet unknown factors in our problem. Black Dinah holds the fort, and
rules the roost for us; and, when she will half-way do her work and treat us
with reasonable civility, we are wont to be satisfied, look leniently upon her
moral delinquencies, and greatly prefer her to any of the foreign tribe.

Langhorne's muddled disdain and fondness for African Americans
was symptomatic of Southern attitudes toward African-American domestics. On the one hand, African-American women were a historically
familiar element of Southern life, raising White children, maintaining
households, and ministering to the needs of White people. On the other,
African Americans remained relatively mysterious to White Southerners who were disinclined to push beyond Black caricatures and consider their shared humanity. Whites were unable or reluctant to acknowledge that African-American domestics possessed an intimate understanding of White lives. Stationed in the midst of White Southern
households of all socioeconomic stations, domestics were in a distinctive
position from which they could dissect the material and social details of
White lives. In 1977, Annapolis chronicler Ruth Keith (1977:153) conceded that "The blacks were aware of the happenings in the city because
their women worked in the homes of the whites. Even those whites in
moderate financial circumstances, could and did afford 'two black hands
in the kitchen.'" Yet she acknowledged that Whites did not have a
remotely comparable understanding of African-American life, and
Whites were silently captivated by the mysteries of African-American
life. Keith noted that an African-American domestic caring for White
children "often took her charges into her own neighborhood." She ventured that those White children relished "the feeling that they were in
forbidden territory and entered into a conspiracy of silence about their
detours to Acton Lane, Gott's Court, Pleasant Street, Washington or
Clay Streets. Through these visits, they did learn something about the
black's way of life." It is unlikely that such forays actually unveiled
African-American culture to White children, but the curiosity betrayed
Whites' attraction and discrepant aversion to African Americans. This
contradictory intimacy and invisibility was perhaps most marked in
domestic labor, but it clearly was central to racialized labor relations, if
not to all social relations between African Americans and Whites.

"Terrapin in Fine Style": African-American Cuisine and Turtle Consumption

Some Americans viewed turtles as lowly reptiles, but terrapin has
been celebrated as one of the Maryland's most esteemed provincial

dishes since the early nineteenth century. White social gatherings regularly featured turtle during the last quarter of the nineteenth century, when turtles prepared by African-American cooks had achieved the status of genteel White delicacy. In July 1877, for instance, "about three hundred people indulged in the free clam chowder lunch at the United States House on Maryland Avenue.... Everybody pronounced this chowder of the first quality, and the turtle soup will no doubt maintain the cook's reputation" ("Turtle Soup Lunch," 1877). In 1885, the *Evening Capital* likewise singled out the revered turtle, noting that "the Arundel Club at their handsome club-room last night enjoyed terrapin in fine style" ("Terrapin Supper," 1885).

Travelers who commented on turtle dishes in the late nineteenth century acknowledged that turtles were uncommon and expensive. In an 1896 account of dining among Washington's elite, Julian Ralph (1896:361) found that terrapins were quite rare and had been replaced by "chicken, veal, and mud-turtle." He observed that a

> Chesapeake terrapin is worth four times what any other terrapin fetches in the market. It is Chesapeake terrapin that the Washingtonians think they eat; but, alas! very few of them, or of us, have tasted terrapin of late. It is so expensive, so rare, that real diamond-back fetches $80 the dozen, and only the rich and the people of Baltimore really get it. (Ralph 1896:361)

In the absence of regional pricing information on terrapin, it is unclear if Ralph's terrapin pricing at the astounding price of $80.00 a dozen is reliable; if it is, terrapin was vastly more expensive than any other meat or Bay food. In 1885, for example, fresh pork (unspecified cut) could be obtained in the late fall in Annapolis markets for 10 cents a pound, with sirloin and porterhouse steak cuts retailing for 14 and 16 cents, respectively ("Linthicums Meat Store Advertisement," 1885; cf. comparable pricing in "Prime Meats Advertisement," 1900). Fresh and salted fish were considerably cheaper, particularly in season: In April and May of 1890, for example, perch bunches cost between 10 and 15 cents, choice crabs cost 35 cents a dozen, and a bunch of ten herring cost 10 cents (e.g., "Fresh Herring Advertisement," 1890; "Soft Crabs Advertisement," 1890). Even if Ralph hyperbolized the real cost, terrapin certainly was more expensive than the vast range of regional foods.

Decreased late-nineteenth century supply and increased cost of terrapin likely enhanced its status as a regional delicacy and decreased its consumption by some households. Nevertheless, consumers routinely purchased small amounts of other costly or uncommon foods to diversify their diets or reproduce longstanding foodways. Consequently, even if turtle was expensive, it likely would have been purchased in modest quantities by some marginalized consumers. This would seem particularly likely among African-American consumers, because terrapin dishes were long a part of African-American cuisine. Supply and cost hold a significant part of the answer to shifting turtle consumption patterns, but price and availability alone did not determine consumption.

The Maynard-Burgess addition contains only a handful of shell fragments (53), so turtle was never a commonly consumed food in the household. However, it was totally absent from every other assemblage in this study. Without further archaeological evidence, it is impossible to determine if antebellum African-American Annapolitans consumed more significant quantities of turtle than late-nineteenth century African Americans (or Whites). The available archaeological remains simply indicate that turtle was quite rare among this series of post-Emancipation African Americans. The evidence does not demonstrate a decline in turtle consumption as much as it indicates very modest turtle consumption in one household and non-existent consumption in the remaining households.

Regardless of the extent of African-American household consumption, African Americans were preparing turtle for White diners using African-American culinary techniques, and popular discourses celebrated the distinctiveness of terrapin dishes. Consequently, the household-consumer symbolism of foods like turtle cannot be entirely disconnected from racialized labor structure or popular discourse. The African-American symbolism for turtle consumption inevitably was influenced by the commodification of culinary techniques, turtles, and African-American cooks themselves.

Turtle consumption presents an apparent dilemma, that of distinguishing between commodification (i.e., terrapin soup as exchanged good) and culture (i.e., terrapin soup as African-American cultural expression). Commodity status and the cultural dimensions of material meaning typically are considered divergent, if not diametrically opposed, phenomena (cf. Miller 1995:24–25), so we are faced with the perplexity of settling how these quite different dimensions of meaning could be accommodated in a single material good. On the one hand, African-American preparation of terrapin could be interpreted as implying that African Americans willingly or grudgingly commodified deeply held cultural practices in an ever-expanding White-controlled marketplace that homogenized all distinction. Conversely, the African-American households that continued to consume turtle in the face of commodification could be painted as sentinels of cultural tradition. The distinction between commodity and cultural property, though, is considerably more ambiguous. African Americans at least equivocally viewed cultural "resources" like culinary practices as commodities as well, with no self-evident division between commodity and cultural practice. The consequences of the White-dominated consumer economy certainly are of profound significance. However, expecting utter resistance hazards reducing all African-American agency in consumer space to either monolithic assimilation or the wholesale reproduction of "authentic" cultural traditions.

The unsettled feeling that African-American cuisine was "sold" caricatures the complexity of consumption shifts and polarizes "fake" mass-consumed materialism to the "genuine" substance of cultural tradition. Certainly, the commodification of once-distinctive turtle-preparation techniques and their extension into White households transformed their African-American symbolism. Yet African-American cuisine never "disappeared": elements of it were transformed and transfigured in regional foodways, just as some Anglo and European culinary techniques were adopted by African Americans. At the same time, we should not assume that every practice archaeologists construct as a "cultural tradition" was of equal symbolic importance. Some African Americans in Annapolis may not have had a particularly fervent attachment to turtles in the first place, so they may not have been averse to consuming other foods in their stead.

"The Duties of a Washerwoman": Laundresses and Consumption Tactics

Many African-American women did laundry or seamstress work in their homes. Much like oyster tongers who worked alone on the Bay, laundresses valued the independence of working at home for practical, as well as personal, reasons. By working at home, a laundress could increase her earning potential by washing garments from several households, and working at home enabled a laundress to complete her own domestic tasks. In 1919, an African American told Frances Taylor Long (1919:42) that she had

> served as a cook in a private home ... [and] as a maid ... but she preferred the duties of a washerwoman to those of either of the other phases of work. She explained that although when she cooked she secured her own meals free, nevertheless she could work for only one family; as a washerwoman, she could work for as many different persons as she had strength to do the washing. Furthermore, she could do her work usually in about five days, giving her Friday and Saturday, in part or entirely, for her work around her home. By doing washing she was also enabled to spend nearly all her time at home, which she preferred.

Like tongers, laundresses valued the absence of persistent surveillance, which was routine in household-based domestic service. Such surveillance could not be totally circumvented, though. An 1881 household manual, for instance, urged mistresses to closely monitor laundresses' work, because "If the laundress is sure this inspection will take place, it is a constant spur to working in the best way" (Campbell 1881:59). Maria Spencer Maynard and sister-in-law Martha Maynard each appeared in the 1860 census as a "washerwoman." Martha and her husband David Maynard lived in an extension of the house and apparently shared a backyard space where she and Maria did laundry together. In 1888, *The Homemaker* described the way most Southern washing was done in spaces like the Maynards' yard, noting that "The washing is done out of doors in a big iron kettle over a fire of 'trash,' amid a great show of teeth and interminable gossip between the laundress and the man who helps her 'pack up water,' and puts out the clothes line" ("Plantation Housekeeping," 1888:46). Although peopled by racial caricatures, this description was likely similar to how washing actually was conducted in many Southern backyards into the twentieth century. In 1933, for example, a study near Charlottesville, Virginia noted that "the washing is done outdoors ... in the same way that was done fifty years ago" (Leap 1933:73). African-American women performed such washing "either in their own home or at the white farmhouse" (Leap 1933:114).

Laundering in the Maynard-Burgess yard is reflected in the 285 buttons recovered at the site, most of which were probably lost during washing. Some of Maria and Martha's customers probably were Naval Academy students or military staff, since the assemblage contains 6 Navy and 2 Army uniform buttons (Bomback 1993). Because the 8 buttons were all manufactured between 1820 and 1852, though, it is possible that they were salvaged from discarded uniforms and used on other garments prior to their loss in the yard. The assemblage likely reflects a mix of reused clothing and buttons, as well as normal losses in washing and domestic use (Figure 16).

Like Maria and Martha, subsequent Maynard-Burgess residents certainly did laundry and seamstress labor for the household, if not White employers. The mechanization of washing and sewing alike impacted such African-American labors, but it did not significantly transform that labor until after World War II. For instance, an automatic bottle machine-produced jar (post-1920) from the backyard bore witness to household sewing. Recovered along an exterior wall of a post-1941 addition, the still-sealed jar contained a household member's sewing kit of fabric fragments, needles, and thread (Mullins and Warner 1993: 51–52). Certainly a vast amount of many Americans' everyday garment maintenance was done by household members with sewing kits like that found at Maynard-Burgess, just as some consumers did their own laundry as a routine part of household labor.

Figure 16. Sometime in the 1860s, this gardener was photographed in Naval Academy clothing with the State House dome and the former home of Declaration of Independence signer William Paca in the background. The gardener may have served the Union cause, but it is more likely these clothes were salvaged from the Academy (courtesy of Maryland State Archives; Special Collections, Mame Warren Collection, MSA SC 985-151).

By the time this sewing kit was buried, African-American laundresses' labor for White households had been dampened by the advent of professional laundries and washing machines. In 1927, a study in Charlottesville, Virginia contemplated laundering's mechanization and commercial laundries' business, and concluded that "Home laundry work will not soon regain its importance as a means of livelihood for Negro women. Many white families have now installed expensive mechanical devices in their homes and are no longer dependent on the colored wash woman" (Brown 1927:113). Yet, contrary to this 1927 prediction of laundresses' demise, a Department of Labor report estimated that 270,000 African-American women were self-employed laundresses in 1930, with another 50,000 in professional laundries (Brown 1989: 468). The report noted that in 1935 "bureau agents were told again and again that commercial laundries, especially in the South, were having a terrific struggle to compete with the Negro washerwomen."

The inconsistent documentation of African-American women's labor renders even the best quantitative analyses provisional. Annapolis' city directories typically recorded only the name and occupation of a male head of household, but they suggest the scope of African-American domestic labor. In the 1910 city directory, 122 African Americans (10.98% of African-American directory entries) appeared as "servants." Only "oysterman" (138 entries; 12.42%) and the catch-all "laborer" (295; 26.55%) categories had more entries. The 1910 census for the Courthouse block identified 19 African-American women as laundresses (Ford 1993). The 104 buttons recovered in preliminary excavations support the census-keepers' record of women's work in the neighborhood. Yet the recording of women's work clearly was uneven: In 1880, the census tallied 108 Black or Mulatto residents on the block, but none of the 55 Black women were labeled laundresses (Ford 1993). The 1900 census enumerator also ignored African-American women's labors: of 98 Black or Mulatto women living on the block, none were called laundresses, and only 1 African-American woman (a dressmaker) had any occupation recorded at all.

Archaeological contexts, in contrast, provide substantial evidence of laundresses' labor. In Washington, D.C., for example, Charles Cheek and Amy Friedlander (1990:55) excavated adjoining African-American-occupied alley and White street-front households and found more than twice as many buttons in the African-American alley contexts. Beyond reflecting the racialization of laundry labor, Cheek and Friedlander's findings demonstrate that the labor roles of African-American and White women differed considerably.

DOMESTIC LABOR AND THE MOVEMENT OF GOODS

White employers forged an illusion of intimacy with (and self-superiority over) their African-American laborers through a variety of material redistribution patterns. Processes such as the provision of discards provided goods to African-American laborers under the guise of benevolence, but Whites believed these practices implicitly pinned obligations on the receiver and confirmed the racial superiority of the supplier. African-American consumption of salvaged White clothing had a particularly long and rich history. On the eve of the Civil War, Frederick Law Olmsted (1968:27) observed in South Carolina that "the greater part of the colored people, on Sunday, seemed to be dressed in the cast-off fine clothes of the white people, received, I suppose, as presents, or purchased of the Jews." In 1860, Olmsted (1970:80) noted an African American in Louisiana who had on a splendid uniform coat of an officer of the flying artillery. After the Mexican war, a great deal of military clothing was sold at auction in New Orleans, and much of it was bought by planters at a low price, and given to their negroes, who were greatly pleased with it.

By ridiculing the quality of African Americans' salvaged goods ("cast off"), deprecating their exchange venues (Jewish merchants), and exoticizing the goods themselves (Mexican military clothing), Olmsted portrayed the consumption of secondhand goods in terms of racial differences and identified salvage as a Black material pattern.

The movement of clothing from Whites to African-American laborers continued unabated after Emancipation. In 1880 *Harper's Weekly* noted that African-American sharecroppers in Alabama customarily were provided shelter, food, and "clothing [which] is usually that cast off by the white family" ("Inside Southern Cabins, Alabama," 1880:781). This racialized material distribution and labor structure reproduced many of the circumstances of slavery, except for chattel status. The transfer of goods between White employers and African Americans routinely was painted as pure White altruism toward the subject race, but the provision of discarded goods to African Americans certainly had implicit costs. In 1933, a budget study unable to quantify African-American clothing expenses concluded that "Clothing costs were very hard to get, practically every [African-American] family has white friends who look after their clothing needs and who pass on their old clothing in return for some small service" (Leap 1933:62). Exactly what "small service" was exacted in return is unclear, but it clearly was not an exchange guided by unadulterated generosity. The domestic-service relationship persisted well into the twentieth century because White superiority was reproduced by patronizing Black domestic laborers. The 1933 study, for instance, noted that "washing and ironing tends to be a regular arrangement, and some of the white families have had the same laundress for many years" (Leap 1933:114).

White employers saw the provision of discards and gifts as the beneficence of the dominant race. In 1896, Julian Ralph found that New Orleans'

> white men and women give their clothing to the colored people—to servants or dependents—when it is no longer serviceable for them.... it seems to me that every man or woman is accustomed to make this use of his or her discarded goods, and that every white family has at least one colored family in charge in this way. The servants look upon this descent of clothing and finery as a right, and the dependents take it for granted that what remains shall be theirs. (Ralph 1896:385)

Ralph did not explore the implications of having "at least one colored family in charge," because such material and labor subordination was the accepted and unquestioned structure for race relations. However, the charitable recycling of White goods certainly was intended to reproduce racialized labor relations and keep White employers "in charge" of African-American domestic laborers. In 1935, a Richmond, Virginia study identified extensive salvage among African Americans and concluded that

> From the point of view of the Negro this is hardly charity. He has come to expect such gifts, and often considers them as part of his just compensation.... from estimates made by a number of employers, we can say that the gifts in food and clothing to domestic servants serve to supplement no little the income derived from their labor. (Harlan 1935:29)

This line of reasoning posed such "gifts" as a mechanism to legitimize low wages, rather than as objects representing Whites' positive reciprocity or a relationship of reciprocal obligation.

Institutions like the Naval Academy and hotels used redistribution to fortify racialized labor structure, much like White households employing domestics, but the range and quantity of goods was considerably greater than that secured in household service. The single largest employer of African-American Annapolitans, the Naval Academy provided a vast volume of discarded goods to its employees. The Academy's scale and bureaucratic organization was utterly unlike the private homes and businesses that employed African-American Annapolitans because it was economically stable, staffed by a large African-American workforce, and extended a pension and benefits rarely offered to African Americans. An African American whose father worked in the Academy for 40 years remembered that for "practically everybody, if you weren't working in a private home, the Naval Academy was the source of employment" (Jopling 1991). However, the sort of work performed in the Academy was indistinguishable from that African Americans performed in private homes and other workplaces: African-American employees at the Academy primarily did service labor, ranging from barbering to cleaning to cooking and serving midshipmen's meals. One woman noted that "the majority of the people in Annapolis, Negroes in Annapolis, worked at the Naval Academy.... Men worked in the laundry and the women worked in the private [officers'] homes" (Warren 1990). The Academy clearly mirrored the racist society that its students were preparing to defend, and its often arrogant treatment of African-American Annapolitans convinced some African Americans to pursue other labor. For example, a man who grew up on South Street admitted that

> I saw the way we were treated as people and all and I just didn't want that. I wanted something better. I saw where everybody was working. Everybody

worked at Carvel Hall [Hotel], the Naval Academy, or they had menial little janitorial jobs. And I said that's not for me.... I always said I would never work at the Naval Academy. (Jopling 1991)

The Academy discarded an enormous volume of goods that were recycled by employees and distributed throughout Annapolis. A woman who grew up in the Gott's Court neighborhood indicated that "the boys who cleaned the midshipmen's barracks ... would bag these clothes and give them to the ladies. The ladies would wash them, bring them home, and give them to the children" (Goodwin et al. 1993:6). One African American who grew up in the Courthouse neighborhood observed that

anyone who worked there was given stuff and they brought home shoes, anything that was worn—shoes, shirts, ties and pants. In the main they would re-do them ... they would take off the buttons and re-do them for good use.... So nearly all of Annapolis was clothed from the Academy. (Jopling 1991)

A South Street man whose father worked in the Academy galley echoed the memory of widespread Academy salvage, noting that "every child in Annapolis had a sailor's hat or a pair of pants" (Jopling 1991). A Bellis Court tenant likewise indicated "I know that you would see somebody and say 'Oh, they've got on those midshipmen shoes'—we never even thought about it" (Jopling 1991).

By becoming so commonplace that some consumers "never even thought about it," the Academy's tacit concession of discards masked its interest in assuaging labor tensions and reproducing its large working-class African-American and White labor force (Figure 17). The systematic, but publicly unacknowledged, movement of goods from the Academy to employees was a subtle, yet significant, mechanism for reproducing that labor force. A pension, job security, a predominately African-American work force, and the occasional receipt of shoes and jackets convinced many African-American Annapolitans to secure employment at the Academy. Discarded goods were acquired by African-American employees at St. John's College and local hotels as well, but the volume likely paled in comparison to that flowing from the Academy.

Thievery and African-American Consumption

The specter of an unmonitored stream of goods flowing from White employers to African Americans fueled the apprehension of some genteel observers. Such commentators criticized redistributive practices like gift-giving and salvage, arguing that they eroded already-tenuous African-American morality and amplified deep-seated Black proclivities for laziness and thievery. An 1884 household manual quoted a

Georgia mistress who melodramatically lamented that " 'The colored servant grows steadily worse. She is uncleanly, wasteful, pilfering, careless, and story-telling. She robs me unsparingly to feed her children, or her sisters, or her friends, or to give away' " (Peirce 1884:171). In the eyes of such observers, Black domestics were untrustworthy and undisciplined laborers requiring persistent and dehumanizing surveillance. The construction of latent Black miscreancy rationalized workplace and public surveillance and contributed to anti-Black violence (or at least condoned public ignorance of such violence).

White ideologues often seized on the "food basket" custom to prove their point. African-American domestics commonly took home discarded food on which some domestics' families depended, but many Whites believed the practice promoted African Americans' natural propensities to deception, laziness, and pilfering (cf. Katzman 1978:198). In 1901, for instance, a Southern mistress told Langhorne (1901:170) that African-American domestics " 'all plunder us, carrying home with them at night all that they can lay their hands on to feed trifling husbands, or children growing up in idleness.' " Langhorne (1901:172–173) launched an attack on the universality of Black thievery, concluding that the

> real injury is to the colored children, permitted to grow up in idleness, depending for their needs upon what they know is taken from others.... How often is the sorrowful story repeated among us of the loving-hearted but unwise mother plundering her employer to feed her offspring, laboring to the extent of her ability to keep her son in idleness and, when broken down by age and infirmity, seeing him who should be the support and comfort of her old age spending his young manhood behind prison bars!

Such hyperbole relied on the belief in universal Black criminality to justify domestics' surveillance, casting the food basket and salvaged clothing as an inevitable step toward degeneracy.

White women were expected to direct the surveillance of African-American domestic laborers, ostensibly so those domestics would internalize genteel discipline and racial deference. However, the surveillance of domestics exerted a discipline on White mistresses as well. An 1889 travel account of life in Florida recounted a mistress' arduous effort to discipline an African-American domestic, a relatively typical passage in manuals that contemplated how White mistresses should negotiate the "domestic problem." The author "soon discovered ... that we had a very fair specimen of a self-willed, untamed savage in our kitchen, and that the task of reducing the same to subjection would require no small

←——

Figure 17. Edwin Dennis went to work for the Naval Academy in 1848 and remained an employee until 1910 (courtesy of Philip L. Brown).

amount of patience and surveillance" (Harcourt 1889:348). Such discourses imposed demanding racial surveillance on African-American women as a means to simultaneously discipline White mistresses to their domestic roles and White subjectivity.

Whites assumed thievery was embedded in Black racial character, so domestics' theft was presumed to reach epidemic proportions. African-American thievery likely was common, but it was mostly insignificant pilfering of food and clothes. The most common targets of theft almost certainly were institutions like the Naval Academy and hotels, where pilfering was materially inconsequential and surveillance was more relaxed than in most private homes. Occasionally, though, thieves were prosecuted by these major employers. In 1898, for instance, the *Anne Arundel Examiner* reported that "William Jones, colored, 19 years old, employed in the commissary store at the Naval Academy, had a hearing Friday ... charged with the larceny of sugar, eggs, meat, and other articles from the store" ("Held for Court," 1898). This was probably a typical purloin for an Academy employee, but the number of such episodes is unclear, since the Academy did not publicize all the mundane thievery that went on within its walls. Eventually, around World War II, the Academy instituted some policies to at least superficially minimize theft and discourage salvaging. One man's father worked in the Academy laundry for 40 years, and "you could take your laundry down and have it done. But then, I think, so many people were beginning to take the Navy stuff, I think they stopped it.... I remember my father took bags of things" (Warren 1990). Whether the Academy instituted such policies to combat the material effects of rampant laundry larceny or simply maintain the appearance of workplace discipline is unclear.

One African-American Annapolitan underscored the complex symbolism and utility of pilfering. He suggested that

> If it wasn't for the Naval Academy and Carvel Hall [Hotel], people would have starved. The food that came out of those two places. People would bring it out, had to ... they would hide it inside their clothes, and they would sell it. You might get six, seven, ten pounds of meat. That's going to last you a long time. Meat, butter, different things, clothes, handkerchiefs, shirts, shoes. (Jopling 1991)

Just as it had been during enslaved laborers' "taking," thievery was a complex fusion of genuine material need, profiteering on pilfered goods, and subversion of racist employers.

There is no way to determine the concrete extent of theft by African Americans or any other laborers. Some theft attributed to African Americans, though, clearly was the work of others who capitalized on the prevalent suspicion of African-American employees. In 1874, for instance, the *Maryland Republican and State Capital Advertiser* was forced to concede that

> for some time past the student's of St. John's College have at various times missed different articles from their rooms, and, very naturally, strong suspicions rested upon the chambermaids and servants. One day last week the thief was discovered to be a fellow-student. ("Sad Depravity," 1874)

However, such admissions that thievery was not racially exclusive were rare, and White criminals were constructed as individuals who had deviated from the White standard; African Americans' crimes, in contrast, were projected onto all African America. *The Bee* lamented this in 1887 when it observed that "the white people blame the whole race for what one does, while on the other hand a white person who commits a crime is held individually responsible" ("Bawdy Houses," 1887). The real magnitude of Black thievery was irrelevant because of the weighty assumption that all African Americans were implicated in a universal, racially based criminal propensity. The assumption of latent criminality or universal petty larceny among African Americans made accusations of violent Black criminality even more convincing, as murder, rape, and assault loomed as mere degrees away from petty theft.

CERAMICS AND COMMUNAL RECIPROCITY

Perhaps no class of historic artifacts has been studied as extensively as ceramics (e.g., Miller 1980, 1991). Ceramics were essential to food preparation, consumption, and preservation, so they are one of the few artifact types found on virtually every domestic archaeological site. In the last quarter of the nineteenth century, Victorian ceramic consumers could purchase wares from many different marketing outlets. Virtually all regional stores carried a wide range of styles, mail-order catalogs hawked extensive lines of pottery, and some vessels were sold by peddlers. As with many other mass-produced Victorian commodities, increased availability, expanded production, and advertising contributed to modest, stable prices. Etiquette books and behavioral counsel in newspapers and magazines further fueled ceramic consumption, fanning consumer demand for the specialized, stylish wares that were considered essential for a genteel table.

Rather than limit ceramic analysis to an examination of wholesale pricing, style, and genteel etiquette, this interpretation of African-American ceramic symbolism focuses on ceramic consumption as a tactic comparable to recycling or pilfering. Archaeological evidence argues that African Americans acquired many of their ceramics outside the mass marketplace through the sort of tactical patterns that flourished among domestics. African-American Annapolitans developed a distinctive ceramic consumption pattern that largely evaded the retail market, yet subtly adopted some dominant dining standards. African-American Annapolitan assemblages are distinguished by aesthetic diversity, including a wide variety of designs and decorative techniques; the ceramics are older than most artifacts in the same assemblage; and most ceramic tableware is heavily worn, indicating extensive use of the vessels.

The decorative diversity of the African-American assemblages in Annapolis directly counters Victorian ceramic consumption counsel. Ceramics produced after the mid-nineteenth century usually were marketed in sets of complimentary vessel forms with identical decorations or molded motifs. An 1885 household manual warned ceramic consumers that they would be compelled to buy sets, indicating that "generally both decorated china and ornamental glass are sold in sets, and dealers are unwilling to supply any single piece" (Corson 1885:99). Price itself did not bar poorer consumers from purchasing sets. In surveying the numerous inexpensive ceramic sets on the market, an 1888 etiquette book concluded that "there are so many pretty attractive designs from which to choose, according to the amount of money at command, that if we were to attempt to review all that are suitable, the subject would be entirely beyond the scope of this book" (Lavin 1888:120–121).

The absence of matching vessels at Maynard-Burgess and in the Bellis Court privy argues that most of these ceramics were acquired in small quantities. Archaeologists have analyzed comparable small-quantity ceramic consumption patterns and concluded that some consumers gradually assembled piecemeal sets of matching or similar wares in lieu of large set purchases (e.g., Klein and Garrow 1984:221; Miller 1974). However, there is no indication of such a strategic consumption pattern in the Annapolis assemblages: There are no consistent colors, decorative preparations, functional types, or wares. The variety of wares in the assemblages does not suggest any long-term acquisition pattern focused on assembling a ceramic set.

This consumption pattern is reflected in the Maynard-Burgess cellar assemblage, which contained a minimum of 42 ceramic vessels. The bottle assemblage from the cellar had a mean production date (1882.10) close to the feature's *terminus post quem* of 1889, suggesting rapid production, consumption, and discard of the cellar's bottles. The cellar ceramic assemblage, in contrast, was dominated by older ceramics. To a certain extent, this is expected: By the late nineteenth century, bottles normally were consumed for their contents and discarded relatively quickly. Ceramics, in contrast, were consumed as commodities themselves and used for longer periods. Manufacturers' marks often provide the most circumscribed chronologies for ceramics, but only two vessels in the Maynard-Burgess cellar had identifiable marks (an 1846–1856 Rockingham spittoon produced by Edwin Bennett and an 1846 Davenport and Company whiteware basin [Godden 1964:189; Kovel and Kovel 1986:173]). Despite the absence of more marked vessels, the cellar did not contain any ceramic with a manufacturing *terminus post quem* after the mid-nineteenth century. The assemblage also included a handful of relatively old ceramic types, such as three pearlware vessels (two circa 1813–1834 shell-edge twifflers and one circa 1795–1830 painted bowl), two mocha whiteware bowls (circa 1820–1840), and an 1841–1857 unscalloped shell edge whiteware plate.

The Maynard-Burgess cellar assemblage suggests that the ceramics were relatively older than bottles from the same household, and older ceramics dominated the 1920 *terminus post quem* Bellis Court privy as well. The Bellis Court ceramics were produced over a long span of time between the middle of the nineteenth century and the 1890s or later. One method used to date the Bellis Court privy assemblage was a mean ceramic date, calculated by averaging the median production date assigned to each sherd (South 1977). Because nineteenth century ceramic dates can be quite broad and some of these sherds came from the same vessel, the mean sherd date is only suggestive. Nevertheless, the privy sherds' mean production date of 1864.95 certainly is considerably earlier than the feature's 1920 *terminus post quem*. A second method used to date the Bellis Court assemblage was the identification of marked ceramics. The privy contained a minimum of 36 ceramic vessels, including 5 vessels with manufacturers' marks. Unlike the sherds' 1864.95 mean date, these marked wares were produced more recently (mean production date 1890.30). Consequently, the assemblage has an early mean sherd date (1864), more recent marked vessels (1890), and a still more recent *terminus post quem* (1920).

While the Bellis Court assemblage includes some mid-nineteenth century wares that probably were not bought new by the household, it also includes some wares that likely were purchased new later in the privy's life. Some of the older vessels in the Maynard-Burgess cellar and the Bellis Court privy may have been purchased new by the households. Yet if a substantial number of the older vessels were purchased new, they survived an amazingly long time. The notion that a significant number of the vessels were display pieces or heirlooms is implausible because the vast majority of the vessels were highly worn, and none were pricy or uncommon wares, which would be the most likely targets

of careful curation. Even if one or two vessels were pieces with idiosyncratic personal value, it is unlikely that the bulk of the assemblage
was purchased new and went unbroken for 40 years or more. Clearly the
age of the Maynard-Burgess vessels and the mix of old and new wares at
Bellis Court suggest that ceramics were acquired in small lots over an
extended period and used for long periods of time.

Neither Maynard-Burgess nor the Bellis Court privy contained
matched wares, but other deposits from the Courthouse Site suggest
that African Americans did discard portions of ceramic sets. In the
uppermost strata of an eighteenth century cellar within a few feet of the
Bellis Court privy, artifacts from subsequent nineteenth century households had accumulated in the settling cellar hole. While that later debris
may have come from any household in the block, virtually all of the block
was occupied by African Americans by the middle of the century, so
those artifacts likely were from the block's African-American households. The cellar slump contained two vessels with a matching 1836–
1864 Palestine pattern, although they were in different colors (red and
brown) (Williams and Weber 1978:156). A third Palestine vessel (in
brown) was recovered from the Bellis Court privy. In 1898, *The House
Beautiful* warned against such apparent mixing of wares, noting that
"the service of each course should be of one kind of dishes. There is
nothing which looks so splotchy and as inelegant as a table covered with
five or six kinds of dishes" ("Notes, Tableware" 1898). Mixing colors in
the same pattern was an uncommon modification of ceramic standards,
but many consumers assembled tableware collections that obeyed some
table codes (e.g., matching designs) and resisted others (e.g., uniform
colors) (cf. comparable color mixing patterns in Larsen and Lucas
1994:6.9; Lucas 1994:7.9). Two matching Charles Meigh and Sons muf-
fins (i.e., seven-inch plates) dating to 1851–1861 also were recovered
from the cellar slump. Consequently, despite the absence of matched
ware in the Bellis Court privy assemblage, it is possible that these and
neighboring households had some sets.

The melange of decorative preparations, age of the vessels, and
heavy wear suggests that many ceramics came into these African-
American households through various forms of non-market exchange,
such as generational gifts, salvage, barter, and positive reciprocity.
One African-American Annapolitan recalled that "I don't remember us
having any good china sets, you know.... I think a lot of stuff was passed
down from grandparents to parents" (Jopling 1991). Another household's ceramics came from a great grandmother who "collected it
through the years" (Jopling 1991). This sort of exchange certainly was
not unknown among other consumers, but African-American reciprocity

tended to remain insular because of racist boundaries. Such communal exchange included numerous other material goods and services. In the Courthouse neighborhood, for example, "a lot of the women did raise flowers. They compared flowers, they exchanged flowers. It was the camaraderie they had amongst themselves" (Jopling 1991). A woman from the neighborhood remembered that "Annapolis was a very friendly town. Your door was never locked and neighbors would come and go, and if they wanted to come and get something from the refrigerator they would come and get that" (Jopling 1991).

The Annapolis assemblages are not prototypical Victorian table settings: Each is relatively small, composed of older wares, and almost entirely mismatched. A starkly contrasting ceramic consumption pattern was identified in Annapolis at the Main Street site, where the 1889 *terminus post quem* privy of a prosperous White physician's family contained 121 ceramic vessels (Mullins 1989). Seventy-three of the 121 vessels were white-bodied and undecorated, and the assemblage contained 6 groups of matching vessels. The white-bodied vessels included 37 hard-paste porcelain and 13 ironstone vessels, wares that were the height of late-nineteenth century ceramic style (Majewski and O'Brien 1987:120). The porcelains also included 2 French plates like those described in an 1883 household manual, which noted that "Dresden, French china, and Japanese are the wares now in vogue" (Pennsylvania Publishing Company 1883:478). These groups of matching vessels were almost certainly purchased together, just as they were marketed in Victorian catalogs and stores.

The contrasting mix of ceramics in the Maynard-Burgess cellar suggests that everyday dining was a context in which the household felt little compulsion to seamlessly reproduce dominant table discipline. The modest quantity of 8 table vessels in the glass assemblage appears to support that interpretation, since an archetypal Victorian table would contain more stemware and table vessels. Main Street, for instance, contained 21 glass tumblers and 8 stemmed glasses. The ceramic and glass tablewares from Maynard-Burgess argue that the household rejected, modified, or simply ignored many dominant dining dictates in their everyday food consumption. This does not mean that they entirely spurned fine tableware, as archaeological assemblages tend to over-represent commonly used goods: "Everyday" ceramics are used more often than "Sunday china," making them more likely to be broken and discarded. Nevertheless, if the household even occasionally used partial matching sets or a small number of pricy table vessels, their ability to prevent any of those vessels from breaking and entering the archaeological record is quite extraordinary.

The absence of aesthetically uniform assemblages does not necessarily indicate that these families did not intimately understand table
etiquette. They may well have adhered to basic everyday table etiquette
and behaved like genteel diners, even if their everyday table ceramics
rejected the showy material trappings of genteel dining. For instance,
even though the Maynard-Burgess assemblage appears to be dominated
by wares obtained outside the marketplace or in small quantities, the
functional make-up of the Maynard-Burgess ceramic assemblage actually was quite similar to that at Main Street. The Main Street assemblage included 47 teaware forms (e.g., handled cups, teapots, saucers;
38.84% of the vessel assemblage). The Maynard-Burgess cellar contained 14 teaware forms (33.33% of the assemblage). This functional
similarity suggests that tea and coffee drinking was common in both
households at a time when one etiquette book observed that "afternoon
teas have become a standard entertainment in American homes" (Everett 1902:383). The quantity of teawares in both assemblages stands in
stark contrast to the Bellis Court collection, however, which included
only 4 deep saucers and no cups (11.11% of the assemblage).

The Maynard-Burgess tea vessels did not match, but of the 14
teaware forms at Maynard-Burgess, 7 vessels were undecorated or
molded and 3 were sparsely painted hard-paste porcelain cups. This
pattern of consuming undecorated or sparsely decorated wares in lieu of
matching sets mirrors a suggestion made in 1885 by etiquette writer
Juliet Corson. Corson advocated purchasing undecorated wares when
sets were too costly, recommending that "when it is necessary to econo-
mize, only plain white china, and glass free from any set ornamentation,
should be bought; because it is far easier to replace plain ware if any is
broken" (Corson 1885:99). Although the runny caramel glaze of the
Maynards' Rockingham teapot would have been quite prominent among
these plain teawares, the undecorated Maynard-Burgess vessels generally would have looked similar.

Informal exchange of ceramics and selective resistance to etiquette
did not utterly ignore prevailing material standards, as consumers
recognized and negotiated dominant consumption patterns. An African
American who grew up in the Courthouse Site neighborhood remembered that his mother "used to pride herself on a set of dishes she bought
at [local retailer] S&N Katz.... The stuff we used through the week was
maybe a lot of odd stuff. You wouldn't have a whole set. The plates might
be different" (Jopling 1991). The son's contrast of his family's sets and
everyday unmatched dishes indicates recognition of genteel table etiquette, even if the household did not strictly adhere to those table
rules and material standards everyday.

Oral testimony indicates that many African Americans reserved distinct ceramics and conventions for particular occasions, shifting from informal to genteel conventions when deemed appropriate. Like the family with matching S&N Katz vessels, a woman who lived on Gott's Court remembered that "we had everyday dishes and then we had special occasion dishes" (Jopling 1992). A man who grew up on South Street noted that his family likewise "had all kinds of dishes and decorated dishes, the kind that you don't use everyday. They were mostly white—you just didn't touch them. They were used for Christmas or some special occasion or sometimes if we had company" (Jopling 1991). Genteel dining rules were reserved for that company, such as "the Minister, of course," illuminating that African-American households clearly had flexible dining etiquette. When the minister and comparable luminaries came to dine, "everything was all special, proper. Naturally you put out the best. Everybody had good linen, napkins" (Jopling 1991).

The division of a ceramic assemblage into everyday and "special" wares was exactly what was dictated in some etiquette books. One circa 1860 manual (Kirby and Kirby ca. 1860:18) even reserved its counsel to "the best china, that is kept on the top shelf of the cupboard, and only comes out on high days and holidays. It is very superior, let me tell you, to the blue and white cups and saucers in the kitchen." A woman who lived on Franklin Street classified her family's ceramic assemblage much as this etiquette book suggested, into kitchen and dining-room wares respectively designed for "everyday and special times.... [Great-grandmother and grandmother] had a lot of things in the cupboard—crystal glasses, bowls, the green set for ice cream. The everyday was in the kitchen. We used the china closet on Sundays and special occasions" (Jopling 1991). She noted that her "great grandmother ... always had the table properly set to know which fork to pick up" (Jopling 1991). Obviously, even if highly structured etiquette was not followed everyday, many African Americans recognized dominant decorum and the material goods associated with such protocol.

TACTICAL MEDIATIONS

African-American consumption tactics mediated a range of social and racial contradictions, some of which were not unique to African America. Indeed, many of these tactics appear among other consumers who shared comparable structural dilemmas. Yet in positions such as that of domestic laborers, African Americans were distinctively situated against Whiteness and within racialized labor. Tactics such as recycling and theft indirectly critiqued the racial and material structure of consumer space by undermining its control of Black materialism. However, such tactics remained mostly enigmatic to White observers, who were utterly dependent on the African-American laborers they excluded as citizens.

The sociopolitical impact of such consumption tactics is somewhat ambiguous. In most cases, the express target of tactical consumer struggles was not dominant structure (e.g., national producers) as much as a host of lived contradictions (e.g., a local employer), so it is tempting to ignore such consumption's impact on a societal scale. Yet the piecemeal African-American transformation of local incongruities worked toward fashioning a sense of being that was denied by racism; that is, it was part of a collective, albeit generally unorchestrated, African-American effort to eliminate anti-Black material, social, and historical dispossession by foiling dominant definitions of Black subjectivity. Certainly many Whites recognized that African-American consumption tactics defied various forms of dominant Black subjectivity, and a few even pondered the syncretism of Black and White subjectivity. However, those tactics and their profound impact on American society usually were ignored. We should approach those seemingly innocuous tactics as deviations within and against White consumer space, efforts to mediate the contradictions that coded the material world as White exclusive. As observers threatened by eroding Whiteness understood, any genuine mediation of those incongruities would yield dramatically new racial subjects. In its most radical implications, such a mediation threatened to undo Whiteness entirely and fashion new African-American and White subjects alike.

Affluent Aspiration
African-American Consumer Desire

In 1919, White academic Francis Taylor Long published a study of African-American labor and economics in Clarke County, Georgia during the recently ended First World War. Long's research was typical of a flood of empirical studies that used emergent social scientific methods to analyze a variety of social, moral, and material dilemmas. Long's study intended to explain the apparent erosion of African-American labor discipline and deference to Whites, a mission that inevitably recycled familiar racist caricatures and projected them onto consumer behavior. A clothing dealer, for instance, informed Long (1919:54) that "he had never before sold so large a number of silk shirts to negroes as during the war.... Negroes had also bought much more largely than ever the highest-priced suits of clothes, shoes and other furnishings." Food, furniture, automobile, and phonograph expenditures increased as well, according to Long, and he reported that "Similar extravagance was shown with reference to rugs, pictures, china, bric-a-brac, and other articles."

Through an analysis of African-American materialism and expenditure patterns, Long laid the blame for deteriorating Black social discipline on elevated African-American wages and the consumption they allowed. Many observers before Long championed the thesis that consumption bred a moral hedonism that was antithetical to labor and social discipline; indeed, similar accusations had been leveled at enslaved African Americans and were routinely directed toward a variety of marginalized American consumers. If anything, it would seem that racial ideologues actually would aspire to ensure that African Americans *were* consumers, as this would reproduce their subordination in a racially structured wage labor system. Yet, oddly enough, the discourse surrounding African-American consumption most often ran in exactly the opposite direction: Most White writers were apprehensive that African-American consumption heralded a disastrous erosion of Black moral, labor, and racial discipline. These observers did not see African-American economic subordination in material consumption; instead, they saw the concession of symbolic and utilitarian privileges that were central to consumer citizenship, a status still denied to Blacks after World War I.

What was perhaps most telling about Long's fevered condemnation of African-American consumption was that it focused on apparently innocuous material goods. The material culture he chose to criticize seems utterly mundane: silk shirts, mahogany chairs, jewelry, brand groceries, and household bric-a-brac. Observers like Long illuminated the social significance of African-American consumption by simultaneously dismissing it and apprehensively warning of its potential implications. On the one hand, many Whites reduced African-American materialism to harmless extravagance; on the other, the same commentators often underlined the threat of African-American consumption on a self-evident, unique White identity. Long (1919:55), for instance, reduced African-American materialism to wastefulness, concluding that "During his heyday in the Great War the negro seems to have been attracted, as is usual with him in times of prosperity, more by the superficialities, the tinsel and glitter of life, than by its permanent benefits and durable satisfactions." This maneuver to construct certain sorts of materialism as "artificial" and opposed to an ambiguous "reality" (e.g., hard work, racial deference) was a familiar discursive strategy. In 1866, for example, traveler Whitelaw Reid observed that in Georgia stores "the show-cases are filled with cheap jewelry, and the thousand knick-knacks which captivate the negro eye" (Reid 1965:122). Much like Long a half-century later, Reid stressed that African-American consumers were entranced by "captivation," a superficial emotional value that was the inverse of reason and logic (cf. Lears 1989:78–80). For much different reasons, genteel African-American scribes often espoused the same sort of self-imposed "thrift" and material asceticism advocated by genteel Whites. They, too, saw a decline in morals and social order resulting from the "easy" satisfaction of desire in consumer space. African-American elite sometimes critiqued consumption simply because it threatened their personal sway over the community, but for many African Americans material asceticism was a strategy to uplift African-American entrepreneurship and unite African Americans socially and materially.

Relatively mundane objects inspired apprehension because they posed the specter of a society in which material culture would not clearly mark subjectivity. This chapter examines why rather commonplace objects were considered pivotal scenes of social struggle to African-American consumers and racist ideologues alike. Confronted by a society in which goods were increasingly more available, disposable income was rising, and leisure time was expanding, genteel ideologues struggled to reproduce their material distinction and authority. The most strident voices came from a cross-section of elites and various moral voices (e.g., churchmen) who saw themselves as social, moral, and, in some cases, racial gatekeepers. In this section, I probe both what these ideologues feared in African-American consumption, and why modest goods and their consumption assumed such significance among many African Americans. The chapter examines how genteel apprehension of consumer culture's democratizing promises was amplified by a pervasive White apprehension of African-American desire and eroding racial boundaries. These apprehensions are illustrated in discourses on Victorian bric-a-brac, goods that are commonly recovered on archaeological sites, but are ignored because of their scarcity and symbolic and functional ambiguity. The chapter then turns to how social and material desire is reflected in the consumption of brand goods and how genteel ideologues attempted to defuse that consumption through their advocacy of thrift. The discourses and symbolism surrounding material culture like bric-a-brac, canned goods, and brand commodities may seem to be of no consequence, or they may simply appear to be reflections of dominant production organization and late-nineteenth century marketing evolution. Instead, I will argue that they were points of struggle that reflect the potential implications of even the most mundane commodity consumption on citizenship and racial subjectivity.

"IT IS YOUR DUTY TO LIVE WELL":
DEMOCRATIZING MATERIALISM

Genteel anguish over the decreasing exclusivity of consumer space (and elite inability to restrict entrance to it) took a number of intertwined forms. A central facet of this anxiety was a class uneasiness that consumer culture's democratizing appeals forbode a mass society without clear status ranking. An 1875 household manual, for example, warned that genteel Americans, like their European counterparts, could soon face the "increased demoralization" of servants caused by "the progress of democratical sentiment. The laboring classes have become too acutely sensible of their equality to submit readily to the obvious forms, at any rate, of an oppressive superiority of position" (Harper and Brothers 1875:126). Some etiquette and household tomes actually counseled Americans to acquiesce to their class and social lot, such as an 1873 manual that observed that "Every one ought to live according to his circumstance, and the meal of the tradesman ought not to emulate the entertainments of the higher classes" (Ellet 1873:37).

Others directed their counsel to prosperous trend-setters who legitimized class deference by displaying a material ideal to the masses. An
1897 manual in this vein argued that "A man has a right to live according
to his means; nay, more, if you have a good income, it is your duty to live
well" (Sangster 1897:411). These sorts of class-apprehensive commentaries revealed a struggle in which elite sought to reproduce their
affluence and authority, seeking new means of distinction or even re-
sorting to absurd pleas to non-elite to accept their appropriate subordination.

A related anxiety about consumption focused on its erosion of
White exclusivity, an uneasiness fanned by Emancipation and ever-
increasing European immigration. Genteel writers exaggerated that it
was becoming impossible to materially differentiate between groups,
and many of these critics pointed to both class instability and the racial
menace posed by an unregulated consumer space. For instance, an 1871
etiquette book noted that

> The uniformity of dress is a characteristic of the people of the United States.
> The man of leisure and the laborer, the mistress and the maid, wear clothes of
> the same material and cut. Political equality renders our countrymen and
> countrywomen averse to all distinctions of costume which may be supposed
> to indicate a difference of caste. The uniformity which results is not pictur-
> esque, and our every-day world in America has, in consequence, the shabby
> look of being got up by the Jews in Chtahma Street, and turned out in a
> universal set of second-hand clothing. (Harper and Brothers 1871:160)

Not by chance, the etiquette book reproached apparent material equality through a stigmatizing Jewish caricature that racialized material
uniformity and threatened White consumers with the disappearance of
clear racial differentiation. Even more distressing was Edward King's
(1875:773–774) analysis that the Civil War had a material and racial
"leveling influence." In place of the stable antebellum continuum of
planter-poor White-enslaved African Americans, King observed, "a middle class is gradually springing into existence, bridging the once impas-
sable gulf between the 'high up' and the 'low down,' and some of the more
intelligent and respectable negroes are taking rank in this class." To
White elite in the North and South alike, the notion of a fluid class
structure without clear racial exclusivity was a chilling prophecy.

The shared element in most critiques of expanding consumption
was an apprehension of desire. In 1908, English traveler Sir Alfred Low
(1974:102) suggested that "There is no limit to ambition in the United
States." Low rhetorically exaggerated the limitlessness of aspiration,
but this sort of comment threatened many elite. Observers were wary
that consumer desire threatened established social order through a
diverse range of implied material, social, moral, and racial effects. Some

Victorian elite had recently secured their own status through ambitious climbs from poverty, so they were slow to reject the potential of hard work and shrewd entrepreneurship. However, most newly moneyed and long-affluent Whites alike did not believe such ambition was open to Blacks. These elite were concerned that conceding ambition to African Americans was tantamount to suggesting genuine equity. In the wake of Emancipation, for example, the *Maryland Republican and State Capital Advertiser* ("Southern Military Despotisms," 1867) launched a typical condemnation of universal Black freedom and civil rights, calling the moment

> the most abominable phase barbarism has assumed since the dawn of civilization.... the blacks in their ignorance are made to believe that not only the "day of jubilee" has come, but that of aggrarianism [sic] or a common distribution of property also. They are now crazy for the promised spoils.

The Annapolis paper's suggestion that African Americans likened Emancipation to a sacred "day of jubilee" captured the distinctive spirituality of African-American desire. In the wake of Emancipation, African-American Christianity harbored a powerful Messianic current that spilled over into partisan politics and economics (Foner 1988:94). Enslaved African Americans had long prophesied Emancipation, and for the Messianically inclined, freedom affirmed African America's preordained destiny. African-American Christians often analogized Emancipation to the Old Testament account of the deliverance of the Children of Israel (Foner 1988:93). One newly emancipated African American concluded that "God planned dem slave prayers to free us like he did de Israelites, and dey did" (Levine 1977:137). Wiley Bates (1928:20) borrowed the same Biblical analogy nearly a half-century later, noting that "the Jews, when liberated, went to Canaan, their own land by lot and inheritance. The Negro, forty-eight years ago, as a race was like the Son of Man—nowhere to lay his head." Rather than repress aspiration, faith and the church were fundamental vehicles for partisan activity, community activism, and entrepreneurship, providing a moral understanding of African-American subjectivity and an institutional foundation for economic and social organization (Rachleff 1989:24). African America had long desired the privileges and opportunities of free citizens, so the rights of consumption were not simply secular or economic concessions; in some African-American minds, they were a measure of spiritual justice that provided hope for the African-American future.

It was critical for Whites to publicly deny the rights of desire to African Americans, undercutting the possibility that African Americans could even entertain the aspirations of White citizens. In 1887, for example, a dime novel on Southern life included a relatively typical

160 Chapter 7

enslaved character whose freedom moved him to entertain White-exclusive privileges: "After the war there came a change. Uncle Ned (Gran'mamy's husband) became possessed of a devil—ambition.... For fifteen years he had done nothing but drive our carriage; but now he believed himself qualified to make a fortune" (Butterworth 1887:222). In 1926, an etiquette writer argued in a similar vein that untenable aspirations undermined the lives of European-born women who resisted domestic labor:

> Why should it be true, that with our thousands of immigrants anxious to make their way in the new land, that these women object so decidedly to taking service in families, where good homes await them and no demand upon their earnings is made but to clothe themselves?... There are many reasons for this, and chief among them in the minds of the newly arrived immigrants is the promise held out to them of a land of equality and independence, where wealth is easily acquired and the hope of being soon enabled to lay aside enough for themselves to own their own homes and be of the employer class and not the employed. (Cushing 1926:230–231)

African-American ambition was materialized in a wide range of forms, including costly material culture (e.g., real estate), as well as relatively inexpensive goods (e.g., household decorative articles). For observers like Long, the silk shirts, brand groceries, mahogany chairs, and parlor rugs in the homes of African Americans were obvious threats to the racial exclusivity and White domination of public space. An 1882 manual on household decorative goods underlined the symbolism inherent in apparently meaningless things when it indicated that it was possible "to carry the 'civilizing influence of the beautiful' even into the homes of the humblest at the minimum of expense" (Facey 1882:vi). Rather than see inexpensive and prosaic goods as insignificant, Long understood that their consumption harbored entrance into what was formerly racially exclusive, "civilizing" symbolism with profound social and racial implications; these goods were indications of deep-seated desires and ambitions that historically were denied to African Americans. Commodities were not simply evidence of African Americans' penetration into White space; they also demonstrated how African Americans could "consume" dominant social ambitions and subjectivity, posing a potentially radical shift in White consumer citizenship.

"TO LIVE IS TO CONSUME!": CONSUMPTION AS EMPOWERMENT

At the turn of the century, economist Simon Patten (1889, 1907) argued that social subjectivity should be forged in consumption rather than labor. Among the most ardent champions of mass consumption, Patten encouraged consumers to acknowledge their desires, rather than suppress them, a sentiment that found an increasingly receptive audience. The embrace of such desires was viewed by many people as a newly empowering privilege with significant social implications. In 1910, for instance, Bertha June Richardson's study *The Woman Who Spends* concluded that the material world had vast social significance that rested on the shoulders of women. Richardson (1910:38–39) boldly swept aside domestic ideology, which already was eroded by women's agency in public consumer space, arguing that "For women ... the problem is not, What shall be produced to supply my needs? but, How shall I spend to satisfy my needs? The greater the opportunities for spending, the wider the field of choice." Household writers Martha and Robert Bruere (1912) echoed Richardson's suggestion that consumption held a measure of women's empowerment: "Time was when the woman who kept house was expected to be high priestess of that dire goddess, How-to-Save-Money, but her metamorphosis from producer to consumer has shifted her worship to the new deity How-to-Spend" (Bruere and Bruere 1912:181).

This rethinking of consumer empowerment did not ignore collective social interests in a fixation on individual desire. Instead, like Patten, Richardson (1910:110–111) cautioned against consumption that did not heed society's shared interests, noting that

> The man whose satisfaction can only lie in the gaining of his own ends, regardless of the aims of others, seeks a dangerous gratification.... Today, these two kinds of satisfaction, the individual and what might be called the group, are constantly pitted against each other in the struggle of life.... The rights of the individual against the good of all! How to reconcile the interests of both is the question the twentieth century has to solve.

For Richardson (1910:113), materialism's social implications demonstrated the "necessity for a new and broader conception of individual satisfaction, for making it a part of the satisfaction of the larger group." This "broader conception" of material desires conceived of consumption in terms considerably more complex than individuals' shopping strategies. The Brueres, for instance, quoted a teacher of the emerging discipline of domestic science who characterized her field as "'a training in relations. It takes up government, and politics, and business, and health, and capital, and labor and the social setting of them all. It is really training the consumer to live.' And to live is to consume!" (Bruere and Bruere 1912:193).

The groundwork for a widespread investment in consumption was laid as observers began to rethink consumption's centrality to social subjectivity. Significantly, Richardson and the Brueres focused their analyses on consumption's empowerment of women marginalized in other public and private spaces: For marginalized Americans, consumption was not a new behavioral discipline, but an opportunity with profound social implications. An 1885 manual, for instance, hailed the "complete revolution in the whole domain of house-furnishing and decoration, a revolution which has thrown opportunities in the way of everybody, rich and poor alike" (Sypher and Company 1885:18). Such "opportunities" implied consumer citizenship, so many Whites resisted extending that status to African Americans. In 1866, a Southern planter employing newly freed African-American tenants told traveler John Trowbridge (1866:366) that he operated his own store for these laborers because "the negroes, if allowed to buy their own supplies, would spend half their time in running about the country for knick-knacks." Such plantation stores suggest the African-American desire invested in seemingly innocuous goods and newly won shopping rights, just as they reveal one of the many White strategies to deny such rights through overpriced goods and market control. The optimism invested in consumption was somewhat unrealistic perhaps, but many Americans clearly were reconsidering the opportunities embodied in the consumption of seemingly meaningless material culture.

"Solid Attractions": Bric-a-Brac and Race

In 1887, household writer Laura Holloway outlined the appropriate furnishings that should be placed in a home's showpiece social space. Holloway (1887:41) noted that this room "should have solid attractions in the form of easy-chairs, sofa-lounges, and ornaments. All the knick-knacks ought to be gathered there, and the room made as pretty as variety and good taste can make it." Knickknacks included a host of statues, vases, figurines, chromolithographs, and assorted curios that featured ambiguous motifs from the colonized world, nature, or a romanticized classical or historical past. Such objects were manufactured and marketed extensively in the late nineteenth century.

On February 22, 1876, William H. Butler and James C. Bishop inventoried the possessions of their neighbor John Maynard, and found a home with genteel furnishings quite comparable to the space Holloway idealized 11 years later (Anne Arundel County Probate Inventories 1876). By his death in July 1875, John Maynard was familiar with many of Annapolis' African-American elite, including men like Butler and Bishop. Butler, who lived a few doors away from the Maynards, was a builder and real estate investor who owned 33 homes and 4 vacant lots in the mid-1870s (Ives 1979:147). In 1873, he became the first African-

American elected official in Maryland when he won a seat on the City Council, and in 1876 his property holdings made him the city's largest private landowner ("William H. Butler," 1987:10). Since the second quarter of the nineteenth century, the Bishop family was among Baltimore and Annapolis' most influential African-American lineages. James C. Bishop apparently was a son of William Bishop, Sr., who ranked among Annapolis' 12 richest individuals in 1860 (Calderhead 1977:18; Gatewood 1990:74). Willard Gatewood (1990:74) identifies James Bishop as a sugar manufacturer who owned a pew in Saint Anne's Episcopal Church, which lay at the center of Church Circle, and a home on the Circle— likely the home built by William Bishop, Sr. (Brown 1994:15).

The household that Butler and Bishop inventoried at 163 Duke of Gloucester Street may have been modest in comparison to their own homes, but its material trappings certainly suggested aspirations to gentility. The bulk of the assemblage's value rested in a group of objects in the Maynards' "Front room," a Victorian term for a showplace domestic space (Schlereth 1991:117–120). The room contained a $3.00 side board, an $8.00 sofa, six mahogany chairs valued at $12.00, and a $6.00 parlor carpet. Amongst these goods was an entry for a lot of "Wat Not" (i.e., "what not") valued at $0.75 and six pictures with a total value of $6.00. The modest $0.75 value of the Maynard's "wat not" indicates it likely was mass-produced decorative goods, most of which retailed for a nickel or less. The six "pictures" probably were chromolithographs, color lithographs marketed since the 1860s and retailed at an average cost of two or three dollars each (Schlereth 1991:194).

Bric-a-brac has been found on each of the African-American archaeological sites in Annapolis. The Maynard-Burgess cellar, for instance, contained two porcelain knickknacks: a match holder and a female peasant figurine. Merely two objects may seem insignificant, but quantity alone cannot provide a definitive measure of symbolic significance. That significance is suggested by the vigilant curation of bric-a-brac. One African-American Annapolitan acknowledged his mother's conscientious care for such objects, observing that

> we had knick knacks in our living room. In fact, we had quite a few of them. We weren't allowed to touch them. My mother didn't like to see her stuff broken up. She was so proud of her things. It was there for you to look at it. We weren't barred from the living room, we just weren't allowed to touch them. (Jopling 1991)

Historical archaeologists commonly find these sorts of trinkets and consign them to the anonymity of a massive artifact catalog, analyzing them in purely functional terms or reducing them to idiosyncratic shows of individual whimsy (for exceptions, cf. Orser 1996:40; and Stewart-

Abernathy 1992:118). Yet many Americans like Long recognized that such objects were highly charged social symbols. The archaeological obliviousness to such objects is a complex confluence of methodological and intellectual quandaries. Methodologically, the dilemma seems almost self-evident: So few pieces of bric-a-brac are recovered that it is assumed that they do not have particularly profound symbolic meaning. Ignoring knickknacks simply because of low quantities, though, is a superficial negation. After all, a paucity of particular items is a way that archaeologists legitimize the focus on many other goods.

A related counter is that they are insignificant because of their inexpensive price. Most mass-produced bric-a-brac did indeed retail for a nickel or less, making it a relatively poor vehicle to celebrate material standing. Yet this equation of bric-a-brac symbolism with exchange value minimizes the desires and social values invested in many inexpensive commodities. As *The Boston Cooking-School Magazine* observed in 1897, "in these days, when the artificer can give us almost perfect copies of the artist's work, at a nominal sum, there is scarcely a home so humble that it may not have a Raphael, a Carot, a Millet, speaking from it walls" (Parker 1897:37). Rather than assume that the symbolism of such prints was determined by their price, they clearly were valued for their construction and reproduction of genteel subjectivity.

As with virtually all commodities, there certainly was some relationship between bric-a-brac's use and exchange values. Despite their modest price, some consumers likely construed bric-a-brac's exoticism and novelty with scarcity and costliness, inferring that the uncommon object necessarily had great exchange value. In 1993, for instance, an African American from the Gott's Court neighborhood inspected an excavated ceramic figurine and concluded that "evidently when you worked for White families they would give you these things. Because I'm more than sure black people did not have the money to buy a lot of expensive things" (Goodwin et al. 1993:11). Clearly such objects could confound perceptions of exchange value and implied status, despite their modest cost. Nevertheless, not all consumers principally defined material symbolism based on an object's cost, and it is unreasonable to reduce an object to a more or less solitary meaning shaped wholly or primarily by its price.

Another analytical approach to bric-a-brac—one common to much archaeological analysis—is to focus on function. This presents the dilemma of determining precisely what "function" entails, a particularly thorny problem with purely decorative material culture like bric-a-brac. Typically, archaeologists view function as a rational union of artifact form and intended purpose, a definition that focuses on an object's utility and considers aesthetic style as a separate category of analysis (Miller 1987:117). Yet fixating on function-utility rationalizes producers' economic values and mystifies (or ignores) consumer symbolism (cf. Baudrillard 1975).

Bric-a-brac is distinctive (albeit not unique) in its capacity to evoke symbolism that stems from the object's enigmatic aesthetics; that is, the symbolism of bric-a-brac is so ambiguous that it seems to be defined almost wholly by the consumer, even though such meanings clearly are not constructed by autonomous consumers. Approaching bric-a-brac symbolism as an amalgam of consumer-endowed meanings and unrecognized dominant structuring influences suggests dimensions of both Simmel's aesthetic value and Marx's fetishism (Orser 1992:97). Aesthetic value springs from an individual's pleasure derived from the feelings associated with the object and its style. This dimension of material meaning is predominately defined by an individual's idiosyncratic perception of a particular object. In a comparable way, the fetishized commodity appears to assume its meaning from its very physicality, but this isolation of the object evades how its symbolic properties are endowed by unrecognized social processes (e.g., conditions of production). These two types of value are not necessarily exclusive; rather than settle on bric-a-brac as one or another type of good, it and other commodities clearly have dimensions of the fetishized commodity and can still accommodate distinctive aesthetic values.

Ironically, consumers likely were attracted to the very symbolic ambiguity that discourages some archaeologists from venturing into bric-a-brac interpretation. In a marketplace of highly standardized commodities, bric-a-brac was quite symbolically and functionally ambiguous. Wholesale catalogs featured bric-a-brac with a vast range of novel motifs, including Japanese fans, Biblical figurines, Boar hunt statues, casts of Lincoln's death mask, and classical cherubs (e.g., Castelvecchi 1885; Linington 1880). In most cases bric-a-brac simply depicted consumer culture's fanciful and xenophobic visions of other peoples, places, and subjects. For instance, one catalog's offerings included "Baskets of Darkies," porcelain figurines of delighted Black children at play (Spelman 1883:137). These baskets of African-American children reflect that the subject of bric-a-brac was the consumer, not the illusory subjects that it depicted: Indeed, much like the Black caricatures in advertising, these figurines posed as imitations of a Black reality that never existed.

Bric-a-brac occupied a particularly complex symbolic terrain: on the one hand, it obliquely celebrated White supremacy, imperialism, and industrial affluence; but, on the other, it simultaneously risked the erosion of its dominant symbolism because its aesthetics were so ambiguous. The central organizing tenet in bric-a-brac style was a sort of prosaic exoticism; that is, producers attempted to circumscribe bric-a-brac's symbolism by objectifying subjects in idealized, non-menacing poses that still retained an exotic, enigmatic air. Bric-a-brac materialized colonized peoples, romanticized histories, fantasized cultures, and natural motifs in a form that was designed to demonstrate White Western society's ability to define and control such alien entities. Bric-a-brac also expressed many consumers' yearning for clear, revitalized roots, particularly in the form of motifs such as mainstream historical figures (e.g., George Washington) and classical design (e.g., pseudo-Grecian statues) (Lears 1994:104). However, even the symbolism of these familiar subjects was flexible, historicized, and situational. These conventional motifs with apparently self-evident meanings amplified the racialization of other objects that ostensibly represented the contemporary world; that is, exotic goods depicted spatial, cultural, and temporal "Others" that contrasted starkly with the historical, social, and racial stability represented by staid George Washington prints and classical statuettes (Stewart 1993:148–149).

Bric-a-brac defied valuations like purchase price or utility, instead functioning as a vehicle of consumers' desire to see themselves within an idealized society and world. An 1885 household manual fancifully envisioned the nationalist, materialist, and racialized dimensions of such consumption, suggesting that Americans

> take a very great interest in other peoples and in other countries, an interest so great that it has affected our whole way of living; not only our houses show it, but our pictures, our amusements, our books, our newspapers, and our dress. In our houses we give our love of adventure free play, and like to be reminded at every turn, of the fact that America, big as is her territory, is but a small part of the world. (Sypher and Company 1885:6)

Objects like the Maynards' peasant girl figurine placed the household within a society whose roots lay in a bucolic agrarian past, a vision that contrasted to the reality of Southern agricultural experiences. The "miracle" worked by such objects was that they appeared to resolve such realities through redefinition, distortion, ignorance, or evasion. The placid peasant girl with a basket of flowers could accommodate utopian aspirations for the shape of society to come, evoke quixotic visions of the oppression that lay behind, or evade the social complexities of late-nineteenth century urbanized industrial America. Bric-a-brac was of no consequence if it did not harbor some resolution of concrete social dilemmas, even if that resolution was a symbolic delusion (cf. Stewart 1993:147).

Household manuals contained extensive counsel on the selection and display of prints like those in the Maynards' front room. In 1869, for example, Catherine Beecher and Harriet Beecher Stowe (1869:84) recommended specific chromos to spur "refinement, intellectual development, and moral sensibility." An 1873 guide also advised consumers that "the subjects of the pictures must be such as we can truly sympathize with, something to awaken our admiration, reverence, or love" (Ellett 1873:21). Historical-themed lithographs and chromolithographs were among the most common motifs in the last quarter of the nineteenth century (Schlereth 1991:193–197). An 1880 trade catalog for C.M. Linington's in Chicago included a standard sample of historically themed "chromo portraits, size 9 × 11, of Lincoln, Grant, Washington and wife, Douglas, Stonewall Jackson" and other figures from the American past and Western civilization (Linington 1880:3–6). African-American marketers soon offered "race" prints to counter the vision of a uniformly White history and present. During World War I, for example, *The Crusader* drew its readers' attention to a firm selling "pictures of the Negro boys in France.... The pictures are beautifully painted in colors and give a vivid idea of how the Negro lads are making history 'over there.' One or more of these pictures should be in every Negro home" ("Pictures That Should Be In Every Home," 1918). A 1940 Works Projects Administration report noted that the homes of African-American Virginians often contained historical pictures of a comparable tenor:

> Pictures adorn the walls—sometimes yellow tintypes of stern-faced fore-bearers, or Biblical scenes, and more often rotogravure pictures of motion picture stars. A popular wall piece in many homes in recent years features the pictures of "great Negro Leaders." (Works Projects Administration 1940:337)

In place of George Washington, these prints depicted African-American personal and collective "race" histories.

The parlors of most turn-of-the-century African Americans contained pictures, continuing a well-established African-American tradition of decorating domestic spaces with graphics of all sorts. In 1880, for example, a *Harper's Weekly* correspondent in Georgia noted that in most African-American homes the walls were "covered with newspaper. *Harper's Weekly* was a great favorite for this purpose, and they begged it eagerly from me, because, I suspect, it served the double purpose of wallpaper and pictures" ("Inside Southern Cabins: Georgia, Part I," 1880: 733). In 1901, William Taylor Thom (1901a:91) reported that in the homes of Sandy Spring, Maryland's African Americans "many of the rooms are carpeted and adorned with prints and pictures on the wall." Robert Park (1969:160) noted in 1913 that an African American setting up house "will probably want to have some pictures on the walls. The thing that strikes his fancy is usually something in a large gilt frame such as one can buy cheap in an auction store." In typical fashion, Park disparaged African-American aestheticism by observing that African-American consumers were driven by "fancy" rather than reason and obtained their "cheap" pictures in auction houses rather than respectable retail stores.

By the late nineteenth century, household manuals and other material discourses began to racialize bric-a-brac consumption. The *Maryland Republican and State Capital Advertiser* pondered bric-a-brac aesthetics in 1880 by comparing American material affluence to constructions of luxury among other "races." The paper observed that "in Ireland, the accompaniment of salt to a potato is a luxury. Among the Cossacks, a clean shirt is more than a luxury" ("Luxury," 1880). In America, in contrast, "torsos, antiquities, and statues are justified in usurping the elbow-room of living men and women. The general charm of knick knacks is unquestionable." The editorial succinctly condensed nationalism and race in a single material aesthetics that was testament to America's profound industrial might and White supremacy. Francis Marion Crawford (1882:91–92) echoed this nationalized racism, observing that "Germans ... are singularly indifferent to the minor adornments of life" and "Italians ... show an utter disregard for what we understand by taste." Crawford distinguished these contrasting racial aesthetics with "American" taste, but she then fractured the American norm along class lines by suggesting that middling Whites had yet to grasp elite taste. Crawford (1882:96–97) exalted the refinement of "American" consumers, but

> Americans, like other rich people with whom wealth has not been very long hereditary, have yet to learn the extent of its uses and the limitations of its power.... It is the misapplication of it [i.e., wealth] that is dangerous, the pouring of it into the hands of vendors of doubtful bric-a-brac and the opening of unlimited credit for the decorator.

The social implications of African-American bric-a-brac display were contested by many White observers who separated appearance and reality. Jacob Riis (1971:118), for instance, believed inexpensive bric-a-brac was used to forge the illusion of affluence in African-American homes, noting that

> The poorest negro housekeeper's room in New York is bright with gaily-colored prints of his beloved "Abe Linkum," General Grant, President Garfield, Mrs. Cleveland, and other national celebrities, and cheery with flowers and singing birds. In the art of putting the best foot foremost, of disguising his poverty by making a little go a long way, our negro has no equal.

Riis' distinction between abundance and impoverishment cast the White-exclusive former as a reality Blacks could, at best, simulate, implying that they were racially unsuited to genuine affluence. Reducing the African-American material world to hollow appearance circumvented the power of material culture, a common tact among genteel anti-materialists. The significance of African-American material culture lay in its transgression of Whiteness. Astute observers like Riis sensed subtle violations of ostensibly White materialism—indeed, Riis' *How the Other Half Lives* was dedicated to dismantling such appearances in racialized New York. Riis devoted profusely illustrated chapters to Italians, Germans, African Americans, and other non-White New Yorkers to construct an unspoken White norm and preserve the sanctity of White material symbolism. Riis obviously felt compelled to address material culture, aware that the distinction between appearance and reality was not as unambiguous as he suggested.

Scholars sometimes pose public and private symbolisms, portraying public materialism as a strategic social display and private symbolism as authentic cultural expression (e.g., Weatherill 1988). Similarly, others see all materialism as public artifice that attempts to compensate for a personal emptiness. E. Franklin Frazier (1997:230–231), for instance, argued in 1957 that

> In seeking an escape in the delusion of wealth, middle-class Negroes make a fetish of material things or physical possessions. They are constantly buying things—houses, automobiles, furniture and all sorts of gadgets, not to mention clothes.... The objects which they are constantly buying are always on display.... The acquisition of objects which are not used or needed seems to be an attempt to fill some void in their lives.

Of course, it is unreasonable to unambiguously distinguish between public display (which is artificial and material) and private symbolism (which is authentic and personal) (cf. Glennie 1997:178–179). The very notion of "display" is an enigmatic concept, even though it appears recurrently in material culture analyses. Display could entail any number of conscious and unrecognized interests and audiences that cannot be modeled through any straightforward public/private dichotomy. At the very least, it seems shortsighted to reduce most, if not all, African-American agency in public space simply to strategic artifice masking some "absence."

African-American bric-a-brac often reflects how racialized labor implicated many African-American women in consumption. Bric-a-brac and various modest gifts routinely were given by White employers to their African-American domestics, typically passing from the White mistress to the laborer. For instance, one Annapolitan's mother received bric-a-brac from White families for whom she did housework: "She would bring them off jobs. People would give them to her. Sometimes the people who she worked for would go away and when they came back they would bring a little gift" (Jopling 1991). It would be naive to think that the trinkets Whites gave to African-American domestics sprang from unadulterated benevolence. Instead, gift-giving was one element within a strategy to legitimize African-American subordination, encourage reliability and devotion, and dissuade domestics from defiance ranging from theft to quitting the job.

NATIONAL MARKETS
AND AFRICAN-AMERICAN CONSUMERS

In the final quarter of the nineteenth century, American shoppers began to consume vast quantities of mass-produced brand-name canned and bottled goods. The shift to brands certainly was a significant element in transforming production organization, marketing, and mass-commodity symbolism (cf. Lears 1994; Strasser 1989; Susman 1984). Yet the appeal of brands was not a monolithic wave that rolled over American consumer space without any connection to consumers' social position. For consumers who confronted persistent prejudice in local markets, nationally and regionally produced brand commodities embodied consumer culture's liberatory potential. National brands; exchange venues, such as chain stores; and new consumption forms, such as mail-order sales, undermined and evaded community merchants' racism by shifting a significant measure of power away from local merchants and onto an ambiguously defined national marketplace. Brand producers, mail-order wish books, and most chains promised uniformity in product quality, superior goods, and competitive prices, all measures of equity that were rarely extended to African Americans. The racial ideologies of national producers and local marketers were not wholly dissimilar, of course; however, in contrast to the lived racism of local marketing, the mass marketplace appeared to pose a more likely possibility of equity and offer a means to circumvent local merchants' deceits.

The sale of goods by brand was a stark break from antebellum marketing. Antebellum advertisements typically were taken out by local merchants selling a variety of goods that were advertised by type (e.g., flour), rather than by manufacturer. In the 1840s, a few specific products began to be sold through repetitive slogans, and consumer familiarity with such slogans provided the seeds for brand advertising (Goodrum and Dalrymple 1990:20). Yet brand symbolism was delayed as a significant market force until the final quarter of the nineteenth century. America's industrial capacity did increase in the years leading up to the Civil War, but on the eve of the war, local and regional producer still could sell their goods far more cheaply than most national manufacturers. Most goods continued to be sold in bulk—loose from merchants' barrels or tubs. However, massive production by postbellum manufacturers and workforce transformations provided increasingly more goods to sell, and advances in print technology provided improved techniques to advertise goods and distinguish individual products. In 1870, only 121 trademarks were registered in the United States, but brand-name marketing and commodity trademark protection mushroomed in the late nineteenth century; in 1906, over 10,000 trademarks were filed (Schlereth 1991:161–162). By 1921, a commercial artist went so far as to proclaim that the shift "from barreling in bulk to individual packaging symbolized the achievement in modern life of a very high civilization" (Lears 1994:304).

Brands were most common for household goods that were difficult to distinguish without labels, such as foods, soaps, and medicines. To distinguish themselves, brands conveyed more than mere product identification. Postbellum producers allied their goods with ambiguously related symbolic qualities to persuade consumers to pay more for a variety of real and imagined commodity attributes, such as higher quality, reliability, and countless other distinctions. For instance, Henry Crowell used the picture of a Quaker on his famous Quaker Oats to invoke virtue and thrift, and Ivory Soap conjured hygenicism by trumpeting its purity. In semiotic terms, brand consumers purchased a sign rather than just a functional good, consuming both oats and the ambiguous Quaker values that the brand embodied.

Like window displays, containers and package aesthetics prolonged consumer anticipation and heightened daydreaming desire by encouraging a consumer to imagine the vast symbolic, as well as functional, benefits in relatively mundane commodities (cf. Willis 1991:1–2). The sales appeals clearly were alluring; by the 1880s etiquette books and household manuals routinely advocated brand purchases and evaluated the quality of various brands. In 1888, for instance, *The Homemaker* evaluated a series of name brand goods and concluded that "we hope that there are other good brands, but of these we are sure" ("Plantation Housekeeping" 1888:44). Brand consumption also was boosted by the passage of the Pure Food and Drug Act in 1906 and a series of related pure food laws that required labels to itemize a product's contents and weight (cf. "Purity in Food," 1910). Such laws did not eliminate bulk sales or adulterated goods; however, compliance was a dilemma for regional manufacturers who did not standardize their products and for community merchants who dealt primarily with local producers (Strasser 1989:257).

African-American consumers clearly favored mass-marketed brand foods. In 1919, a White grocer reported to Long that his

> negro customers now invariably demand only fancy groceries of the very best brands he has. A negro customer who would formerly buy a cheap grade of flour, or haggle very much about paying the difference between the cheaper grade and the better, now asks for the best grade of fancy flour and pays for it without hesitancy. (Long 1919:54)

The National Negro Business League's Secretary agreed in the 1920s, when he noted that "in proportion to his income, [the African American] buys more high grade, trade-marked goods than any other group in America" (Cohen 1990:152).

Paul Edwards (1969:52) examined brand-name food consumption in 1932 and emphasized the scope and persistence of brand consumption among African Americans. Edwards demonstrated that bulk food composed a very small portion of the African-American diet in the late 1920s. He found that most African Americans purchased national brands of staple foods like coffee, baking powder, and flour (Table 7). For instance, of 977 African-American households consuming baking powder, 84.45% purchased brand-name baking powder, and 75.15% purchased brand-name flours (Edwards 1969:53–57). Edwards expected clear class differences, so he analyzed his interviewees in three groups, each sharing comparable occupations and wealth. For most goods, though, he only identified slightly higher brand consumption among the most wealthy "business and professional" class. For example, 88.4% of the wealthiest consumers purchased brand baking powders, and 85.3% of the poorest households purchased such "high-grade" baking powder (Edwards 1969:53). No significant difference was noted between brand consumption patterns in the four cities Edwards (1969:54) tested most

Table 7. African-American Brand Consumption by Good, 1929–1930

Standing	Brand coffee consumers	Brand flour consumers	Brand baking powder consumers
Common and semi-skilled labor	79.99%	71.42%	82.89%
Skilled labor	77.04%	82.00%	86.25%
Business and professions	92.26%	81.81%	86.88%
All respondents	82.68%	75.15%	84.42%

Source: Edwards 1969:53–57.

extensively (Nashville, Birmingham, Atlanta, and Richmond). Lizabeth Cohen's (1990:152) analysis of African-American brand consumption in 1920s Chicago suggests that there were no radically contrasting Northern and Southern brand consumption patterns.

African Americans' "tremendous preference for the higher-priced brands" certainly was not propelled by lower cost: Brand names universally were more expensive than bulk goods (Edwards 1969:56). Instead, African-American brand consumption had two basic functions. First, brand goods provided product "security" by tactically evading the deceits of local marketers who sold goods in bulk. Unlike sealed, nationally produced brands, bulk goods were packaged and priced by individual marketers, providing local merchants the opportunity to include lower quality wares, misweigh products, adulterate goods, and launch innumerable other schemes that cheated African-American customers. African Americans were not the sole target of such fraud, but they certainly were systematically subjected to it. In contrast to barrels of loose goods of unknown origins, nationally packaged commodities promised superior and consistent quality. No longer was a consumer dependent on a merchant's assessment of the quality of goods or the purchaser's best judgement; now a consumer could rely on a predictable and proven brand. In 1936, *The Brown American* argued that brand devotion provided a mechanism that domestics used to reward or punish racist grocers and national producers. The journal noted that:

> There is another important group of these market-going Brown women; they are the less fortunate sisters, who have gone into Domestic Service. What of their buying power? It will not be hard for one to realize that they must have powerful voice in the spending of many more millions by those who are really able to buy. Any slight suffered by one of these faithful domestics, whether it be intentional or unintentional, on the part of a million dollar concern or the neighborhood grocer, may serve to swing hundreds and even thousands of dollars another way each year, for a product disliked by a cook seldom reaches a table twice.

This vision of brand consumption's potential strategic influence reflected the personal and collective empowerment some observers saw in brand consumption.

Brand consumption had a second more symbolic appeal to African Americans: Brands harbored the prospect of consumer and civil citizenship. In 1932, for instance, Paul Edwards (1969:98–99) concluded that for African Americans "to possess garments bearing the trademarks of well-known advertisers, sold for the most part in the better stores, is a further important indication of status." Since the 1880s, product labels and advertising exploited nationalism, genteel values, and American abundance to sell goods, proclaiming the superiority of American goods and the virtues of affluence. Uneeda Biscuit, for instance, advertised in Yiddish in turn-of-the-century Jewish newspapers, stressing that civilized American life was symbolized in their crackers (Heinze 1990:168–169). Such advertising invitations to consumer citizenship virtually never were extended to African Americans, though; any African-American inference that a share of citizen privilege was conveyed or implied by brand consumption was idealistic. Indeed, in Edwards' estimation, advertising itself contributed very little to African Americans' brand-name devotion in the 1920s. Edwards (1969:194) reported that many African Americans were "absolutely ignorant of the existence of some of the most widely advertised brands of types of consumer products entering into even the poorest houses." He believed that

> what information the majority of Negro consumers have about these brands may be traced in most instances to quite passive influences. The Negro housewife's knowledge of brands of grocery products is limited largely to those "pushed" by the corner grocer, and to those used in the white home where she works as cook or maid. (Edwards 1969:194)

Edward's findings suggest that perhaps African-American consumers most valued the power brands gave them in the act of shopping itself; that is, brands provided African-American consumers sway over local merchants by investing decision-making power in the consumer, rather than the merchant. This does not discount the impact of brand advertising, but it does argue that African-American brand consumption was more complex than wholesale submission to dominant brand advertising symbolism. The process of evaluating brands in use, weighing the judgement of trusted marketers, establishing loyalties to certain brands for product superiority as well as racial symbolism, and pondering package and point-of-sale symbolism likely were all factors in African-American brand favor.

The Maynard-Burgess household established a relatively early attachment to brand-name goods. The bottle assemblage contained 26 nationally advertised brands, including 8 bottles of Udolpho Wolfe's Aromatic Schiedham Schnapps, 4 Rumford's baking powder vessels, 6 mineral water bottles from New York and New Jersey, and single examples of Hamlin's Wizard Oil, Bromo Seltzer, and an unidentified Heinz food (Mullins 1996:580–586). The remaining African-American sites in Annapolis all contained brand bottled goods as well. Gott's Court contained Bromo Seltzer and Rumford vessels, as well as examples of Dr. Bull's cough syrup, Dr. Kilmer's Swamp Root Kidney Remedy, Hires Root Beer extract, and Heinz sauce (Goodwin et al. 1993:120). Yard refuse around Bellis Court included 2 Potter Parlin baking powder vessels, a Heinz bottle, a Superlative baking powder vessel, and a Vaseline bottle. The Cathedral Street privy contained single bottles of Vaseline, Drexel's Bell cologne, and a sauce or food packaged by New York bottler J.W. Beardsley.

Brand-name consumption apparently decreased the purchase of locally produced bottled goods. For instance, of 87 vessels recovered from the Maynard-Burgess cellar, none were embossed by Annapolis area bottlers or pharmacists. In an assemblage of 54 glass bottles and table vessels at Gott's Court, no Annapolis pharmacists or bottlers were included either. Some unembossed vessels likely were used to bottle local preparations, but the short manufacture-deposition lag and narrow range of production dates suggests that few vessels were recycled extensively (Table 8). Subsequent excavations (Goodwin et al. 1993:120) at Gott's Court identified a single bottle of Parlett and Parlett's Indian Rock Ginger Ale, a World War I era West Street bottler ("Parlett and Parlett Advertisement," 1916). The Cathedral Street privy also contained 2 early twentieth-century vessels from Annapolis bottlers (Mullins 1996:603-605). Yet the absence of more local or regional bottled goods and predominance of nationally produced goods suggests that the brand-name adherence that Paul Edwards saw in the 1920s South began in African-American Annapolis by the 1890s.

RACIALIZING THRIFT

The consumption of brands and nationally produced goods did not pass unnoticed by genteel observers. During the late nineteenth and early twentieth centuries, some White ideologues used the seasoned ideology of "thrift" to cast much African-American consumption as improvidence that was symptomatic of deep material, moral, and racial dilemmas. These genteel moralists updated puritanical thrift ideology by projecting race and class onto "waste," a concept that became a malleable antithesis to idealized White consumption. The racialized

Table 8. Comparative Glass Manufacture–Deposition Lag

Assemblage	Mean production date	Manufacture–deposition lag
Maynard-Burgess cellar (1920 *TAQ*)	1882.10	37.48
70 Franklin Street privy (1940 *TAQ*)	1899.33	40.77
Bellis court privy (1939 *TAQ*)	1904.35	34.65

class aspersions cast on certain consumption patterns and goods attempted to stigmatize such consumption and fortify the class and racial exclusivity of consumer space.

Thrift was a central, avowed focus of budget studies since the 1870s, and the fundamental currents of Victorian thrift ideology were inherited from antebellum moralists (Horowitz 1985:1–12). White reformers' interest in African-American frugality belied their apprehension that African-American consumption of mainstream goods provided a foothold into American society. To deny that foothold, many commentators and studies focused upon "waste" in African-American consumption and reduced it to various unalterable racial attributes. In 1886, for example, *Harper's Weekly* found "that the negroes who are beginning to earn money have much yet to learn in the way of thrift, and that most of them are improvident, spending their earnings as soon as they get them" ("The Industrial South," 1886:791). In an 1898 study in Farmville, Virginia, W.E.B. Du Bois (1898:38) acknowledged the pliability of the concept of thrift and moral interpretation in general when he noted that one "visitor might tell us that the Negroes of Farmville are idle, unreliable, careless with their earnings, and lewd; another visitor, a month later, might say that the Farmville Negroes are industrious, owners of property, and slowly but steadily advancing in education and morals." Du Bois did not contest the presence of "lazy and criminal" African Americans, but he attacked the projection of such traits "without reservation" onto all African Americans.

One class of material goods examined by thrift ideologues was canned food (Figure 18). Modest amounts of canned foods were produced around the Civil War, and the country had less than 100 canneries in 1870 (Heite and Heite 1989:106). By 1889, though, 20 million cases of vegetables alone were produced in the United States (Heite 1990:19). Fruits, vegetables, and oysters were canned throughout the Chesapeake, including Annapolis. For instance, the Annapolis Canning Company opened in 1873, and by 1880 it was "shipping largely to England and the continent of Europe where their brand is in high favor" ("Annapolis Canning Company," 1880). By the turn of the century, many cookbooks advocated the use of such canned goods because they were inexpensive, widely available, and of reliable quality. One 1912 household manual even resolved that "the modern housekeeper is in the throes of metamorphosis from producer to consumer.... To make jelly is ceasing to be an important part of housekeeping—to eat jelly is, let us hope, the unending privilege of all" (Bruere and Bruere 1912:180).

For some observers, seemingly innocuous canned food consumption epitomized the destabilization threatened by consumer goods: The con-

Figure 18. A 1914 photograph of B.C. Britton's store shows a line of canned goods along the wall to the right, as well as freshly butchered meats and a barrel of loose goods (courtesy of Maryland State Archives; Special Collections, Annapolis, I Remember Collection, MSA SC 2140-253).

sumption of canned food undermined home production, which reproduced gendered domestic labor; their cheap cost and ready availability posed the unsettling democratic accessibility of mass consumer space; and canning (like all mass production) inevitably threatened to diminish the quality of material goods. Commentators began to disparage profligate canned food consumption in the 1880s, and those critiques were laden with racial stigmatizations. In 1886, for instance, *Good Housekeeping* noted that

> the poorest classes do much to keep themselves in poverty by their almost invariably uneconomical shopping.... [Their diet] is a feast at times, to be followed by long deprivation, just as members of the lower races, Indians, aboriginal Mexicans and the like, when they have earned a few dollars, will feast on canned oysters and other delicacies, and then go on short and poor rations for weeks. ("Family Marketing," 1886:250)

Good Housekeeping's critique shrewdly evaded blaming material inequalities on dominant market conventions or labor disparities; instead, irrational, racially based consumption practices were the source of non-Whites' material dilemmas. By situating those dilemmas within caricatured class and Black foils, the shortcomings of consumer culture loomed as non-Whites' failure to reproduce genteel consumer discipline. Such discourses rationalized inequality by blaming it upon Blacks and other outliers whose inability to adhere to genteel consumer discipline belied consumer culture's theoretical equality.

A current of thrift discourse focused on canned food consumption and home food preservation, both of which can be examined archaeologically. An estimate of the number of cans in the Maynard-Burgess cellar would be unreliable because of advanced metal deterioration, but the feature contained 792 fragments conclusively identified as cans. However, the cellar contained little evidence of home food production. The assemblage included only 2 glass preserving jars and a single crock, indicating that little home food canning was going on in the household by 1889 (Mullins and Warner 1993:105). No preserving jars were recovered among 53 glass vessels at Gott's Court (Warner 1992). A minimum vessel count for the Cathedral Street privy identified only 2 preserving jars in an assemblage of 26 vessels, and the Bellis Court privy included just 1 jar (and 3 lid liners) in an assemblage of 56 bottles (Aiello and Seidel 1995:1:224–226). The possibility that such a small number of preserving jars was being used for extensive canning seems unlikely because the mean manufacture dates are so recent for the few preserving jars. For instance, the 2 jars at Maynard-Burgess had median manufacture dates of 1889 and 1893, in contrast to an assemblage mean production date of 1882.10; persistently recycled vessels, on the other hand, should be older than other vessels in the assemblage, not more recent. Those 2 vessels may well have been purchased earlier than the mean manufacture date and used repeatedly, but 2 vessels in an assemblage of 87 vessels does not constitute compelling evidence for extensive home food production. The notion that these households preserved foods in other glass vessels also is unlikely because the remaining vessels virtually all were small-mouthed bottles, which only could accommodate liquids.

The decline of home food production and preservation in these households apparently was common to many American consumers, despite the persistent genteel advocacy of thrift. Juliet Corson's aptly titled 1888 volume *Family Living on $500 A Year* emphasized economizing and prudence, yet even she concluded that "in these days when factories for canning fruits and vegetables are scattered all over the country ... home preservation would seem superfluous" (Corson 1888: 51). The widespread availability of inexpensive canned foods hastened the decline of home food preservation. Home food preservation persisted longer in some contexts, particularly in rural communities and among cash-poor tenant farmers who were restricted to credit in a landlord's commissary store (cf. Holland 1990:68; McDaniel 1984; Orser 1988:132). Yet even commissary consumers purchased canned foods whenever possible. In 1901, for instance, William Taylor Thom reported that African Americans in Litwalton, Virginia "live on supplies obtained from the stores of their employers, and under the modern system of canned meats and vegetables but little housekeeping is needed" (Thom 1901b:1154).

Some commentators candidly acknowledged that the demise of home canning was a welcome end to one of womens' most arduous labors. In her 1908 household manual *The Housekeeper's Week*, Marion Harland did not reject home canning, but she admitted that

> there are many reasons why it is no longer advisable to put up the huge quantities of these things that our mothers and grandmothers did. The drudgery of putting them up is great and the much larger variety in nutritious foods now on the market makes dependence on such supplies less necessary than formerly. It is now possible to buy good canned fruit and jellies from the factories though one must know and be sure of the brand. (Harland 1908:258)

In 1898, *The Boston Cooking-School Magazine* noted that its menus included canned goods because "Canned vegetables, in a high state of perfection, can now be had at very reasonable prices.... as tomatoes, kornlet, peas, and beans in cans may be bought by the dozen, and the cost be lessened accordingly, all these will be found in the menus" ("In Reference to Menus" 1898:241).

During World War I, resource conservation programs capitalized on the opportunity to revive thrifty values like frugality and self-control, and some directed those ideologies at African Americans (cf. Horowitz 1985:114). In 1917, for instance, a "canning and preserving" contest was held for

> the Colored Women of Anne Arundel county.... Each exhibitor must first submit all of her work to the school teachers in her neighborhood for inspection before bringing a sample of each kind of work (such as canned vegetables, meats and fruits, and preserves, jellies, and pickles) to Annapolis. ("Exhibition," 1917)

The overt concern for African-American thrift was a thinly veiled ideological ruse to instill social and labor discipline. In 1918, for example, a War Stamp rally was held for the "Colored Folks" of Annapolis, and a speaker informed the crowd that " 'Training in thrift is a moral training.... The difference between the savage and civilized man lies very largely in the fact that the savage cannot look very far into the future and provide for the future'" ("Colored Folks," 1918). This moralizing intensified and became laden with racist xenophobia during and after World War I, when nativist sentiment and Americans' disposable incomes simultaneously swelled. Long's study of wartime African-American materialism observed that "never before have merchants sold negroes so many fine clothes, shoes, and firearms; never before have they spent so much money traveling about aimlessly; never before have they bought such expensive and luxurious articles of food" (Long 1919:52). Long directly attributed the independence of African-American laborers to elevated World War I wages and an improved standard of living that intensified vexing Black traits. He believed "high wages on the farm and in the towns have encouraged the negro's natural tendency to idleness," and a local farmer verified that "'extra high wages such as we had during the war and still have create idleness'" (Long 1919:37, 53). Long concurred that "the negroes did not work as well nor were they as easily managed during the war as before," reviving lingering romanticism for slavery a half century after Emancipation (Long 1919:37–38).

To verify Black affluence, Long demonstrated extensive African-American consumption of mass-produced goods. However, he cast African America's consumption as selfish profligacy by contrasting it with a protracted empirical study of Black Liberty Loan patronage during the war. Long's highly suspect analysis concluded that Blacks did not widely support such programs, instead choosing to satisfy selfish material desires. This implied to Long that African Americans did not support "American" values. The overt racism of Long's tract and the radically contrasting wartime support of African Americans in other cities argue that he grossly misrepresented genuine nationalist sympathy among African Americans. In Annapolis, for example, the normally bigoted *Advertiser Republican* admitted in 1918 that

> when the war is over, and stock is taken of the loyalty of the negro race, there will be much to be carried to the credit side of the ledger on their behalf.... The whole country has been surprised at the wonderful showing made by the colored people in subscribing to the various Liberty Loans and in the purchase of War Savings Stamps. Reports are frequently coming that indicate the good fighting qualities of the American negro in battle. ("Colored Men Loyal," 1918)

Clutching at revived racism and nativist xenophobia, though, Long hoped to construct a vision of universally self-centered Black laborers and consumers who were unable to accommodate affluence. In a period that witnessed the Red Scare, the revival of the Ku Klux Klan, race riots, and the pinnacle of eugenics, Long's contorted racial philosophizing clearly resonated in White America (cf. Cohen 1990:36–37; Gossett 1963:340–341).

Thrift discourses often advocated a measure of material self-sufficiency by championing restrained consumption, home production, saving, and other puritanism. Ostensibly, such measures buttressed moral discipline, but they were intended to reproduce White privilege by convincing African Americans to remove themselves from consumer space. The effort to convince African Americans to willingly forsake consumption was a fruitless bid to negotiate the eternal White dilemma of keeping African America outside White public space, while African Americans continued to provide American society's essential labor and racial footing. By the 1920s, such thrift ideology had become transparent and bankrupt to most African Americans. For instance, in 1925 E. Franklin Frazier (1968:337) noted that most prosperous African Americans chose to secure managerial positions rather than their own businesses because they had "little faith in the acquisition of wealth by thrift and the sweat of his brow." These entrepreneurs recognized the material insecurity of African-American business ownership and the fallacy that thrift and hard work inevitably brought affluence.

Despite the oppressive intent of genteel thrift discourses, some African Americans clung to thrift because they interpreted it as a moral, social, and material means to achieve race and class independence. To many African Americans, the ambition of frugality was African-American sovereignty, not the thinly veiled dependence that genteel White ideologues pursued in the same guise. In some quarters, material conservatism still remains a powerful symbol of African-American autonomy. For instance, a woman from the Gott's Court neighborhood fondly recalled extensive home canning, remembering that her mother "made everything: watermelon rinds, brandy pears, applesauce. People didn't buy stuff in the store" (Goodwin et al. 1993:11). Archaeological material culture does not reveal such widespread home food preservation among African-American Annapolitans; oral history, though, accords it symbolic status that the archaeological record does not reflect in artifact quantities (cf. comparable oral historical significance accorded to preservation in Holland 1990:68). The interpretation of canning in the minds of present-day African-American Annapolitans probably reflects a generational rethinking of home food preservation. Oral histories indicate that home preserving primarily was associated with generations prior to our interviewees, none of whom were born before World War I. Significantly, most African Americans who remember home food

canning did not do that canning themselves, even though they consumed the products of that labor. For example, the grandfather of a
man in the Courthouse neighborhood "used to make wine," but the
grandson acknowledged that "I don't know what the process was ... I
never watched" (Jopling 1991). Another woman noted that her grandmother preserved extensively, "mostly jellies and jams," but "I wasn't
around when she was doing the canning. It was just there" (Jopling
1991). Canning apparently was not as commonplace as these Annapolitans remember, but today there appears to be renewed symbolic
significance to the self-sufficiency of previous generations' home production. The archaeological paucity of preserving jars suggests that late
nineteenth and early twentieth century African Americans were not
particularly attached to canning and the labor and preparation experience which it demanded. Nevertheless, the knowledge required to can
foods, the elaborate preparation canning demanded, and the material
independence it implied made a definite impression on subsequent
generations.

ASPIRATION AND
AFRICAN-AMERICAN CONSUMPTION

In 1924, E. Franklin Frazier (1968:339) repudiated the effort to
attribute African-American consumption to inherent racial traits. Frazier instead concluded that "two hundred and fifty years of enforced labor,
with no incentive in its just rewards, more than any inherent traits,
explain why the Negro has for so long been concerned chiefly with
consumption rather than production." Frazier recognized that labor
inequality, racist codes, and economic marginalization compelled African America to pursue civil privilege and social self-determination in
consumer space. Material goods and consumer space harbored possibilities that played on affluence, democratization, and nationalism, and
lurked within a rich range of accessible objects and flexible symbols.
    Such aspirations certainly were expressed in the consumption of
costly and inaccessible material goods like real estate, yet even apparently innocuous commodities witnessed the contestation of racial subjectivity. African Americans' very aspirations to consumer citizenship
and a potentially equitable footing with White shoppers were significant
because they politicized consumer space and illuminated the illusions of
White consumption. Many African Americans undermining the White
consumer archetype harbored a desire to at least provisionally satisfy
the image of gentility; they were not intent on dismantling race itself,

and they sometimes were unaware of the penetrating threat such aspirations posed to White privilege. African Americans often internalized the genteel discipline associated with material culture such as bric-a-brac, yet the vast majority of African Americans clearly were not aspiring to White bourgeois assimilation. Instead, they hoped to secure the material and social self-determination promised by consumer discourses, fighting to purge genteel subjectivity of its anti-Black racism. As Frazier suggested, White social and material domination compelled African America to formulate and pursue many such aspirations in commodity consumption, a politically precarious position from which to launch a truly radical social reconstruction. Nevertheless, many White observers were apprehensive of these innocuous objects because they threatened to unseat a White-exclusive genteel consumer subjectivity.

Double Consciousness, Whiteness, and Consumer Culture

In 1931, an editorial in *The Crisis* concluded that "advertisement and installment buying have made the nation blind and crazy. We think we must buy whatever is offered. The orgy must be stopped and no group is strategically better placed than the American Negro" (Du Bois 1972: 393). Indeed, African America's liminality provided a unique position from which African Americans observed, participated in, and critiqued consumer society. African Americans confronted all of the archetypal dilemmas of consumer society: They wrestled with the moral implications of materialism; negotiated the tension between prudent economizing and material hedonism; contemplated consumer culture's capacity to deliver its grandiose promises; and probed the contradictions between class inequality and a theoretically egalitarian mass consumer culture. Despite these relatively standard consumer contradictions, African-American consumption and material discourse was charged with a distinctive urgency that variously tolerated, evaded, minimized, or resisted the racist injustice that underlay consumer culture. African Americans celebrated many of the hopeful possibilities of consumer society, but they were hard-pressed to ignore their paradoxical marginalization by Jim Crow racism. African America stood at the heart of consumer space as laborers, marketers, and consumers, but African America's centrality to consumption and impression on White subjectivity was evaded or ignored by White America. Torn by the incongruities of racialized inclusion and exclusion, African Americans both obliquely and explicitly debated how to appropriately construct their relationship to consumer culture in ways that circumvented racism. Laden with sociopolitical implications, African-American consumption and material discourse confronted consumer society's racist boundaries, challenged America's racialized labor structure, and envisioned how African America could secure civil and consumer citizen rights through material consumption.

African America's unique social position both within America, yet outside it, was described in W.E.B. Du Bois' now-classic formulation of double consciousness. Du Bois argued that the permanent contradictions of African America's position yielded a divided self with a heightened critical vision of American life (Lewis 1993:281). Double consciousness was described by Du Bois (1969:16–17) as a "second-sight in this American world—a world which yields him no true self-consciousness, but only lets him see himself through the revelation of the other world." The underside of this heightened "second-sight" vision was that it was formulated through the veil of race, which "only lets him see himself through the revelation of the other world"—a racialized White world that stifled African-American self-consciousness. For Du Bois, this yielded a struggle in which African Americans constantly negotiated the contradictions of "two-ness, an American, a Negro; two souls, two thoughts, two unreconciled strivings; two warring ideals in one dark body whose dogged strength alone keeps it from being torn asunder."

When this idea appeared in *The Souls of Black Folk* in 1903, it was an astounding notion that envisioned an African-American subjectivity that could be African as well as American. Du Bois believed struggle would produce an African-American subjectivity that comprehended its Africanness and unique historical experience, as well as its American identity. He confronted the fundamental contradiction of all public space when he observed that African America

> would not Africanize America, for America has too much to teach the world
> and Africa. He would not bleach his Negro soul in a flood of white American-
> ism, for he knows that Negro blood has a message for the world. He simply
> wishes to make it possible for a man to be both a Negro and an American,
> without being cursed and spit upon by his fellows, without having the doors
> of Opportunity closed roughly in his face. (Du Bois 1969:4)

Du Bois appreciated that struggle would precede an African-American subjectivity that reconciled the African experience and the implicitly White American ideal. Certainly a syncretic African-American subjectivity existed when Du Bois surveyed turn-of-the-century America. Yet Du Bois' focus upon struggle inevitably destabilizes any neat definition of African-American subjectivity. Situating struggle at the heart of African-American subjectivity circumvents the assumption that essential cultural identity, imposed socioeconomic conditions, or some other preexisting attribute is the sole or predominant source of subjectivity. Instead, African-American culture is a constantly emerging hybrid forged through struggle against racism, and it is a subjectivity that can both affirm and challenge dominant social conditions. It seems unlikely that such struggle against racism would yield unambiguous evidence of, for instance, monolithic African affinities, utter assimilation into mainstream America, a frontal assault on anti-Black racism, or a wholly separatist Black nationalism. All of those were real possibilities in African-American experience, but none alone can capture the complex mechanisms through which African-American subjectivity was forged and contested. The only dimension of African-American subjectivity that can lay even a provisional claim to a universal—and even then it is a complex universal—is this heritage of anti-racist struggle. African Americans shared an experience of resistance against structures that aspired to disempower them, a struggle that encompassed a common cultural, social, and material history, yet never completely dismantled racialized categories.

In 1947, Earl Conrad suggested that a struggle much like that Du Bois described was still being waged in all public space. Conrad (1947: 231) concluded that:

> The resistance in the Negro is one which utilizes all the weaknesses in the economy, politics, philosophy, and religion of the dominant group. On the one hand, it drives the Negro to integrate himself as fully as possible into the broad national fabric, and on the other hand compels him to create a world of his own in his ghettos and in the areas of the South where he is massed. He builds his own economy, while battling to penetrate the white man's economy. He fights for realization as a national or mass group of his own, yet concurrently seeks to join the nation's mainstream. I find that both these processes are historical and inevitable, and not contradictory, inevitable to a greatly outnumbered group which must seek all methods of advance.

Conrad soberly understood that African-American struggle was a tactical negotiation that preyed on racism's interstices. Within racism's ideological fissures African America fashioned a material, social, and cultural foothold that was both within and apart from American society. Racialization never utterly vanquished African-American aspiration or cultural integrity, but it always compelled African Americans to warily survey the ambiguous distinction between empowering incorporation and escalated subordination.

Consumer space certainly was a scene of struggle, yet it yielded no African-American politics that was strategically structured, explicitly articulated, focused on universal goals, or became a philosophy or morals unto itself. Nevertheless, African-American consumption contributed to a politicized consciousness of the ideological interests of White racism, the benefits and drawbacks of commodity consumption, and African Americans' power to define critical elements of their lives despite racism. Consumer space was itself so complex in its economic and labor organizations, marketing possibilities, and local racist dynamics that it is infeasible to outline a universal African-American consumption pattern. However, there are strong consistencies in African-American consumption that suggest how African Americans negotiated common structural conditions and constantly transformed a shared heritage. Much as Du Bois argued, the focus of African-American consumption was a rejection of Black and American as incongruous identities. African Americans' desire for citizen privileges took many different forms, including the consumption of bric-a-brac, bottled and canned goods, political knickknacks, or mass-marketed foods. I have traced some consistencies in consumption by African Americans in one community, but the identification of a pattern in objects themselves is simply the initial element of interpretation. Rather than ponder the patterning of things, we are interested primarily in the patterning of *ideas* that were projected onto, reflected in, and emanating from these material goods. When the limits of function, cultural identity, and market structure are eliminated as the mechanisms determining consumption meaning, there are few ways to see material objects as anything other other than ever-unfolding social ideas. Those ideas and consumption choices negotiated contradiction and social position based on objective structural conditions as well as on conscious desires and subjectivity.

By necessity, there must be some dominant social structure that circumscribes possible social ideas. If we define an overarching systemic framework for consumers after the mid-nineteenth century, it is infeasible to place anything other than Whiteness and its myriad racist surveillance mechanisms in such a position. It is difficult to see how all consumption choices and agency were not ultimately negotiations of racism, whether perceived as such or not. This is not to deny that race itself is a complex lived phenomena with many local faces: In the northeast, racial subjectivity is a much different social construct than it was in the contemporary South, for many historical, material, and demographic reasons. Whiteness contains a dimension of racism, as well as class, patriarchal, and regional inequalities that were materialized in many different forms. Clearly all these forms of material and social inequality were closely allied, but it is striking that they almost universally assume White supremacy.

The ideas that seem to recur throughout African-American material assemblages in Annapolis revolve around a persistent African-American desire for full citizen privileges. The aspiration for such citizenship in the face of anti-Black racism was expressed in many contexts, so we cannot expect that simply studying consumption patterns in isolation will reveal African America's politics. Perhaps what commodities reflect most clearly is the utopian aspirations of African Americans; that is, the desires for membership and affinity vested in seemingly innocuous material forms that had a tenuous capacity to actually fulfill such desires. In this respect, the material world does not so much reflect what society was like, but how consumers hoped it would be.

Initially, it seems odd that African Americans would place such profound hopes in consumer space, but consumer culture held out a powerful promise to many disenfranchised Americans. In the wake of Emancipation, African Americans placed great conviction in the capacity of commodities to improve their lives, and they recognized the symbolic privilege of entering consumer space with the status of consumer citizenship. This commitment to consumption was heightened by the collapse of Reconstruction, retrenched public racism, and the arrival of Jim Crow codes that circumscribed the potential to effect significant change in politics, business, or labor. African Americans were not alone in the projection of politicized aspirations onto seemingly meaningless objects: By the 1920s, consumption itself appeared more fundamental to mass American identity than once-dominant ideological formations such as religion and nationalism.

The impact of African-American consumer desire certainly was felt outside shop floors. The transactions enacted in retail spaces, open-air markets, and streets were simply the culmination of struggles in other labor and public spaces, just as they were the precursor to subsequent struggles of the same sort. Yet any scholar hoping to trace self-evident cause-and-effect relationships between consumer patterns and social changes likely will be frustrated. Heuristically, broad relationships can be traced between consumption patterns and production structure, economic and market organization, and shifting labor formations, but those patterns took many different local forms. Even though Whiteness was central to consumer culture, White privilege was forged and resisted in a very wide range of forms that are unlikely to yield a universal consumption pattern or politics.

Black and other non-White caricatures continually have displayed what it means to be "not White," so we might reasonably look at WASP, European, and African-American assemblages alike and ask how consumers were attempting to appropriate the empowering dimensions of genteel subjectivity by avoiding such non-White caricatures. That is, people consumed elements of idealized White subjectivity in the material world by evading its polarized caricatures, even though many consumers certainly resisted various connotations of White malice. Every material object and assemblage was racialized and can be interpreted as a negotiation of community racial contours and dominant structural conditions.

Historical archaeology has made a significant effort to confront racism in the material record and reflect on the presentation of the African-American past, but the discipline has been slower to probe the enigma of Whiteness. Various forms of anti-Black racism, such as economic marginilization, seem quite clear in the archaeological record. Nevertheless, race remains more or less an implicitly African-American research topic, not clearly connected to White subjectivity. Certainly the ambiguity of Whiteness and the implications of admitting archaeologists' footing in White supremacy have slowed our entry into research on race and Whiteness. Methodologically and intellectually, the means to conduct such research is not self-evident: Of necessity, an archaeology of Whiteness is compelled to confront its enigmatic nature, since few people can identify how and why they "became" White, are unable to recognize that they remain so, or simply do not comprehend precisely what it means (cf. Sacks 1984).

Framing scholarship as a mechanism to discuss race and White supremacy is a sticky dilemma in which all social scientists, not simply historical archaeologists, are mired. Michael Blakey (1997:141) elevates archaeology's capacity to confront Whiteness when he argues that archaeology may well "assist Euroamericans in transcending the state of denial which fails our common understanding and reconciliation." Blakey suggests that archaeologists should confront social contradiction, rather than evade "sticky" issues like White supremacy. Complicity in White superiority is a complex phenomenon that is difficult to confront, so it is more often than not sidestepped; the consequence of this evasion is that racism looms as the injustice wreaked on African America in the past by deviant Whites. However, Whiteness cannot be reduced to either a creation of aberrant individuals or a consciously deployed campaign against non-White peoples. Whiteness instead provides a backdrop that assumes that the privileges of decision-making by White people are "normal" and ostensibly open to all appropriately disciplined individuals. To acknowledge this in the past and present is to acknowledge the profound role of race in American history, an essential first step toward rethinking the impression of White supremacy on consumer space, workplaces, material symbolism, and every other space or subject. To evade the impact of race on American society seems at best a naive vision of the past, and at worst a dangerous message to deliver to contemporary America.

References

Abel, M.H.
 1927 *Successful Family Life on the Moderate Income.* 2nd ed. J.B. Lippincott, Philadelphia.
Abelson, E.S.
 1989 *When Ladies Go A-Thieving: Middle-Class Shoplifters in the Victorian Department Store.* Oxford University Press, New York.
Advertisements that insult
 1918 *The Crusader,* September. 1918, p. 9.
Afro-Americans building towns
 1906 *Afro-American Ledger,* May 26. 1906, p. 1.
Agnew, J.
 1990 Coming Up for Air: Consumer Culture in Historical Perspective. *Intellectual
   History Newsletter* 12:3–21.
 1989 A House of Fiction: Domestic Interiors and the Commodity Aesthetic. In *Consuming Visions: Accumulation and Display of Goods in America, 1880–1920,* edited
   by S.J. Bronner, pp. 133–156. Norton, New York.
Aiello, E.A., and J.L. Seidel
 1995 *Three Hundred Years in Annapolis: Phase III Archaeological Investigations of
   the Anne Arundel County Courthouse Site (18AP63), Annapolis, Maryland.* 2 vols.
   Archaeology in Annapolis, Annapolis, Maryland.
The alley law
 1918 *The Bee,* February 2. 1918, p. 4.
The American race problem: The Negro's solution
 1918 *The Crusader,* November. 1918, pp. 12, 14.
Annapolis Canning Company
 1880 *Maryland Republican and State Capital Advertiser,* May 15. 1880, p. 3.
Annapolis Hebrews help
 1905 *Anne Arundel Examiner,* December 1. 1905, p. 5.
Annapolis notes
 1898 *Afro-American Ledger,* December 10. 1898, p. 1.
Anne Arundel County Certificates of Freedom
 1831 John T. Maynard Certificate of Freedom. 1831–1845 Certificates Folio 7. Mary-
   land Hall of Records, Annapolis, Maryland.
Anne Arundel County Chattel Records
 1857 Purchase Record for Phebe Ann Spencer. Chattel Records Folio 318. Maryland
   Hall of Records, Annapolis, Maryland.
 1839 Purchase Record for Maria Maynard, 1839. Chattel Records Folio 38. Maryland
   Hall of Records, Annapolis, Maryland.
Anne Arundel County Manumission Records
 1857 Phebe Ann Spencer Manumission Record, 1857. Manumission Records Folio 112.
   Maryland Hall of Records, Annapolis, Maryland.

1840   Maria Maynard Manumission Record. Manumission Records Folio 609. Maryland Hall of Records, Annapolis, Maryland.
Anne Arundel County Probate Inventories
1876   John T. Maynard Probate. Maryland Hall of Records, Annapolis, Maryland.
Anonymous letter writer says he is Brandon murderer
1919   *Evening Capital Maryland Gazette*, March 3. 1919, p. 1.
Babson, D.W.
1990   The Archaeology of Racism and Ethnicity on Southern Plantations. *Historical
Archaeology* 24(4):20–28.
Bates, W.H.
1928   *Researches, Sayings and Life of Wiley H. Bates*. City Printing Company, Annapolis, Maryland.
Baudrillard, J.
1983   *Simulacra and Simulations*, translated by P. Foss, P. Patton, and P. Beichtman.
Semiotext(e), New York.
1975   *The Mirror of Production*. Telos Press, St. Louis, Missouri.
Bawdy houses
1887   *The Bee*, June 25. 1887, p. 2.
Bayliff, W.H.
1971   Natural Resources. In *The Old Line State: A History of Maryland*, edited by
M.L. Radoff, pp. 267–307. Hall of Records, Annapolis, Maryland. Originally published
1957.
Beaudry, M.C., L.J. Cook, and S.A. Mrozowski
1991   Artifacts and Active Voices: Material Culture as Social Discourse. In *The Archae-
ology of Inequality*, edited by R.H. McGuire and R. Paynter, pp. 150–191. Basil
Blackwell, Cambridge.
Beecher, C., and H.B. Stowe
1869   *The American Woman's Home; or, Principles of Domestic Science*. J.B. Ford,
New York.
Beidleman, D.K., W.P. Catts, and J. Custer
1986   *Final Archaeological Excavations at Block 1191, Wilmington, New Castle County,
Delaware*. DelDOT Archaeological Series No.39. Delaware Department of Transpor-
tation, Dover.
Berlin, I.
1974   *Slaves Without Masters: The Free Negro in the Antebellum South*. Pantheon,
New York.
Big funeral closes last Snowden chapter
1919   *Evening Capital*, March 3. 1919, p. 1.
Bilotta, J.D.
1992   *Race and the Rise of the Republican Party, 1848–1865*. Peter Lang, New York.
The Black fiend
1875   *Maryland Republican and State Capital Advertiser*, June 12. 1875, p. 2.
Black mammies
1912   *Afro-American Ledger*, October 5. 1912, p. 4.
A Black skin remover advertisement
1898   *The Bee*, March 5. 1898, p. 5.
Blakey, M.L.
1997   Past is Present: Comments on "In the Realm of Politics: Prospects for Public
Participation in African-American Plantation Archaeology." *Historical Archaeology*
31(3):140–145.
Bomback, R.
1993   Button Inventory. In *Final Archaeological Investigations at the Maynard-*

Burgess House (18AP64), An 1850–1980 African-American Household in Annapolis, Maryland, edited by P.R. Mullins and M.S. Warner, Appendix V, pp. 194–205. Archaeology in Annapolis, Annapolis, Maryland.

Borchert, J.
1982   *Alley Life in Washington: Family, Community, Religion, and Folklife in the City, 1850–1970*. University of Illinois Press, Urbana.

Boskin, J.
1986   *Sambo: The Rise and Demise of an American Jester*. Oxford University Press, New York.

Brackett, J.
1969   *The Negro in Maryland*. Johns Hopkins University Press, Baltimore. Originally published 1889.
1890   *Progress of the Colored People of Maryland since the War*. Johns Hopkins University Press, Baltimore.

Bronner, S.J.
1989   Reading Consumer Culture. In *Consuming Visions: Accumulation and Display of Goods in America, 1880–1920*, edited by S.J. Bronner, pp. 13–53. Norton, New York.

Brottman, M.
1997   "The Last Stop of Desire": Covent Garden and the Spatial Text of Consumerism. *Consumption, Markets, and Culture* 1(1):45–80.

Brown, J.C.
1989   The Negro Woman Worker. In *Black Workers: A Documentary History from Colonial Times to the Present*, edited by P.S. Foner and R.L. Lewis, pp. 465–469. Temple University Press, Philadelphia. Originally published 1938.

Brown, P.L.
1994   *The Other Annapolis, 1900–1950*. Annapolis Printing Company, Annapolis.

Brown, W.H.
1927   *The Education and Economic Development of the Negro in Virginia*. University of Virginia Phelps-Stokes Fellowship Papers, No. 3. University of Virginia, Charlottesville.

Bruere, M.B., and R.W. Bruere
1912   *Increasing Home Efficiency*. Macmillan, New York.

Building in progress
1907   *Evening Capital*, February 1. 1907, p. 4.

Busbey, K.G.
1910   *Home Life in America*. Methuen, London.

Butterworth, H.
1887   *A Zigzag Journey in the Sunny South; or, Wonder Tales of Early American History*. Estes and Lauriat, Boston.

Calderhead, W.L.
1977   Anne Arundel Blacks: Three Centuries of Change. In *Anne Arundel County Maryland: A Bicentennial History, 1649–1977*, edited by J.C. Bradford, pp. 11–25. Anne Arundel County and Annapolis Bicentennial Committee, Annapolis, Maryland.

Campbell, C.
1987   *The Romantic Ethic and the Spirit of Modern Consumerism*. Basil Blackwell, Oxford.

Campbell, H.
1881   *The Easiest Way in Housekeeping and Cooking*. Fords, Howard, and Hulbert, New York.

Capital jottings
1896   *Evening Capital*, August 1. 1896, p. 1.

Castelvecchi, L.
1885 *Catalogue and Price List of Antique, Grecian, Roman, Medaeval and Modern Plaster of Paris Statues, Statuettes, Busts, Etc.* L. Castelvecchi, New York.
Cheek, C.D., and A. Friedlander
1990 Pottery and Pig's Feet: Space, Ethnicity, and Neighborhood in Washington, D.C., 1880–1940. *Historical Archaeology* 24(1):34–60.
Chesapeake and Potomac Telephone Company
1932 *Annapolis Telephone Directory.* Chesapeake and Potomac Telephone Company, Baltimore.
Christensen, N.
1969 Fifty Years of Freedom: Conditions in the Seacoast Region. In *The Negro's Progress in Fifty Years*, edited by Emory R. Johnson, pp. 58–66. Negro Universities Press, New York. Originally published 1913.
Circuit Court meets
1907 *Anne Arundel Examiner*, April 19. 1907, p. 5.
The city drug store
1893 *Evening Capital*, April 1. 1893, p. 3.
City is to have up-to-date canning plant
1918 *Annapolis Advertiser*, August 1. 1918, p. 1.
Clayton, R.
1987 *Free Blacks of Anne Arundel County.* Heritage Books, Bowie, Maryland.
Codfish catch
1885 *Evening Capital*, February 2. 1885, p. 2.
Cohen, L.
1990 *Making a New Deal: Industrial Workers in Chicago, 1919–1939.* Cambridge University Press, Cambridge, England.
Coleman, R.W.
1925 *The First Colored Directory of Baltimore City.* R.W. Coleman, Baltimore.
The colored citizen's part
1919 *Evening Capital*, February 19. 1919, p. 1.
Colored folks hold war stamp rally in city
1918 *Annapolis Advertiser*, July 13. 1918, p. 1.
Colored Literary Association
1900 *Anne Arundel Examiner*, October 4. 1900, p. 5.
Colored men in business
1908 *Afro-American Ledger*, August 15. 1908, p. 2.
Colored men loyal
1918 *The Advertiser-Republican*, September 19. 1918, p. 4.
Conrad, E.
1947 *Jim Crow America.* Duell, Sloan and Pearce, New York.
Co-operation
1890 *The Bee*, January 18. 1890, p. 2.
Corson, J.
1888 *Family Living on $500 A Year: A Daily Reference Book for Young and Inexperienced Housewives.* Harper and Brothers, New York.
1885 *Miss Corson's Practical American Cookery and Household Management.* Dodd, Mead, and Company, New York.
Cozzens, F.M.
1888 *Saratoga Springs: Its Mineral Fountains, Drives, Hotels, and Other Items of Interest.* Jacob Leonard and Sons, Albany.
Crawford, F.M.
1882 False Taste in Art. *North American Review* 308:89–98.

Curtis, S.
1991 *A Consuming Faith: The Social Gospel and Modern American Culture*. Johns
Hopkins University Press, Baltimore.
Cushing, E.F.
1926 *Culture and Good Manners*. Students Educational Publishing Company, Mem-
phis.
Davis Collection
1849 James W. Sullivan's Collector's Tax Book for the Year 1849. Maryland Hall of
Records, Annapolis, Maryland.
de Certeau, M.
1984 *The Practice of Everyday Life*. University of California Press, Berkeley.
De Cunzo, L.A.
1998 A Future After Freedom. *Historical Archaeology* 32(1):42–54.
Deetz, J.
1990 Landscapes as Cultural Statements. In *Earth Patterns: Essays in Landscape
Archaeology*, edited by W.M. Kelso and R. Most, pp. 1–4. University of Virginia Press,
Charlottesville.
1977 *In Small Things Forgotten*. Doubleday, New York.
Denning, M.
1987 *Mechanic Accents: Dime Novels and Working-Class Culture in America*. Verso,
London.
De Voe, T.F.
1867 *The Market Assistant*. Hurd and Houghton, New York.
A disgrace
1906 *Anne Arundel Examiner*, December 28. 1906, p. 4.
Du Bois, W.E.B.
1996 *The Philadelphia Negro: A Social Study*. University of Pennsylvania Press,
Philadelphia. Originally published 1899.
1972 *The Emerging Thought of W.E.B. Du Bois: Essays and Editorials from The Crisis*.
Simon and Schuster, New York.
1969 *The Souls of Black Folk*. Dodd and Mead, New York. Originally published 1903.
1935 *Black Reconstruction in America*. Harcourt Brace, Cleveland.
1899 *The Negro in Business*. Atlanta University Press, Atlanta.
1898 The Negroes of Farmville, Virginia: A Social Study. *U.S. Department of Labor
Bulletin* 14:1–38.
The Dutch to invade Maryland
1899 *Anne Arundel Examiner*, April 6. 1899, p. 3.
Eagleton, T.
1990 *The Ideology of the Aesthetic*. Basil Blackwell, Cambridge.
Edsforth, R.
1987 *Class Conflict and Cultural Consensus: The Making of a Mass Consumer Society
in Flint, Michigan*. Rutgers University Press, New Brunswick, New Jersey.
Edwards, P.K.
1969 *The Southern Urban Negro as a Consumer*. Negro Universities Press, New York.
Originally published 1932.
Eighth District Items
1873 *Maryland Republican and State Capital Advertiser*, March 15. 1873, p. 3.
Ellet, E.F.
1873 *The New Cyclopaedia of Domestic Economy and Practical Housekeeper*. Henry
Bill Publishing Company, Norwich, Connecticut.
Enlargement of the Naval Academy
1873 *Maryland Republican and State Capital Advertiser*, March 1. 1873, p. 3.

Epperson, T.W.
1990   Race and the Disciplines of the Plantation. *Historical Archaeology* 24(4):29–36.
Everett, M.
1902   *The Etiquette of Today: A Complete Guide to Correct Manners and Social Customs in Use among Educated and Refined People of America.* Henry Neil, location unknown.
Evitts, W.J.
1974   *A Matter of Allegiances: Maryland from 1850 to 1861.* Johns Hopkins University Press, Baltimore.
Ewen, S.
1988   *All Consuming Images: The Politics of Style in Contemporary Culture.* Basic Books, New York.
1976   *Captains of Consciousness: Advertising and the Social Roots of Consumer Culture.* McGraw Hill, New York.
Exhibition of the work of colored women of county
1917   *The Advertiser-Republican,* December 6. 1917, p. 8.
Extensive fish packing
1885   *Evening Capital,* May 7. 1885, p. 4.
Facey, J.W., Jr.
1882   *Elementary Decoration: A Guide to the Simpler Forms of Everyday Art as Applied to the Interior and Exterior Decoration of Dwelling-Houses Etc.* Crosby Lockwood and Company, London.
Family marketing
1886   *Good Housekeeping,* September 18. 1886, pp. 249–250.
Ferguson, L.
1992   *Uncommon Ground: Archaeology and Early African America, 1650–1800.* Smithsonian Institution Press, Washington, D.C.
Fields, B.J.
1985   *Slavery and Freedom on the Middle Ground: Maryland During the Nineteenth Century.* Yale University Press, New Haven.
Fischer, R.A.
1988   *Tippecanoe and Trinkets Too: The Material Culture of American Presidential Campaigns, 1828–1984.* University of Illinois Press, Urbana.
Fogel, R.W.
1989   *Without Consent or Contract: The Rise and Fall of American Slavery.* Norton, New York.
Foner, E.
1988   *Reconstruction: America's Unfinished Revolution, 1863–1877.* Harper and Row, New York.
Ford, B.P.
1993   1880–1910 Census Tables. In *Phase I-II Archaeological Investigations on the Courthouse Site (18AP63), An African-American Neighborhood in Annapolis, Maryland,* edited by M.S. Warner and P.R. Mullins, Appendix I, pp. 97–114. Archaeology in Annapolis, Annapolis, Maryland.
Foucault, M.
1984   What is an Author? In *The Foucault Reader,* edited by P. Rabinow. Pantheon, New York. pp. 101–120.
1980   Truth and Power. In *Power/Knowledge: Selected Interviews and Other Writings, 1972–1977,* edited by C. Gordon, pp. 109–133. Pantheon, New York.
Fox, R.W. and T.J.J. Lears (editors)
1983   *The Culture of Consumption in America.* Pantheon, New York.

Franklin, J.H.
   1967   *From Slavery to Freedom: A History of Negro Americans*. 3rd ed. Alfred A. Knopf, New York.
Fraser, N.
   1989   *Unruly Practices: Power, Discourse and Gender in Contemporary Social Theory*. University of Minnesota Press, Minneapolis.
Frazier, E.F.
   1997   *Black Bourgeoisie*. Free Press, New York. Originally published 1957.
   1968   Durham: Capital of the Black Middle Class. In *The New Negro: An Interpretation*, edited by A. Locke, pp. 337–343. Arno Press, New York. Originally published 1925.
   1924   Some Aspects of Negro Business. *Opportunity* 2(22):293–297.
Freehling, W.H.
   1984   Franklin Pierce. In *The Presidents: A Reference History*, edited by H.F. Graff, pp. 225–234. Charles Scribner's Sons, New York.
Fresh herring advertisement
   1890   *Evening Capital*, April 10. 1890, p. 3.
Frissell, H.B., and I. Bevier
   1899   Dietary Studies of Negroes in Eastern Virginia in 1897 and 1898. *U.S. Department of Agriculture Bulletin* 71:1–45.
Gaines, K.K.
   1996   *Uplifting the Race: Black Leadership, Politics, and Culture in the Twentieth Century*. University of North Carolina Press, Chapel Hill.
Gardner, K.B., and L.A. Adams
   1926   *Consumer Habits and Preferences in the Purchase and Consumption of Meat*. United States Department of Agriculture Bulletin No. 1443. United States Department of Agriculture, Washington, D.C.
Gatewood, W.B.
   1990   *Aristocrats of Color: The Black Elite, 1880–1920*. Indiana University Press, Bloomington.
Genovese, E.
   1972   *Roll, Jordan, Roll: The World the Slaves Made*. Vintage, New York.
Giddens, A.
   1991   *Modernity and Self-Identity: Self and Society in the Late Modern Age*. Polity, Cambridge.
Gilroy, P.
   1987   *"There Ain't No Black in the Union Jack": The Cultural Politics of Race and Nation*. University of Chicago Press, Chicago.
Glennie, P.
   1995   Consumption Within Historical Studies. In *Acknowledging Consumption: A Review of New Studies*, edited by D. Miller, pp. 164–203. Routledge, New York.
Godden, G.
   1964   *Encyclopedia of British Pottery and Porcelain Marks*. Crown, New York.
Goldstein, E.L.
   1991   *Surviving Together: African Americans and Jews in Annapolis, 1885–1968*. Ms. on file, Historic Annapolis Foundation, Annapolis, Maryland.
Goodrum, C., and H. Dalrymple
   1990   *Advertising in America: The First 200 Years*. Abrams, New York.
Goodwin, R.C., S.L.C. Sanders, M.T. Moran, and D. Landon
   1993   *Phase II/III Archaeological Investigations of the Gott's Court Parking Facility, Annapolis, Maryland*. City of Annapolis, Annapolis, Maryland.

Gossett, T.F.
1963   *Race: The History of an Idea in America.* Schocken, New York.
Gottdiener, M.
1997   *The Theming of America: Dreams, Visions, and Commercial Spaces.* Westview, Boulder.
Gould, F.E., and P.R. Halleron
1910   *Annapolis City Directory.* Gould and Halleron, Annapolis.
Glut of herring
1885   *Evening Capital,* April 20. 1885, p. 4.
Grand dragon "lost" on road but Klan held demonstration
1924   *Evening Capital,* August 7. 1924, p. 1.
Hair artist
1890   *The Bee,* March 1. 1890, p. 3.
Handsman, R.G.
1995   The Still-Hidden Histories of Color and Class: Public Archaeology and the Depot Village of West Kingston, Rhode Island. Unpublished paper presented at the Conference on New England Archaeology, Sturbridge, Massachusetts.
Harcourt, H.
1889   *Home Life in Florida.* John P. Morton and Company, Louisville.
Harlan, H.H.
1935   *Zion Town—A Study in Human Ecology.* University of Virginia Phelps-Stokes Fellowship Papers, No. 13. University of Virginia, Charlottesville.
Harland, M.
1908   *The Housekeeper's Week.* Bobbs-Merrill, Indianapolis.
Harper and Brothers
1875   *The Bazar Book of the Household.* Harper and Brothers, New York.
1871   *The Bazar Book of Decorum.* Harper and Brothers, New York.
Harris, J.B.
1995   *The Welcome Table: African-American Heritage Cooking.* Simon and Schuster, New York.
Harrison, F.V.
1995   The Persistent Power of "Race" in the Cultural and Political Economy of Racism. *Annual Review of Anthropology* 24:47–74.
Haynes, G.E.
1968   *The Negro at Work in New York City: A Study in Economic Progress.* Arno Press, New York. Originally published 1912.
Heinze, A.R.
1990   *Adapting to Abundance: Jewish Immigrants, Mass Consumption, and the Search for American Identity.* Columbia University Press, New York.
Heite, E.F.
1990   *Archaeological Data Recovery on the Collins, Geddes Cannery Site.* Delaware Department of Transportation, Dover.
Heite, L.B., and E.F. Heite
1989   *Archaeological and Historical Survey of Lebanon and Forest Landing, Road 356a, North Murderkill Hundred, Kent County, Delaware.* DelDOT Archaeological Series No.70. Delaware Department of Transportation, Dover.
Held for court
1898   *Anne Arundel Examiner,* March 31. 1898, p. 5.
Henderson, C.R.
1897   *The Social Spirit in America.* Chautaqua-Century Press, New York.

Hill, S.H.
1982 An Examination of Manufacture-Deposition Lag for Glass Bottles from Late Historic Sites. In *Archaeology of Urban America: The Search for Pattern and Process*, edited by R.S. Dickens, Jr., pp. 291–327. Academic Press, New York.
Historical and industrial edition
1908 *Evening Capital*, May 1. 1908, p. 1.
Holland, C.C.
1990 Tenant Farms of the Past, Present, and Future: An Ethnoarchaeological View. *Historical Archaeology* 24(4):60–69.
Holloway, L.C.
1887 *The Hearthstone; or, Life at Home*. L.P. Miller and Company, Chicago.
Holt, M.F.
1992 *Political Parties and American Political Development from the Age of Jackson to the Age of Lincoln*. Louisiana State University Press, Baton Rouge.
Home Owners' Loan Corporation
1941 *Valuation Analysis and Conclusions: Extension U.S. Naval Academy*. Ms. on file, Maryland Hall of Records, Annapolis, Maryland.
Horowitz, D.
1985 *The Morality of Spending: Attitudes toward the Consumer Society in America, 1875–1940*. Johns Hopkins University Press, Baltimore.
Howson, J.E.
1990 Social Relations and Material Culture: A Critique of the Archaeology of Plantation Slavery. *Historical Archaeology* 24(4):78–91.
Hoy, D.C.
1986 Power, Repression, Progress: Foucault, Lukes, and the Frankfurt School. In *Foucault: A Critical Reader*, edited by D.C. Hoy, pp. 123–148. Basil Blackwell, New York.
Hurst, H.W.
1981 The Northernmost Southern Town: A Sketch of Pre-Civil War Annapolis. *Maryland Historical Magazine* 76:240–249.
Hutton, F.
1992 Social Morality in the Antebellum Black Press. *Journal of Popular Culture* 26(2):71–84.
Ignatiev, N.
1995 *How the Irish Became White*. Routledge, New York.
Immigration
1870 *Maryland Republican and State Capital Advertiser*, December 3. 1870, p. 2.
Immigration, labor, etc
1870 *Maryland Republican and State Capital Advertiser*, December 17. 1870, p. 2.
Ingersoll, E.
1882 *The History and Present Condition of the Oyster Industry*. United States Department of the Census, Trenton, New Jersey.
Ingraham, J.H.
1860 *The Sunny South; or, The Southerner at Home*. G.G. Evans, Philadelphia.
The Industrial South
1886 *Harper's Weekly*, December 4. 1886, p. 791.
Inquest
1875 *Maryland Republican and State Capital Advertiser*, April 10. 1875, p. 3.
Inside Southern Cabins: Alabama, Agricultural Negroes
1880 *Harper's Weekly*, December 4. 1880, pp. 780–782.

Inside Southern Cabins: Charleston, South Carolina
1880   *Harper's Weekly*, November 27. 1880, pp. 765–766.
Inside Southern Cabins: Georgia, Part II
1880   *Harper's Weekly*, November 20. 1880, pp. 749–750.
Inside Southern Cabins: Georgia, Part I
1880   *Harper's Weekly*, November 13. 1880, pp. 733–734.
Insulting Advertisements
1918   *The Crusader*, December. 1918, pp. 4–5.
Ives, S.
1979   Black Community Development in Annapolis, Maryland, 1870–1885. In *Geographical Perspectives on Maryland's Past*, edited by R.D. Mitchell and E.K. Muller, pp. 129–149. Department of Geography, University of Maryland, College Park.
Johnson, C.S.
1923   Negroes at Work in Baltimore, Md. *Opportunity* 1(6):12–19.
Johnson Publishing Company
1896   *Johnsons' Annapolis Directory, 1896–1897*. Johnson Publishing Company, Wilmington.
Jopling, H.
1998   Remembered Communities: Gott's Court and Hell Point in Annapolis, Maryland, 1900–1950. In *Annapolis Pasts: Historical Archaeology in Annapolis, Maryland*, edited by P.A. Shackel, P.R. Mullins, and M.S. Warner, pp. 49–68. University of Tennessee Press, Knoxville.
1992   Interview Transcripts from Focus Group Interviews with Gott's Court Residents. Ms. on file, Archaeology in Annapolis, College Park, Maryland.
1991   Interview Transcripts from Archaeology in Annapolis African-American Archaeological Project. Ms. on file, Archaeology in Annapolis, Annapolis, Maryland.
Judge Lynch
1886   *Evening Capital*, April 1. 1886, p. 2.
Kasson, J.F.
1978   *Amusing the Million: Coney Island at the Turn of the Century*. Hill and Wang, New York.
Katzman, D.M.
1978   *Seven Days A Week: Women and Domestic Service in Industrializing America*. University of Illinois Press, Urbana.
Keith, R.
1977   Social Life. In *Anne Arundel County Maryland: A Bicentennial History, 1649–1977*, edited by J.C. Bradford, pp. 152–170. Anne Arundel County and Annapolis Bicentennial Committee, Annapolis, Maryland.
King, E.
1875   *The Great South: A Record of Journeys*. American Publishing Company, Hartford.
Kirby, M., and E. Kirby
circa 1860   *Aunt Martha's Corner Cupboard; or, Stories about Tea, Coffee, Sugar, Rice, etc*. DeWolfe, Fiske, and Company, Boston.
Klein, T., and P.H. Garrow
1984   *Final Archeological Investigations at the Wilmington Boulevard, Monroe Street to King Street Wilmington, New Castle County, Delaware*. Delaware Department of Transportation, Dover.
Kovel, R., and T. Kovel
1986   *Kovels' New Dictionary of Marks*. Crown, New York.

Ku Klux Klan in full garb out on parade
1922 *Evening Capital*, October 30. 1922, pp. 1, 5.

Langhorne, O.
1901 Domestic Service in the South. *Journal of Social Science* 39:169–175.

Larsen, E.L., and M.T. Lucas
1994 Minding Your Own Business: The Harpers Ferry Hotel of the 1830s. In *Archaeological Views of the Upper Wager Block, A Domestic and Commercial Neighborhood in Harpers Ferry*, edited by J. Halchin, pp. 6.1–6.27. National Park Service, Harpers Ferry, West Virginia.

Lavin, E.M.
1888 *Good Manners*. Butterick Publishing Company, New York.

Leach, W.R.
1993 *Land of Desire: Merchants, Power, and the Rise of a New American Culture*. Pantheon, New York.

Leap, W.L.
1933 *Red Hill—Neighborhood Life and Race Relations in a Rural Section*. University of Virginia Phelps-Stokes Fellowship Papers, No. 10. University of Virginia, Charlottesville.

Lears, J.
1994 *Fables of Abundance: A Cultural History of Advertising in America*. Basic Books, New York.

Lears, T.J.J.
1989 Beyond Veblen: Rethinking Consumer Culture in America. In *Consuming Visions: Accumulation and Display of Goods in America, 1880–1920*, edited by S.J. Bronner, pp. 73–98. Norton, New York.
1983 From Salvation to Self-Realization: Advertising and the Therapeutic Roots of the Consumer Culture, 1880–1930. In *The Culture of Consumption: Critical Essays in American History, 1880–1980*, edited by R.W. Fox and T.J.J. Lears, pp. 1–38. Pantheon, New York.

Leone, M.P.
1984 Interpreting Ideology in Historical Archaeology: The William Paca Garden in Annapolis, Maryland. In *Ideology, Power and Prehistory*, edited by D. Miller and C. Tilley, pp. 25–35. Cambridge University Press, Cambridge.

Leone, M.P., P.B. Potter, Jr., and P.A. Shackel
1987 Towards a Critical Archaeology. *Current Anthropology* 28:286–302.

Leone, M.P., P.R. Mullins, M.C. Creveling, L. Hurst, B. Jackson-Nash, L.D. Jones, H.J. Kaiser, G.C. Logan, and M.S. Warner
1995 Can an African-American Historical Archaeology be an Alternative Voice? In *Interpreting Archaeology: Finding Meaning in the Past*, edited by I. Hodder, A. Alexandri, V. Buchli, J. Carman, J. Last, and G. Lucas, pp. 110–124. Routledge, New York.

Let out and lynched
1885 *Maryland Republican*, June 6. 1885, p. 2.

Levine, L.
1993 *The Unpredictable Past: Explorations in American Cultural History*. Oxford University Press, New York.
1977 *Black Culture and Black Consciousness*. Oxford University Press, New York.

Lewis, D.L.
1993 *W.E.B. Du Bois: Biography of a Race, 1868–1919*. Henry Holt, New York.

The lily Whites
1907   *The Bee*, January 26. 1907, p. 4.
Linington, C.M.
1880   *5 and 10 Cent Counter Supplies*. Franz Gindele, Chicago.
Linthicum's Meat Store advertisement
1885   *Evening Capital*, November 9. 1885, p. 3.
Lipsitz, G.
1995   The Possessive Investment in Whiteness: Racialized Social Democracy and the "White" Problem in American Studies. *American Quarterly* 47:369–387.
Little, B.J.
1996   People with History: An Update on Historical Archaeology in the United States. In *Images of the Recent Past: Readings in Historical Archaeology*, edited by C.E. Orser, Jr., pp. 42–78. Altamira Press, Walnut Creek, California.
The Lockwoodsville property
1874   *Maryland Republican and State Capital Advertiser*, January 10. 1874, p. 4.
Logan, G.C.
1998   Archaeologists, Residents, and Visitors: Creating a Community-Based Program in African American Archaeology. In *Annapolis Pasts: Historical Archaeology in Annapolis, Maryland*, edited by P.A. Shackel, P.R. Mullins, and M.S. Warner, pp. 69–90. University of Tennessee Press, Knoxville.
Long, F.T.
1919   *The Negroes of Clarke County, Georgia, During the Great War*. University of Georgia, Athens.
Longstreth, R.
1997   *City Center to Regional Mall: Architecture, the Automobile, and Retailing in Los Angeles, 1920–1950*. MIT Press, Cambridge.
Lott, E.
1995   *Love and Theft: Blackface Minstrelsy and the American Working Class*. Oxford University Press, New York.
Low, Sir A.M.
1974   *America at Home*. Arno Press, New York. Originally published 1908.
Lucas, M.T.
1994   Where Public and Private Meet: A Community Baker and Confectioner in Nineteenth-Century Harpers Ferry. In *Archaeological Views of the Upper Wager Block, A Domestic and Commercial Neighborhood in Harpers Ferry*, edited by J. Halchin, pp. 7.1–7.14. National Park Service, Harpers Ferry, West Virginia.
Lunt, P.K., and S.M. Livingstone
1992   *Mass Consumption and Personal Identity*. Open University Press, Buckingham.
Luxury
1880   *Maryland Republican and State Capital Advertiser*, April 3. 1880, p. 1.
Madam Agnes Smith's Electrical Hair, Face and Skin Culturist Shop
1916   *The Bee*, March 4. 1916, p. 2.
The Magic Shampoo Drier and Hair Straightener advertisement
1909   *The Bee*, November 6. 1909, p. 5.
Majewski, T., and M.J. O'Brien
1987   The Use and Misuse of Nineteenth-Century English and American Ceramics in Archaeological Analysis. In *Advances in Archaeological Method and Theory*, edited by M.R. Schiffer, pp. 97–209. Academic Press, Orlando, Florida.
Marchand, R.
1985   *Advertising the American Dream: Making Way for Modernity, 1920–1940*. University of California Press, Berkeley.

The Maryland Hotel
1881 *Maryland Republican and State Capital Advertiser*, December 3. 1881, p. 2.
Marylanders who have made good
1921 *Afro-American Ledger*, March 25. 1921, p. 9.
Marx, K.
1959 *Economic and Philosophic Manuscripts of 1844*. Laurence and Wishart, London.
Masonic emblem presented
1905 *Afro-American Ledger*, January 7. 1905, p. 1.
In the matter of business
1902 *Afro-American Ledger*, October 11. 1902, p. 4.
McConnell, R.C.
1971 The Black Experience in Maryland, 1634–1900. In *The Old Line State: A History of Maryland*, edited by M.L. Radoff, pp. 405–432. Hall of Records, Annapolis, Maryland. Originally published 1957.
McDaniel, G.W.
1982 *Hearth and Home: Preserving a People's Culture*. Temple University Press, Philadelphia.
McKearnin, H., and K.M. Wilson
1978 *American Bottles and Flasks and Their Ancestory*. Crown, New York.
McWilliams, J.W.
1991 *Historical Title Search and Documentation, 163 Duke of Gloucester Street*. Ms. on file, Historic Annapolis Foundation, Annapolis, Maryland.
Meier, A.
1964 *Negro Thought in America, 1880–1915: Racial Ideologies in the Age of Booker T. Washington*. University of Michigan Press, Ann Arbor.
Midnight's musings
1905 *Afro-American Ledger*, April 1. 1905, pp. 1, 5.
Miller, D.
1995 Consumption as the Vanguard of History: A Polemic by Way of an Introduction. In *Acknowledging Consumption: A Review of New Studies*, edited by D. Miller, pp. 1–57. Routledge, New York.
1987 *Material Culture and Mass Consumption*. Basil Blackwell, Cambridge.
Miller, G.L.
1991 A Revised Set of CC Index Values for Classification and Economic Scaling of English Ceramics from 1787 to 1880. *Historical Archaeology* 25(1):1–25.
1980 Classification and Economic Scaling of 19th-Century Ceramics. *Historical Archaeology* 14:1–40.
1974 A Tenant Farmer's Tableware: Nineteenth-Century Ceramics from Tabbs Purchase. *Maryland Historical Magazine* 69:197–210.
Mordecai, S.
1860 *Virginia, Especially Richmond, In By-Gone Days*. West and Johnston, Richmond.
Movement among Southern colored people
1878 *Maryland Republican and State Capital Advertiser*, August 24. 1878, p. 2.
Mullins, P.R.
1998 Expanding Archaeological Discourse: Ideology, Metaphor, and Critical Theory in Historical Archaeology. In *Annapolis Pasts: Historical Archaeology in Annapolis, Maryland*, edited by P.A. Shackel, P.R. Mullins, and M.S. Warner, pp. 7–34. University of Tennessee Press, Knoxville.
1996 *The Contradictions of Consumption: An Archaeology of African America and Consumer Culture, 1850–1930*. PhD. dissertation, University of Massachusetts-Amherst. University Microfilms, Ann Arbor.

1989   *A Review of Ceramics Recovered from Main Street Site*. Ms. on file, Historic
Annapolis Foundation, Annapolis, Maryland.
Mullins, P.R., and M.S. Warner
1993   *Final Archaeological Investigations at the Maynard-Burgess House (18AP64),
An 1850–1980 African-American Household in Annapolis, Maryland*. Archaeology in
Annapolis, Annapolis, Maryland.
The Naval Academy
1890   *Evening Capital*, July 1. 1890, p. 1.
The Negro in business
1909   *The Bee*, July 3. 1909, p. 4.
A Negro to die
1896   *The Bee*, June 6. 1896, p. 4.
A Negro funeral
1875   *Maryland Republican and State Capital Advertiser*, December 4. 1875, p. 1.
The Negro woman goes to market
1936   *The Brown American*. 1936, p. 13.
Negroes for a show
1888   *The Bee*, December 8. 1888, p. 2.
New Goods
1873   *Maryland Republican and State Capital Advertiser*, April 26. 1873, p. 4.
"Niggers"
1879   *Maryland Republican and State Capital Advertiser*, December 6. 1879, p. 1.
Norton, J.Y.
1917   Center Market, Washington. *The Boston Cooking-School Magazine* 21:510–511.
Not sold
1873   *Maryland Republican and State Capital Advertiser*, June 7. 1873, p. 3.
Notes, tableware
1898   *The House Beautiful*, November. 1898, p. 234.
Novelty store
1904   *Evening Capital*, September 1. 1904, p. 1.
Now is your chance
1890   *The Bee*, November 22. 1890, p. 2.
Oak, V.V.
1949   *The Negro's Adventure in General Business*. Antioch Press, Yellow Springs, Ohio.
Officers elected
1900   *Anne Arundel Examiner*, October 11. 1900, p. 5.
Olliffe, C.
1964   *American Scenes: Eighteen Months in the New World*. Lake Erie College Press,
Painesville, Ohio. Originally published circa 1850.
Olmsted, F.L.
1970   *A Journey in the Back Country*. Negro Universities Press, New York. Originally
published 1860.
1968   *A Journey in the Seaboard Slave States, With Remarks on Their Economy*. Negro
Universities Press, New York. Originally published 1856.
On money
1916   *Afro-American Ledger*, August 5. 1916, p. 4.
Oppress him
1904   *The Bee*, December 24. 1904, p. 4.
Orser, C.E., Jr.
1996   *A Historical Archaeology of the Modern World*. Plenum, New York.
1992   Beneath the Material Surface of Things: Commodities, Artifacts, and Slave
Plantations. *Historical Archaeology* 26(3):94–104.

1988   *The Material Basis of the Postbellum Tenant Plantation: Historical Archaeology in the South Carolina Piedmont.* University of Georgia Press, Athens.

Our merchants
1870   *Maryland Republican and State Capital Advertiser*, October 1. 1870, p. 2.

Our oyster trade
1873   *Maryland Republican and State Capital Advertiser*, September 27. 1873, p. 3.

Our weakness
1912   *The Bee*, October 5. 1912, p. 4.

Our woman's column
1900   *The Bee*, August 4. 1900, p. 4.

Owned by Jews
1911   *The Bee*, December 2. 1911, p. 4.

Page, H.E.
1990   Lessons of the Jackson Campaign: Discursive Strategies of Symbolic Control and Cultural Capitalization. In *The Social and Political Implications of the 1984 Jesse Jackson Presidential Campaign*, edited by L. Morris, pp. 135–153, Praeger, New York.

Park, R.E.
1969   Negro Home Life and Standards of Living. In *The Negro's Progress in Fifty Years*, edited by E.R. Johnson, pp. 147–163. Negro Universities Press, New York. Originally published 1913.

Parker, C.H.
1897   The Use and Abuse of Ornamentation in the House. *The Boston Cooking School Magazine* 2(4):238–242.

Parlett and Parlett Bottlers advertisment
1916   *The Advertiser-Republican*, June 1. 1916, p. 8.

Patten, S.N.
1907   *The New Basis of Civilization.* Macmillan, London.
1889   *The Consumption of Wealth.* University of Pennsylvania, Philadelphia.

Paynter, R.
1990   Afro-Americans in the Massachusetts Historical Landscape. In *Politics of the Past*, edited by D. Lowenthal and P. Gathercole, pp. 49–62. Unwin Hyman, London.
1988   Steps to an Archaeology of Capitalism: Material Change and Class Analysis. In *The Recovery of Meaning: Historical Archaeology in the Eastern United States*, edited by M.P. Leone and P.B. Potter, Jr., pp. 407–433. Smithsonian Institution Press, Washington, D.C.

Peirce, M.F.
1884   *Co-operative Housekeeping: How to Do It and How Not to Do It.* James R. Osgood and Company, Boston.

Pennsylvania Publishing Company
1883   *The Successful Housekeeper.* Pennsylvania Publishing Company, Harrisburg, Pennsylvania.

The people aroused
1891   *The Bee*, November 14. 1891, p. 2.

Perdue, C.L. Jr., T.E. Barden, and R.K. Phillips (editors)
1976   *Weevils in the Wheat: Interviews with Virginia Ex-Slaves.* Indiana University Press, Bloomington.

Perry, W., and R. Paynter
1999   Artifacts, Ethnicity, and the Archaeology of African Americans. In *I, too, am American*, edited by T. Singleton. University of Virginia Press, Charlottesville. (in press)

Pictures that should be in every home
1918   *The Crusader*, November. 1918, p. 21.

Plantation housekeeping
    1888   The Homemaker, October. 1888, pp. 43–46.
Polk and Company
    1924   Polk's Annapolis, Maryland Directory, 1924–1925. R.L. Polk and Company, New
            York.
Potter, P.B., Jr.
    1994   Public Archaeology in Annapolis: A Critical Approach to History in Maryland's
            Ancient City. Smithsonian Institution Press, Washington, D.C.
Praetzellis, M., and A. Praetzellis
    1992   "We Were There, Too": Archaeology of an African-American Family in Sacramento,
            California. Sonoma State University Cultural Resources Center, Rohnert Park, Cali-
            fornia.
Pratiau Hair Straightener advertisement
    1895   The Bee, August 3. 1895, p. 1.
Prejudice
    1889   The Bee, September 28. 1889, p. 2.
Prime Meats advertisement
    1900   Evening Capital, April 2. 1900, p. 4.
Purity in food
    1910   Evening Capital, January 18. 1910, p. 4.
Purser, M.
    1992   Consumption as Communication in Nineteenth-Century Paradise Valley, Nev-
            ada. Historical Archaeology 26(3):105–116.
A question of business
    1902   Afro-American Ledger, September 6. 1902, p. 4.
Race pride and cosmetics
    1925   Opportunity 3(34). 1925, pp. 292–293.
The race problem
    1892   The Bee, April 9. 1892, p. 2.
Rachleff, P.
    1989   Black Labor in Richmond, 1865–1890. University of Illinois Press, Urbana.
Ralph, J.
    1896   Dixie, or Southern Scenes and Sketches. Harper and Brothers, New York.
Randolph, A.P.
    1919   Lynching: Capitalism Its Cause; Socialism Its Cure. The Messenger 2(7):9–12.
    1918   The Negro Business Man. The Messenger 2(1):13–14.
Recent parade of Ku Klux Klan, letter to editor
    1922   Evening Capital, November 1. 1922, p. 2.
In reference to menus and recipes
    1898   The Boston Cooking-School Magazine. 1898 (2), pp. 238–242.
Reid, W.
    1965   After the War: A Tour of the Southern States, 1865–1866. Harper and Row, New
            York. Originally published 1866.
Richards, T.
    1990   The Commodity Culture of Victorian England: Advertising and Spectacle, 1851–
            1914. Stanford University Press, Stanford.
Richardson, B.J.
    1910   The Woman Who Spends: A Study of Her Economic Function. Whitcomb and
            Barrows, Boston.
Riis, J.A.
    1971   How the Other Half Lives. Dover, New York. Originally published 1890.

Robinson calmly goes to his death saying he is innocent
  1921   *Evening Capital Maryland Gazette*, April 1. 1921, p. 1.
Robinson's illiterate note to public before execution
  1921   *Evening Capital Maryland Gazette*, April 1. 1921, pp. 1-2.
Rodgers, D.T.
  1974   *The Work Ethic in Industrial America, 1850–1920*. University of Chicago Press, Chicago.
Roediger, D.R.
  1991   *The Wages of Whiteness: Race and the Making of the American Working Class*. Verso, New York.
Rorty, R.
  1989   *Contingency, Irony, and Solidarity*. Cambridge University Press, New York.
Russo, J.
  1990   *Analysis of Annapolis Tax Assessments*. Ms. on file, Historic Annapolis Foundation, Annapolis, Maryland.
  1987   *Annapolis Transit Center Preliminary Historical Research*. Ms. on file, Historic Annapolis Foundation, Annapolis, Maryland.
Sacks, K.B.
  1994   How Did Jews Become White Folks? In *Race*, edited by S. Gregory and R. Sanjek, pp. 78–102. Rutgers University Press, New Brunswick, New Jersey.
Sad depravity
  1874   *Maryland Republican and State Capital Advertiser*, November 28. 1874, p. 3.
Sanborn Insurance Company
  1903   Insurance Maps for Annapolis, Maryland. Sanborn Insurance Company, New York.
Sangster, M.E.
  1897   *Home Life Made Beautiful in Story, Song, Sketch and Picture*. Christian Herald, New York.
Sanitary Meat Market advertisement
  1908   *The Advertiser-Republican*, November 12. 1908, p. 3.
Scarcity of fish
  1900   *Evening Capital*, March 28. 1900, p. 3.
Schlereth, T.J.
  1991   *Victorian America: Transformations in Everyday Life, 1876–1915*. Harper, New York.
  1989   Country Stores, County Fairs, and Mail-Order Catalogues: Consumption in Rural America. In *Consuming Visions: Accumulation and Display of Goods in America, 1880–1920*, edited by S.J. Bronner, pp. 339–375. Norton, New York.
Schuyler, R.L.
  1988   Archaeological Remains, Documents, and Anthropology: A Call for a New Culture History. *Historical Archaeology* 22(1):36–42.
Scott, J.W.
  1992   "Experience." In *Feminists Theorize the Political*, edited by J. Butler and J.W. Scott, pp. 22–40. Routledge, New York.
Seventh Street raid
  1915   *The Bee*, November 6. 1915, p. 4.
Shanks, M.
  1996   Style and Design of a Perfume Jar from an Archaic Greek City State. In *Contemporary Archaeology in Theory: A Reader*, edited by R.W. Preucel and I. Hodder, pp. 364–393. Basil Blackwell, New York.
Silver's Department Store advertisement
  1900   *The Negro Appeal*, February 16. 1900, p. 3.

Singleton, T.A.
    1995   The Archaeology of Slavery in North America. *Annual Review of Anthropology*
                24:119–140.
Smith, W.W.
    1989   *Anti-Jacksonian Politics Along the Chesapeake*. Garland Publishing, New York.
Sobel, M.
    1988   *Trabelin' On: The Slave Journey to an Afro-Baptist Faith*. Princeton University
                Press, Princeton.
Soft crabs advertisement
    1890   *Evening Capital*, May 16. 1890, p. 3.
Some sound sense
    1900   *The Negro Appeal*, February 16. 1900, p. 2.
South, S.
    1977   *Method and Theory in Historical Archaeology*. Academic Press, New York.
Southern military despotisms
    1867   *Maryland Republican and State Capital Advertiser*, November 9. 1867, p. 2.
Southgate, H.
    1875   *Things a Lady Would Like to Know Concerning Domestic Management and
                Expenditure*. 2nd ed. William P. Nimmo, London.
Spelman, W.A.
    1883   *Spelman's Fancy Goods Graphic*. W.A. Spelman, Chicago.
A stag tendered a colored physicial [sic]
    1910   *Evening Capital*, June 9. 1910, p. 4.
Star Theatre advertisement
    1922   *Evening Capital Maryland Gazette*, June 1. 1922, p. 5.
Stewart, S.
    1993   *On Longing: Narratives of the Miniature, the Gigantic, the Souvenir, the Collec-
                tion*. Duke University Press, Durham, North Carolina.
Stewart-Abernathy, L.C.
    1992   Industrial Goods in the Service of Tradition: Consumption and Cognition on
                an Ozark Farmstead before the Great War. In *The Art and Mystery of Historical
                Archaeology: Essays in Honor of James Deetz*, edited by A.E. Yentsch and M.C.
                Beaudry, pp. 101–126. CRC Press, Boca Raton.
Stieff, F.P.
    1932   *Eat, Drink and Be Merry in Maryland: An Anthology from a Great Tradition*. G.P.
                Putnam's Sons, New York.
Straighten the hair
    1910   *The Bee*, March 5. 1910, p. 4.
Strasser, S.
    1989   *Satisfaction Guaranteed: The Making of the American Mass Market*. Smithson-
                ian, Washington, D.C.
Susman, W.I.
    1984   *Culture as History: The Transformation of American Society in the Twentieth
                Century*. Pantheon, New York.
Sweetman, J.
    1979   *The U.S. Naval Academy: An Illustrated History*. Naval Institute Press, An-
                napolis.
Sypher and Company
    1885   *The Housekeeper's Quest: Where to Find Pretty Things*. Sypher and Company,
                New York.

Tate, C.
1992   *Domestic Allegories of Political Desire: The Black Heroine's Text at the Turn of the Century*. Oxford, New York.
Terrapin supper
1885   *Evening Capital*, March 25. 1885, p. 4.
Thom, W.T.
1901a   The Negroes of Sandy Spring, Maryland: A Social Study. *U.S. Department of Labor Bulletin* 32:43–102.
1901b   The Negroes of Litwalton, Virginia: A Study of the "Oyster Negro." *U.S. Department of Labor Bulletin* 37:1115–1170.
Tilley, C.
1990   Michel Foucault: Towards an Archaeology of Archaeology. In *Reading Material Culture: Structuralism, Hermeneutics, and Post-Structuralism*, edited by C. Tilley, pp. 281–347. Basil Blackwell, Cambridge.
1989   Archaeology as Socio-political Action in the Present. In *Critical Traditions in Contemporary Archaeology*, edited by V. Pinsky and A. Wylie, pp. 104–116. Cambridge University Press, Cambridge.
Todorich, C.
1984   *The Spirited Years: A History of the Antebellum Naval Academy*. Naval Institute Press, Annapolis, Maryland.
Trowbridge, J.T.
1866   *The South: A Tour Of Its Battlefields and Ruined Cities*. L. Stebbins, Hartford.
Turtle soup lunch
1877   *Maryland Republican and State Capital Advertiser*, July 7. 1877, p. 3.
United States Bureau of the Census
1900   *Abstract of the Twelfth Census of the United States*. Government Printing Office, Washington.
United States Census Population Schedules
1900   Annapolis, Maryland.
United States Department of Commerce
1969   *Negroes in the United States, 1920–1932*. Kraus, New York. Originally published 1935.
1933   *Census of American Business Retail Distribution: 1933*. 8 vols. Government Printing Office, Washington, D.C.
1913   *Benevolent Institutions 1910*. Bureau of the Census Bulletin No. 43. Government Printing Office, Washington, D.C.
Upton, D.
1996   Ethnicity, Authenticity, and Invented Traditions. *Historical Archaeology* 30(2): 1–7.
The use of cosmetics
1919   *The Crusader*, March. 1919, p. 19.
Utilizing the herring
1885   *Evening Capital*, April 27. 1885, p. 4.
Wage slavery
1906   *The Bee*, October 6. 1906, p. 5.
Waiters at the adjunct
1918   *Annapolis Advertiser*, October 1. 1918, p. 3.
Ward, A.
1886   *The Grocer's Handbook and Directory for 1886*. Philadelphia Grocer Publishing Company, Philadelphia.

Warner, M.S.
1998 *Food and the Negotiation of African-American Identities in the Chesapeake.* Ph.D. dissertation, University of Virginia. University Microfilms, Ann Arbor.
1992 *Test Excavations at Gott's Court, Annapolis, Maryland (18AP52).* Archaeology in Annapolis, Annapolis, Maryland.
Warner, M.S., and B. Ford
1990 Interview Transcripts from Archaeology in Annapolis African-American Archaeological Project. Archaeology in Annapolis, College Park, Maryland.
Warner, M.S., and P.R. Mullins
1993 *Phase I-II Archaeological Investigations on the Courthouse Site (18AP63), An African-American Neighborhood in Annapolis, Maryland.* Archaeology in Annapolis, Annapolis, Maryland.
Warren, M.
1990 Interview Transcripts from Annapolis I Remember Project. Ms. on file, Annapolis I Remember Collection, Maryland Hall of Records, Annapolis, Maryland.
Warren, M., and M.E. Warren
1984 *Maryland Time Exposures, 1840–1940.* Johns Hopkins University Press, Baltimore.
Weakness of the colored American citizens
1885 *The Bee,* November 14. 1885, p. 2.
Weatherill, L.
1988 *Consumer Behaviour and Material Culture in Britain, 1660–1760.* Routledge, London.
Weathorford, W.D.
1910 *Negro Life in the South: Present Conditions and Needs.* Young Men's Christian Association Press, New York.
What the colored people of Annapolis, Md. are doing
1897 *The Bee,* January 9. 1897, p. 8.
W.H. Bates, grocer
1897 *The Bee,* January 9. 1897, p. 1.
White, C.M., Sr., and E.K. White
1957 *The Years Between: A Chronicle of Annapolis, Maryland, 1800–1900.* Exposition Press, New York.
Wilkie, L.A.
1997 Secret and Sacred: Contextualizing the Artifacts of African-American Magic and Religion. *Historical Archaeology* 31(4):81–106.
William H. Butler Sr., another Black political pioneer
1987 *The Maryland Pendulum,* 5(1). 1987, p. 10.
Williams, P., and M.R. Weber
1978 *Staffordshire Romantic Transfer Patterns.* Fountain House East, Jeffersontown, Kentucky.
Williams, R.
1982 *Dream Worlds: Mass Consumption in Late Nineteenth Century France.* University of California Press, Berkeley.
Willis, S.
1991 *A Primer for Daily Life.* Routledge, New York.
Wolf, E.R.
1982 *Europe and the People without history.* University of California Press, Berkeley.
Woolson, A.G.
1873 *Woman in American Society.* Roberts Brothers, Boston.

Works Projects Administration
1940   *The Negro in Virginia*. Hastings House, New York.
Wright, R.
1991   *An Architectural Analysis of 163 Duke of Gloucester Street, Annapolis, Maryland*. Historic Annapolis Foundation, Annapolis, Maryland.
Wylie, A.
1996   The Interplay of Evidential Constraints and Political Interests: Recent Archaeological Research on Gender. In *Contemporary Archaeology in Theory: A Reader*, edited by R.W. Preucel and I. Hodder, pp. 431–459. Blackwell, Cambridge, England.
Yentsch, A.E.
1994   *A Chesapeake Family and Their Slaves: A Study in Historical Archaeology*. Cambridge University Press, Cambridge.

Index